When It Rains In Hell

Harry R.(Randy) McCoy

ISBN: 1-4792-6767-8
ISBN-13: 9781479267675
LCCN: 2012916855
CreateSpace Independent Publishing Platform
North Charleston, South Carolina

Dedicated To

All The Men And Women Who Served In

Southeast Asia

And

To

The Families That Waited Patiently At

Home, Hoping And Praying They Would

Not Receive The Dreaded Telegram

Informing Them Of The Death Of

Their Loved One

In Loving Memory Of

Lori Ann Wanex McCoy
July 19, 1962-Sept. 2, 2000

Table Of Contents

acknowledgements: I want to thank the members of the Falcon and Juliet Recon platoons for living this adventure with me and helping me to survive and to God for seeing to it that most of the members in the two platoons survived our one year in a most dangerous place.

Thanks to the former Wanda McCoy for waiting patiently at home for me and trying her hardest to exorcise the demons that war left me with, and to my daughter Christy Lynn McCoy for her continuing love and her overlooking of the less pleasant aspects of my character that the memories of war caused.

Thanks to my second wife, Lori Ann McCoy, for taking on the challenge of a man she knew was not quite back from combat, and for the love and understanding she showed me. Thanks also for the love and support shown me by my family through the years.

The only reason this book was finally written was the pressure exerted by my good friend CR Webster, a writer herself. When I mentioned that I had tried to write the book forty years ago and quit because of the pain, she suggested that perhaps this was a way to finally ease the pain and disappointment I felt in my country. She was right. The more I wrote the better I felt.

She pushed and prodded me the eight months it took me to write this book. She made sure I stayed on track and finished it in half the time I originally estimated. She took on the task of editing the chapters and trying to mold this fledgling assembler of words into a real writer. She did the best she could with what she had to work with. I owe her a debt of gratitude that I can never repay.

I did not want to be a soldier; I had no desire to fight another country's war. My country called and I grudgingly answered. I was no hero; I did the best I could in each situation I encountered. I lived through the year and now have my story to tell. I hope that I have done my job well enough that the reader will find my tale interesting and informative.

Every soldier that served in Viet Nam has his own story to tell. Many will not, and over fifty-eight thousand cannot tell theirs. Their story is on a black granite monument in Washington, D.C. It is left to the survivors to try to explain the hardships and horrors we faced. I can only hope that I have done a sufficiently creditable job.

Many names have been changed in this book to protect the privacy of the individuals and their families. I have tried to be as factual as I can while writing from memory. Any errors or omissions are mine and mine alone; the things written about in this book occurred almost a half century ago.

foreword: I recall hearing about the Viet Nam war, but remember very little of the details. I was a junior in high school and war was the farthest thing from my mind. I did not see the need for war or understand the politics, but whether I did or not, that war came anyway, taking with it many young men.

Randy McCoy, a first time author, has expressed himself so well in this book, that I found it difficult to stop reading. Each page is decorated with such graphic descriptions of the war that the reader begins to feel as if he is standing right beside him.

I could feel his emotion as he said goodbye to his new wife and family. I could sense his rebellion at not wanting to be drafted. His less than perfect childhood did not give him any enthusiasm to become a soldier.

His details of boot camp were harsh and almost unbelievable, yet in his 19-year old mind, he came to understand the reasoning of the drill sergeants. This grueling training would save his life.

I was able to feel the chill of the rice paddy waters, to hear the roar of choppers, to sense the dangers in the tunnels, saw the beautiful stars on cool nights, and cried when he lost his best friend.

I learned the sensitivity of the author as he and his platoon never burned down the villages of the Vietnamese civilians after invading their domain to check for contraband.

His survival tactics amazed me. Randy was a fighter, determined to live and go home.

As I read through the pages, I became aware that a small town country boy had become a man, whether he desired this route or not, such was his lot. Randy made it home unscathed, or did he?

This book is for any veteran or civilian to read. We need to know the sacrifices that were made by these young men. I never fully understood until Randy wrote this book.

War is real. War is hell. When It Rains In Hell is a must read.

C.R.Webster

Chapter 1

The Army Wants Me but I Do Not Want Them

Deal Island, Md.-August 1967.

I stare at the letter one more time, willing the message to go away. It does not. The short, formal letter has my address on it. It invites me, Harry R. Mc-Coy, to a meeting at the Crisfield Armory in a week. It further states that I will be bussed to Fort Holabird in Baltimore, Maryland. At that base, I will receive testing that might lead to possible induction into the U.S. Army. I have a sinking feeling that possibly means most likely.

This could not have come at a worse time. Eight months ago, I quit working at DuPont in Seaford, Delaware. It was an okay job, but I felt it was a going-nowhere job. The shift work and the long drive to the job meant I was working, sleeping or driving.

The money was not that great. I had a burning desire to get out into the world and make my mark, while making a load of money at the same time.

I leased a gas station in Chance, Md. This was more like it! I was only nineteen and I had my own business. The hours were long and the work frequently dirty, but I was headed upward. I was making good money for that time period, especially when compared to my DuPont earnings.

I had recently met Wanda, whom I considered the love of my life. We had been inseparable from the moment we met. I tore myself away from my job when I could to see her, but I was frequently late to pick her up for dates. She understood that I was trying to build my business and I felt my life was near perfect.

Staring at the letter, all I could think about was that this pretty much sucks. My father said to stay in college, but I just had to have a four-speed Pontiac GTO. I worked hard and now I have it. However, it looks like the army is trying to break up my happy home.

I wonder if I can flunk the tests again, I think. The last time on the bus trip to Baltimore, I took a twenty-four count box of Clark Bars with me. I managed to eat my way through over half the box before my stomach told me that enough was enough. A doctor had mentioned that it might affect your blood sugar enough to flunk an important test. I flunked that test and was sent back home. Will it work again, I ask myself?

Now, please do not judge me too harshly. I was only nineteen, an age when your decisions are often not sound ones. I felt that I was as patriotic as the next person. If the enemy landed in Ocean City, I would be there in two hours. I would be carrying a rifle in my arms and a knife in my belt. However, the idea of fighting for some God-forsaken little country halfway around the world did not fit into my plans. I felt that some wars were necessary and just, like World War II. I read everything I could on the war and I really admired the men who fought in it.

The country of Viet Nam could not even defend itself from what I was reading and seeing. Why should I waste my time on it? I had money to make and a good life to live. Let the people defend themselves. I felt that my country had no right to ask me to do this. They were not even asking politely, they were forcing me to do this.

Leasing the station was my start. I felt that with enough sweat and hard work, a man could make of himself whatever he wanted to be. I wanted to make a million dollars before I was thirty, marry Wanda, and make some more money. I did not mind the long hours, even when it cut into my dating time. I was driven and I knew the hard work would pay off in time.

I remembered the discussions on the war at the college while I was there. I thought of the small demonstrations behind Holloway Hall that I attended. At one, a reporter suddenly thrust a microphone in my face and asked me what I thought of the war. Not quite sure of what my opinion was at that time, I managed to stammer out that I thought it best to stay out of other country's internal politics.

I was at a strategic moment in my life. My business and Wanda were on one side of the scale, and the considerable might of the army was on the other. I briefly considered going to Canada, but discarded that idea immediately. That felt like quitting, but I was no quitter. Besides, I could not make that million in Canada.

Wanda and I discussed the problem. She said she would stick by me and we would face the outcome together. I played the hand dealt to me and had my part-time employee cover for me on the day of the tests.

We had a tearful parting that night, but we were in love. In the mind of a nineteen year old, love would conquer all problems. I look back at this time with the benefit of age-acquired common sense and wonder how I could have been so stupid. As the wise man once said, to be old and wise, you must first be young and stupid.

A friend from Wenona and I drove to Crisfield. We joined the ranks of young men standing in line. We stood there, all of us certain we would not be seeing our families anytime soon. I had a five-pound bag of sugar with me for the bus ride. I could not take the idea of another Clark Bar. I loved them, but was unable to look one in the eye since that last bus trip.

After some paperwork, they loaded the bus and we headed north. I went to work on that bag of sugar and soon hated it as much as the candy bars. When I was sure I could handle no more I gave it to several other young men. That bag of sugar was long gone by the time we reached Ft. Holabird.

At the base, we quickly found out that the army was serious this time. Evidently, they really needed cannon fodder. It appeared that if you could see good enough to get off the bus and had all four appendages, you were army bound. I flunked the hearing test on purpose, being careful not to do too good a job. It did no good, as they were wise to that ploy. They told me I was sound of mind and body and was just what they needed.

Within an hour of walking into the base, they led us in small groups into a room. A very large sergeant read a notice. We were now members of the United States Army. He further stated that we should take one step forward to signify that we understood and accepted. The rest of the men stepped forward, but I resolutely stood my ground and refused to move. This had obviously happened before. They solved the problem quite simply. The large sergeant beckoned to the doorway, and two burly six-footers stepped over to me. They weighed at least two hundred and fifty pounds each and positioned themselves on each side of me. Four meaty hands grabbed me by the belt and shoulders, lifting me off the ground. They moved me forward a foot and deposited me, none too gently, back on the floor. Now I knew why all these sergeants were so big.

My last lame card played, I am now a Private E-3 in the U.S. Army. This was probably the lowest point in my life, up to that day. Many more were to follow in the next two years, some much worse. I am glad that I had no way to see what fate would send me down the road.

Now that we were in the army, the treatment from the sergeants became much worse. They cursed us and called us the lowest form of life on the planet. They said they doubted we would be usable as soldiers. I agreed with them on this and told them I was willing to call the whole thing a waste of both of our times. Just let me head to the bus and they would never see me again.

As I suspected, this did not work. They lined us up and headed us down a gauntlet of soldiers equipped with inoculation guns. These gave you two shots in each arm. They did both arms at the same time, seeming to relish the opportunity. As they pulled the guns away, blood ran down the arms of most men.

With obvious glee, they told us that some of us might have adverse reactions. We have to keep an eye on the person right in front of us. If that person started to sway, you were to grab him and lower him to the floor to keep him from falling. Several men did just that. They crashed to the floor, legs kicking out like demonized rag dolls. The thought ran through my mind that these people giving us shots are sadists. *Dear God, what have I gotten myself into today?*

As I struggled to recover from multiple entry wounds to my arms, I thought of my dad. He told me to stay in college. He was right. My dad and I had never gotten along very well, but in that moment, I realized one thing; he was a lot smarter than I gave him credit for, whereas I was pretty much an idiot.

After more poking, prodding, and filling out paper work, they allowed us to get dressed. They had been herding us along totally naked and making crude jokes about our bodies. I found this to be normal treatment all through the induction and the training that followed. They did their best to convince us that we were a useless piece of dung, but they used another word. They tried to break us down, to remove our individuality and feeling of well being. They told us that only under their expert guidance would we ever have a chance of being a real soldier.

I decided right then that I would endeavor to remain myself, that I would not fold under this obvious psychological attack on my mind. They had my butt for two years and I could do nothing to cure this problem. I would have to put up with their crap but I would not become folded, spindled and mutilated. I would not give in. I would accept the mistreatment, but I would find ways to defy their authority whenever I could. It is only two years, I tell myself. At that time, however, those two years seemed to be an eternity.

A sergeant herded us out to another bus, which they crammed until every seat was full. I noticed that several other enlisted men followed us out to make sure there was no mutiny on the way. The bus headed south to Fort Bragg, North Carolina. Everyone on the bus was stunned and dispirited, sitting there in shock. We talked little, feeling like cows heading to the slaughterhouse. The cows had a better time of it. They did not know where they were going. We did know this.

The arrival at Fort Bragg was another revelation. Mean looking drill sergeants formed a double line at the door. I thought that the verbal abuse in Baltimore was bad but this was much worse. They pointed out that we were the vilest looking, queerest group of men they had ever seen. They insulted our families; called our moms whores, and told us our girlfriends would shortly be making their money after dark. I could not beat the hell out of these sergeants, so I just let it roll off my back.

I did not understand what was happening then. It took me several months with much harsh verbal and physical treatment before I understood the beauty of their plan. It burst out of my brain one night while I was lying on my bunk. I was thinking of the slowest, most painful way to kill Drill Sergeant Cooper. My God, I thought. How did I miss this? They were teaching me pure, unadulterated hate for a human being. They were making me think about killing a person. They were turning me into a killer so skillfully that I had not even realized it. I thought of most of the drill sergeants as just down home country boys with an IQ of sixty on a good day. Instead, it turned out I was the dummy.

The next trial we faced was a battery of tests that took up the evening and half of the next day. This was unexpected and at least as comprehensive as the S.A.T.s I took before college. I was always reasonably smart and I must have done well. It did not even occur to me to flunk them on purpose. I thought if I showed a little intelligence they might find something for me to do that involved staying out of combat.

After the tests, a lieutenant called me into his office. He asked me to sit down. He explained that I had scored well. He noted that I had some college education and said the army could put me into accelerated classes and then OCS (officer's candidate school). I would come out as a second lieutenant and never have to see combat. To do this I would have to sign up for three more years in the army. I smelled a rather large rat. The army would also need officers in Viet Nam. I explained that he would have to do this on my two years in the army or no deal. His demeanor totally changed. He told me he had no more time to waste on me and to send in the next person in the line outside his office as I left.

Yes, lieutenant, this is all I dream about, the chance to sign up for three more years of this unholy treatment. I was lying on my bunk last night just praying to get the chance to sign up for three more years. I washed my face this morning, looked in the mirror, but saw no signs of "idiot" written on my forehead.

They were not through with me yet. Several hours later, I was ushered into another officer's room. The ploy this time was that I had the intelligence to be a rotary wing pilot. Sign up for only two years and the training would start. In a year, I would be piloting choppers and never have to worry about Viet Nam. Excuse me, but I do believe they use many choppers in that country. I can understand how they would never send me over there, though. I would be much too valuable an asset. Yeah, right.

I was later to meet quite a few men in Viet Nam that had signed up for OCS or pilot's school with the attending extra years tacked on. Their universal lament was that no one told them how hard their training was going to be. They washed out and wound up in combat training. The real bitch of the poor deal they made was this; they now had enough time to serve twice or maybe even three tours of combat. I feel for those people, but they brought it on themselves.

After this, they divided us up, sending us to various basic training companies on one side of the base. They housed us in wooden two-story barracks. Each barracks had about eighty men on the two floors, and we had to keep them spotless. We swept the floors every morning at 0500 hours before we went for chow. Every night, before lights out at 2100 hours, we had to mop the floors and wax them. Then we hauled the buffer out of the closet and buffed them. The sergeant had to see his face in the floor or we were in trouble. Other men were making the communal bathroom spotless at the same time.

We entered into an eight-week course of training which was grueling. The day started at 0500 hours with a half hour of exercises, and then breakfast. There were monkey bars at the entrance to the mess hall, so you had to swing through these before you could eat. If you could not do a certain amount fast enough they made you do it over. If you failed this, you did not eat. We got five minutes to eat and a sergeant stood inside the door to make sure we did not exceed this time.

The rest of the day brought more exercises and classroom lectures on weapons and war craft. We spent a lot of time learning marching and the various commands associated with it. They also threw in a lot of one or two-mile marches, always carrying a pack. The packs were loaded down with at least thirty pounds of equipment. As the weeks progressed, the short marches became longer. By the end of basic training, our marches were up to fifteen miles long, and no one could stop. If someone quit or fainted, the sergeants would march us around in a big circle. Several of us had to drop out, pick up the man, and carry him on our shoulders until he recovered. The sergeants did it this way to shame men, so they would not quit.

More than once, I have helped carry a man while telling him he had several minutes to recover and rest. Then we would put him down and tell him he had better walk. Some of the heftier people gave us a lot of trouble. This went away as they lost weight and became better conditioned.

We also spent time on the rifle ranges firing M-14 rifles. We practiced with them several days a week and learned to shoot accurately at up to three hundred yards. This culminated with a shooting test that gauged your ability with the rifle. The best shots earned expert status and good shots received the title of sharpshooter. Lower scoring men were marksmen. This was finally something I enjoyed. I also knew I was going to wind up in combat, so I applied myself carefully. I knew ability with the rifle was important and might save my life. I was quite happy when my score was among the highest in our group and I received the expert medal.

The training was brutal and went on from sunup to almost dark. I was in good shape when I entered the army. As the weeks passed, I got stronger and so did my fellow soldiers. We had to take PT (physical training) tests weekly to test our ability. We worked hard on these tests because we knew if we scored low, they sent you back to week one. They would transfer you to a platoon just starting training. Eight weeks of this crap was quite enough. No one wanted to have to start over. The army carefully structured their training to make the soldier work harder.

The big day finally arrived. We were graduating from basic training. I was happy to have basic ending, but I also knew that the training was far from ending. After this, we were going to another fort for AIT. (Advanced Infantry Training) I hoped that it would be easier, but knowing the army, I doubted it.

Graduation day was a simple ceremony that entailed a lot of marching on a large parade ground in the hot sun at rigid attention. The drill sergeants had warned us that the heat might affect some men. If we saw anyone wavering, we had to hold him up from behind. As usual, the drill sergeants were not concerned with the soldier's problem. They just wanted the formation to look good to the officers who attended. They would gladly march a platoon in the hot sun until some suffered heat exhaustion. We knew they were hardening us up for the rigors of combat, but we felt that they took it just a little too far. We were not human beings to them; merely chess pawns that they could move around the board as they saw fit.

After the graduation parade, we went back to the barracks and received our orders for our new posting. We knew we were destined for more training. The only question was where were we going? Now we knew. We all received orders for Fort Polk, Louisiana.

We would leave the following day by bus. There were no handshakes or "good job, men" from the drill sergeants. They were there just long enough to make sure we packed everything up and that we left the barracks spotless. Once they took care of this task, they departed with never a kind word or a look back. We were already gone from their memory, just another faceless group of men to pass through the base. The war called and they cranked us through as fast as they could.

I was careful to remember each hated drill sergeant and his face, in case I made it back home and might someday run across one of them. Later, in Viet Nam, I realized their training might have saved my life. It definitely made me meaner and more tenacious and those qualities were a necessity in a war zone. I took them off my—*I want to kill this man when I get home* list.

We arrived at Fork Polk after a twenty-hour bus ride, tired and stiff. We had stopped several times but only had time to purchase soft drinks and snacks and then rush back to the bus. Any thoughts of an easier life at this base went away as soon as I saw the group of hated drill sergeants assemble by the bus door. It was more of the same. They insulted moms, our girlfriends, and us. Not being happy with that, they disparaged our religion and asked if there were any "queers" or "Jew-boys" among us. The blacks received their share of attention, too, as they had at our former base. Even the black drill sergeants used the N word repeatedly.

They marched us to our new barracks and I was stunned to see that it looked virtually the same as our former base. There were the same beige-painted barracks, the same mess hall, and the company dayroom. Low fences made of old artillery shell cases half buried in the dirt separated them. Chains connected the shells to protect the neatly trimmed grass areas. It was an almost carbon copy of our old base.

Even the drill sergeants looked the same. They were certainly just as foul-mouthed. The company area looked almost the same. I knew it was going to be another eight weeks of the same old drill. Viet Nam was starting to sound better all the time.

Surprisingly, they left us alone the rest of the afternoon and let us settle in and rest. I was not deceived, however. Sure enough, they woke us up at 0500 hours the next morning and the same old drill started again. Do exercises for a half hour, a quick breakfast with the same run through the monkey bars, and off on a five-mile march. Is that the best you can do, only five miles? They must think we are sissies or something.

The training stretched on, increasing in intensity. They introduced us to "punji sticks." These were six-foot long wooden poles, lightly padded on the ends, which were our imaginary rifles and bayonets and allowed hand-to-hand and simulated bayonet practice without anyone getting hurt. They could really sting, however. If the drill sergeant detected that we were not using them with enough enthusiasm, he would step in and really ring our bell with the sticks.

Then we received training on silent killing. They taught us to sneak up from behind a sentry. We would put our hand over his mouth to keep him quiet and then insert a knife into his back. We turned the blade sideways, so it would slip between the ribs instead of hitting them. This had to happen quickly to be effective, and then we gently lowered him to the ground. On the other hand, we could put our forearm against his throat, punch him sharply in the kidney, and kick our legs out backwards. As he fell backwards, our shoulder would contact the back of his head. This would break his neck as we hit the ground. All well and good, but how could I use this training when I got back home?

The next training was in the .45 caliber semi-auto pistol, the standard army side arm at the time. As soon as I got one in my hands, I loved it. This was no wimpy .22 caliber pistol. It was a big hand-filling hunk of machined steel. It kicked like a small mule. This was serious stuff. I applied myself again and took the firing test with my fellow soldiers. I again scored near the top of the class, achieving 380 points out of a possible 400. I was now a double expert.

Then came training on the M-16 rifle. I hated it as soon as I picked one up for the first time. It was short and made of aluminum and steel. Black molded fiberglass formed the stock and forearm. This was not a proper weapon. It was ugly and highly inaccurate compared to an M-14. The instructors taught that it was for close quarters and you sprayed a burst of rounds at the target. I just did not understand this weapon and did not try very hard. When qualification day came around my obvious distaste for the weapon could be seen in my final score. I barely earned enough points to be termed a marksman.

Despite my original misgivings about the weapon, I was to find later on in Viet Nam that my opinion was wrong. I found the weapon ideally suited for the close quarter, intense but quickly over firefights. It was half the weight of an M-14 and the relatively tiny .223 caliber bullets tended to corkscrew when it encountered flesh. This turned a minor wound into a man-stopping one. An added advantage was the weight of the bullets. We could carry twice the ammo for the same weight. This was highly important in a combat zone. The VC quickly nicknamed them "The Black Death" soon after they became available in Viet Nam.

It is true that the early M-16s quickly gained a reputation as unreliable and could easily get jammed. The cure was modifications to the chamber and a return to the type of powder originally specified. By the time I arrived in early 1968 the problems had disappeared. I can only say that my own personal M-16, serial number 918409, never failed me one time in the three months I carried it every day and the nine months I carried it at times. I still consider it the finest weapon ever designed for jungle fighting.

Halfway through training, Drill Sergeant Harris came into our barracks and told us our platoon would receive training on the 106mm recoilless rifle. Our platoon had a large percentage of men who had fired expert. This was another weapon that interested me very much. I looked forward to learning more about that big long-barreled weapon we occasionally saw mounted on jeeps.

This weapon had an eleven foot long barrel that overhung the front and back of a jeep. It had a single shot machine gun mounted on the top. We aimed and fired the machine gun first. If the round struck the target then we fired the five-foot long main projectile. The noise was deafening and the explosion extremely impressive. Everyone in the platoon liked this weapon and we all did our best to master it. When the firing tests came up most of the platoon did well and my score was again near the top of the class.

We finished the eight weeks with training on map and compass reading and live fire training where we walked up a hillside in a line. We fired live ammo and drill sergeants walked behind us, keeping us in line. That way, no one could drop behind or get out in front. Being shot could be the result if the line distorted too much.

In the final week, we faced a few more challenges. We had to cross a hundred-foot wide river on a rope strung across it. We went across with our legs wrapped around the rope, using our hands to propel ourselves. The drill sergeants made it interesting by grabbing the rope and trying to shake us into the river.

On another day, we had to crawl through a one hundred yard long sand pit as they blew small charges of C-4. The explosive was contained in small bunkers, so it would only blow sand on us if we were close when the explosion occurred. To make it even more fun they shot machine guns over our heads using live ammo. It was five feet in the air, but we could see the tracers coming toward us and hear the bullets cleaving the air above our heads. The drill sergeants did give us some helpful advice.

"Do not stand up, assholes, or you will die," was the helpful advice given by Sgt. Harris. Aw, sergeant, I did not think you really cared about us poor soldiers.

It is finally over. We go through the same graduation ceremony we did when we graduated from basic training. The only difference now is that it is late December. Instead of risking heat stroke, we stood at attention and shivered in our uniforms. We are wearing our dress uniforms now in perfect parallel rows on the field. Hundreds of little tin soldiers, but they would not allow us to wear overcoats and mess up the looks of the perfectly spaced formation.

As with the last graduation, they gather us together in the barracks one final time. They hand out our orders from a tall pile. Surprise! Everyone is going to Viet Nam. Not all to the same outfit there, but all of us will be heading west over the Pacific. The drill sergeants make us tidy the barracks in our dress uniforms one last time. No need to, we left the barracks spotless this morning. This is just one more twist of the screw, one last chance to make us miserable. The sergeants march us out to the trucks that will take us to the airport. Again, they turn and leave. They do not say goodbye. They do not wish us luck. They have fulfilled their obligations and we are now soldiers. Like yesterday's newspaper, they forget us and walk away. The real pisser of the situation is that I see smirks and grins on most of their faces.

We all have thirty day's leave before we report to California for the flight west. Once I get to the airport, I find that my travel voucher will not cover the full cost of a flight back to Maryland. What a perfect end to a lousy eight weeks! Finding a way back to the base and getting this straightened out will eat up valuable leave time. I hail a cab and have him take me to the bus station.

The bus is much cheaper, so I will have money left from the voucher. I will also spend considerable time on that Greyhound. I climb on the bus about five pm on Friday and arrive in Princess Anne, Maryland late Sunday afternoon. I have seen half the small towns in Louisiana, Georgia and Alabama on the way home. We also stopped at most of them. I have not taken a long trip on a bus since.

My parents pick me up in Princess Anne. I have been gone four months and it is good to away from the hardships of the army training. I change to civilian clothes as soon as I get in the door and just sit back in the living room, enjoying the quiet and the lack of anything green.

The orders to Viet Nam hang around my neck like a millstone. I force it to the back of my mind. I am going to enjoy the twenty-seven days I have left of my leave. I will enjoy being with my family and being able to stay at the dinner table as long as I want.

My Pontiac GTO is long gone. The payments were $120 a month and I am making about $80 a month in my new rank of Private First Class. The bank in Princess Anne has refused to lower the payment so I can afford it, and my father told them to come and get the car. I cannot fault him for this because he had to pay the payments after the army drafted me, once my bank account was depleted. Losing that car hurt me deeply but it is water over the dam. Funny, but the bank was a lot more cooperative when I was running my business and maintaining two accounts there.

I call Wanda and we have a joyous reunion. We have been apart four months and we are both in heaven. We ride to the Oaks Drive Inn in Salisbury for burgers. I have been really missing their deluxe cheeseburgers and french fries. In the joy of the moment, I speed through Fruitland a little too fast, and a town cop pulls me over. He gives me a stern lecture and pulls out his ticket pad. I tell him he can give me a ticket if he wants, but I will not be around to pay it. You see, Mr. Policeman, I have this little trip planned to a sunny, hot country far away and I will be staying there a year. He relents and puts his ticket book away. He wishes me luck and tells me I can go. I am stupefied. This is the first time that being in the army has accomplished anything good for me. It will likely be the last, I think.

The leave passes quickly. When I am not enjoying spending time with my family, Wanda and I are together. The Viet Nam cloud hangs above our heads but we try to brush it away. We talk about the future and our plans for our lives. We never talk about the war.

We stop by a favorite hangout for young people in Princess Anne. We have burgers at Peaky's restaurant and reach a pivotal moment in our young lives. Wanda has a best friend named Gail and she comes in and sits down with us. We pour out our tale of woe to her, the shadow that haunts us. To her teenage mind, the solution is simple and she quickly points it out to us.

"Why don't you two get married?" Gail asks us. Wanda and I look at each other. It does not solve the Viet Nam problem, but it feels comfortable. It feels right. We discuss it all day and decide it is the thing to do. Wanda says I have to go to her parent's house to ask for permission to marry her.

Wanda's parents, Albert and Joan Carmean are great people and seem to like me. It does take a lot of courage to ask them if we can get married. To our amazement, they say yes and the planning starts before they can change their minds.

"It's your life, son," my father says when we broach the question to my parents. He gives me the same stern glare he gave me when I quit college. It seemed to say that he thought I was a complete idiot, but he knew I was determined to go through with the wedding.

Three days later, we were married in a simple ceremony at Wanda's house. Both families attended the wedding along with Gail. Wanda looked stunning in her simple white dress, and me; well, I looked like a soldier in my dress uniform. Wanda insisted I wear the uniform though it was not my preference. Young girls of that time seemed gaga over military uniforms. I did not know why. A couple days of basic training would cure them of that proclivity.

We had a brief, extremely happy one week as a married couple at my parent's home. It ended far too quickly. Now it was time to pay the piper. Wanda and the families escorted me to the Salisbury airport for my flight to California. We had a tearful goodbye in the lobby and I hoisted my duffel bag and headed for the commuter. I forced my feet up the ramp and turned for one final look and wave.

I watched Salisbury disappear under me from the plane window. Many changes have happened to me in four short months. I have gone from the driven, but happy-go-lucky young man to a married one headed across the country to my meeting with destiny. *Would I survive that meeting, I wondered?*

Chapter 2
My First Mortar Attack

Tan An-Feb. 1968.

This is the seventh day in this country and we are at a small base several hours south of Long Binh. We initially arrived there and had several days of in-country training. We are taught how to distinguish booby-traps, to fire and maneuver, and how to treat the civilians. It is a rehash of our training in the states.

"Don't want you newbies to get your brains splattered all over the countryside just yet, we want you to kill a few gooks before you do," says a sergeant in the characteristic loving and concerned manner that most of the training personnel exhibit toward us poor privates. I wonder if and when I will get any respect and if I will live long enough to see it happen. *When does that magical day happen, when you become a combat veteran, get some respect and stop being the butt of crude comments from everyone with a higher rank than you? Not any bloody time soon, I tell myself, so learn to live with it for the time being.*

This camp does not appear to have any name and we do not think to ask. It is merely an overnight stop for the convoy we are riding on to our duty base. No one seems to pay any attention to us, or ask us any questions. We are pointed out a wooden platform equipped with mosquito nets, and the location of the mess hall by a bored looking Spec. 4, who appeared to have very little ability to carry on a conversation. He mentions that the convoy will be heading south tomorrow morning and we need to be on it.

Therefore, we sleep under the stars that night, glad that it is the dry season with one hundred degree days and a nice comfortable seventy-five or so at night. O'Brian and I stayed up late that night and decided that since no one was paying any attention to us, missing the convoy in the morning would be a good thing. This seems to be a safe and secure area to pass some time. We have almost a year to serve here, so wasting a couple of days sounds like a good idea.

We find out that the mosquito nets are an absolute necessity here. I feel sorry for O'Brian, because he swatted the little pests all night long and cursed. I grew up on an island lousy with mosquitoes, so they seemed to bother me less.

We managed to evade the convoy for two days, but a buck sergeant corralled us on the third day and pointed out the back of a waiting two and a half ton truck, known to all in the army as a deuce-and-a-half. A convoy of about fifteen trucks and attending convoy escort vehicles are on the road. The escort vehicles are jeeps with .30 caliber machine guns or 106mm recoilless rifles mounted on them. The convoy has been loading all morning and we failed to make ourselves scarce at the right time so we are heading out on the convoy.

The recoilless rifles especially interested us, because that is our MOS, the term the army uses for the exact job they train you to do. We were infantrymen foremost, or as our sergeants liked to point out, cannon fodder. We were assigned the MOS 11H20, or direct fire crewman, and taught how to fire the recoilless rifle and the .50 caliber bolt action mounted on top of the weapon. It fires a single shot each time the firing handle is pulled.

Recoilless rifle was quite a misnomer, used because the gun's shell was actually like a rocket about three feet long with a perforated casing. When fired the force from the burning powder was transmitted out through the holes in the casing to a swelled area around the chamber and back through outlets situated around the chamber and then rearward. The force backward exactly balanced the force of the shell going out the barrel, hence there is no recoil other than a slight jolt at the eyepiece of the sight.

The shell is about five inches in diameter, the barrel about eleven feet long, and with the tripod weighs around a thousand pounds. It can only be carried on a vehicle to make it mobile, or fired from a fixed position.

The weapon was designed after the Korean War to replace the older bazooka, which was designed to kill tanks. As tank size and armor thickness grew, the larger weapon was needed. The .50 caliber gun on top was aimed through the same sight as the main gun, and the theory is that you sight in on a tank with the little gun first and fire. If you hit the tank, then you fire the big gun to disable the tank.

The only fly in the ointment, we were taught in training, is that a tank has a system to acquire a target very quickly, usually in thirty seconds or less. If we hit with the little gun or have a close miss and the tank crew notices, we better send that big round downrange and get a hit in thirty seconds or less, or we are dead.

The weapon has a deadly effect when it is fired, as the back blast coming out the rear kills anyone behind it in a triangle starting at the breech and extending back over one hundred and fifty feet. Careful coordination between the loader and the firer is required.

I remember one day at the range the drill sergeant held up his hand, pointed at me and asked, "Okay, McCoy, you just fired a spotter round and have a near miss and now the turret on the tank is swinging around. What are you gonna do?"

Totally unable to resist, and fully knowing better I said, "Drill sergeant, I'm gonna jump off the jeep and run like hell." This brought a big laugh from the class, but the sergeant just fixed me with his steely glare.

The Drill Sergeant said, "Drop and give me fifty, McCoy," referring to pushups. Unfortunately, I heard that request often during the five months of training, so I dropped and ripped them off quickly, barking out each number loudly. Anything less would have resulted in a request for another fifty.

"Going down to the Ninth Division in Rach Kein, I see. Beaucoup VC down that way," the sergeant allows after perusing our orders. He hands us a metal box loaded with a thousand rounds of M-16 ammo, caliber .223. I grab it and fervently hope we will not need all this today.

He points out the tailgate of a waiting truck and ends with, "Load up your mags boys, but keep your rifles on safe and keep your eyes open once you clear the gate." I am a little amazed because the sarge is treating us like soldiers. I wonder if this is when the respect starts, when you head out the gate and have to load a rifle. I quickly decide that he is just glad that it is us headed out to no-man's land, and that is why he cut us some slack. Well, whatever the reason, we just got a little slack and that does not happen often to a Pvt. First Class.

I am happy temporarily as we climb up over the tailgate and grab the ammo can that O'Brian swings up to me. The can reminds me, though, that this may not be a nice quiet ride through the countryside, courtesy of Uncle Sam. *Not that I expected anything different, but a guy can hope, can't he?*

We settle in and the truck moves off with a clash of gears and a jolt. I am somewhat disconcerted to notice that we are sitting on several hundred white pine boxes of artillery shells, 175 mm, two each, according to the stencils on the boxes. I do a rough tally of the explosives contained within and immediately determine that we are sitting on a very large bomb. If something sets it off, it is going to be a very quick death. I now regret the demolition training I received at Fort Polk, Louisiana during my last several weeks of AIT, or Advanced Infantry Training. Thanks to this training, I can now easily figure how big a boom a given amount of explosives will make and my zero chances of surviving. Had I known, I might have given serious thought about Canada being on my extremely limited list of options.

We grind on through the countryside, one green, wet rice paddy after another. Vietnamese bend over their hoes and Papa-San guides his water buffalo through the foot of water and mud surrounding the rice plants. It is still, hot and dusty to the extreme, with clouds of yellow dust wafting back from the vehicles in front of us and billowing up into the bed of the truck. I am convinced that it is so hot the devil would be looking for a shade tree. I feel the sweat running down my face and armpits, while picking up the dust and slowly turning our skin yellow. It is not bad enough that my country has sent me over here to kill people that have done me no wrong, but they have thrown in this infernal heat, to boot.

O'Brian yells over the din, "I hope Rach Kein comes up soon, this dust is killing me." I respond with a shrug of my shoulders, too miserable to speak, and tie a handkerchief over my face to ward off the dust. O'Brian quickly follows suit.

On and on the paddies disappear into the dust behind us, and we pass through dust-coated villages where the children pause and holler, "Hello, G I." The older people often join them in the greetings and I immediately start to like these people. They are obviously worn down by the heat and hard labor, but always ready for a quick smile. I see many brown, lined faces, old before they are thirty. I also see the shadow of those hardships on those faces, half hidden, but there nonetheless. We later learn their smiles are a universal reaction all across the country and have as much to do with the hope that you will throw them some food, as it does to actually liking you. The food will probably be sold in the village, or bartered. I think that it is significant that we see no fat-bodied Vietnamese; they are a race of very slim people, and it is not because they diet.

Late afternoon comes along and I am worn out fighting the heat and the dust. My arms are tired from tightly gripping my rifle and swiveling my body in every direction looking for the enemy. Maybe it is a little too hot for him to bother with sniping at the convoy. About the time I start to get worried about the coming dusk, we turn onto a real paved road and the pace picks up considerably. I am new to a combat zone, but I know it is not a good idea to be out here after dark.

Fifteen miles down the road, we turn off onto another dirt track again and I see the lights of a sizable base camp shining ahead of the convoy. We roll along parallel to a paved runway and swing through a gate. All the men on the truck remove the magazines from their weapons, and eject the round out of the chamber as we have been taught in training. In base camps, you always carry a loaded magazine in your weapon, but never a round in the chamber and the rifle is always on safe. It is not unusual to have a noncom check your rifle, and woe to the fellow caught disobeying this rule. If the person is lucky, all he will wind up with is several days of KP duty in the mess hall, and they usually reserve a few big, extremely dirty pots for just such miscreants. The mess halls cook in bulk, and some of the pots are big enough for a small kid to climb into for a bath.

O'Brian and I swing down from the truck and join another twenty or so men who made the trip on the trucks. They are like us, new replacements on their way to the first duty stations.

We hear, "Welcome to Tan An. Hey new meat, what's happening back in the states?" from the locals, but they are smiling. They point out the mess hall so we can eat before it closes for the evening. The meal is hot and welcoming, roast beef and potatoes, carrots and peas, and all the cold milk we can drink in waxed paper quart containers. I try to wash away the day's dust by drinking several quarts, but quickly become stuffed.

O'Brian looks across the table, grins and comments. "The food sure is good for a combat zone."

I counter with, "Sure is. I guess they are fattening us up for the kill." We are surprised at the good food, but find later that it is the norm except at the very forward bases.

It is dark now and we are shown to a barracks we can use for the night. We pass through a small square surrounded by unpainted, rough wooden buildings with sandbags stacked around the walls about three feet high. I know it is used to stop shrapnel and small arms fire, but the quantity of sandbags amazes me and I, ever the quick study, know now that I will be up close and personal with many empty sandbags this year.

Another amazing thing is that I hear the unmistakable sound of the Beatles, the Sgt. Pepper's Lonely Hearts Club Band album coming from a record player. All around the square groups of people are sitting down, leaning back against the sandbags drinking what appears to be cold beer. Is that beer? Is it cold? I'll be damned! We sure wound up at the right place tonight. After stowing our meager belongings, we beat feet back to the square.

"Hey you guys, grab a beer. What are your names? Where are you from in the states?" comes from a chorus of voices, and with cold beer in our hands we lean back against the sandbags and survey the scene. I realize that many of the people are nurses, good-looking nurses, even in their OD fatigues. I light up my pipe and inhale a big, intoxicating whiff of Cherry Blend. Everything is suddenly all right with the world.

I look over at O'Brian and say, "Hey, man, we came looking for a combat zone and find party central, at least for tonight. Party hearty!"

The locals explain that Tan An is a hospital as well as a base and choppers bring the wounded in on the airstrip and observation planes also use the strip. Many operations are flown out of this base; with men being carried out when Charley is spotted, and Cobra gun ships are stationed here to support them when they get in a bind.

No one is charging us for the beer and they are good and cold. Our new friends keep them coming and the party is great. I look back at that surreal night in Tan An and remember just how good that beer tasted. It was probably the best I will ever taste in my life. I had no idea that I would be visiting the hospital later several times as a patient. I just enjoyed the night, the music, and all my newfound friends.

Later on, we call it a night and head to the barracks. In the night, I wake up and listen. Something is wrong, but I cannot quite put my finger on it. I am trying to break through the fog of sleep and a little too much liquid refreshment, and with my eyes clearing I see that it is still pitch black outside. Somewhere a loud siren is blaring in the night. A muted, whirring noise passes over the barracks and through the window I can see the darkness split by a bright red light. A loud concussion quickly follows and I hear the thwack and crunch of metal slicing through the barrack walls.

My over-taxed brain finally puts all the clues together and I bolt straight up off the cot screaming.

"Mortar attack, mortar attack," I scream. Now, I have never been in one up to now, but this is sure as hell what they sound like, I am quite convinced.

Another shell rumbles over and turns the dark night into day. I am again treated to the most amazing sounds of metal against wood and metal roofing. The sounds are hard to describe, but very scary when you realize how close you are to them. All around me, dark shapes are stirring and heading for the door. O'Brian is up now, awakened by the din and my frantic shaking of his arm. We follow the crowd out the door and I hope they know where the bunker is and that it is not far away.

A long undulating line of people are running past the barracks and we hear the unmistakable whoosh of another shell passing overhead. Almost as one, we drop to the hard sand and finish our thirty-yard dash on our knees. I can see the bunker doorway ahead now; some brave soul has his arm out the door and he is holding of all things, a candle, a beacon in the night.

We pile into the back wall of the bunker, and I hear the whoosh of air expelled from a set of lungs. I quickly offer my apologies as I am run into from behind and forced harder against the person that I have already half squashed. Several people have candles burning now and the flickering light reveals a mass of humanity all jammed together. I see that half of them are nurses, so I quickly get my arms up over my head to make sure they do not wind up in the wrong place by mistake, since everyone is jammed together.

We are all talking now and no one seems to be hurt, so after a few heart-felt jabs at Charley, as the VC are called, and suggestions as to the occupation of his mother, we introduce ourselves all around.

Monica is the nurse I half squashed and she is from Indiana. Laurie from San Diego is on my other side, and Cliff from Chicago is the person that steam-rollered me from behind. The discussions of home and the people we left behind slowly wane and that siren finally shuts off. We all settle in for a little shut-eye before dawn. Things start very early on an army base, and a mortar attack is not considered a good reason to be sleepy-eyed the next day.

I am surrounded by the heady smells of several different perfumes, still a little buzzed by the beer and falling asleep surrounded by a dozen or more women. Even though no touching or sex is involved, it is just a great place to be. I remind myself that I am a married man, but I have done nothing wrong as bouncing off that nurse was totally accidental, and sleep claims me.

I wake up very early the next morning, the first rays of the sun coming through the open door into my eyes. I am feeling very stiff and my head is pounding. Glancing around I see the bunker is almost empty and as I rise one knee really hurts. Looking down, I realize that my mad midnight dash has worn through one pants leg, and it is now glued to my kneecap with dried blood. I give it a big yank and add more to my pain.

Others are stirring now and O'Brian and I head for the mess hall. I am not sure if I can handle any food this morning, but if I can find a big enough container of coffee and it is not too hot, I just may submerge my head in it. I surprise myself, because the food smells really good and we both shovel it down, not wanting to face that long road on empty stomachs. We empty our canteens and fill them with coffee and head back to the barracks for our belongings, because the convoy is already forming on the road.

This camp will always hold a special place in my heart, because I think we made the transition last night. We came to the base as mere recruits and we are leaving today as soldiers. The training is all in the past, we were in harm's way last night and I think we now deserve the title of soldier. I do not know what will happen in the future, what we will face in the coming year, but I only hope that I can face it squarely and not be found wanting in my duties. The great unknown hangs out there in the future for me and I know a daunting task remains to be faced. I am here in this country ten thousand miles from home and there is no going back for a year. I know there is only two ways to get out of this country. Either I will walk up those stairs into the plane for the flight home, or they will load me into another quite dissimilar one, where all the inhabitants will make the trip back lying horizontally.

I reflect that last night was great, except for the mortar attack, but I do not think my head could handle two nights in a row here. We climb up on the truck, heading for our first duty station, and many new adventures, and unfortunately, many new horrors.

358 days left in country.

Chapter 3
Our First Duty Station

Rach Kein-Feb.1968.

The convoy leaves Tan An and rolls east on Highway Four, one of the few paved roads in the Mekong Delta. O'Brian and I, perched high up on the back of a loaded truck, are treated to a kaleidoscope of new sights and smells. Rice paddies border both sides of the road and stretch far into the distance, as far as our eyes can see. *These people sure grow a lot of rice!* In the rice fields, we can see people everywhere bent over in the hot sun, planting the small rice shoots that will later feed their families through the year with enough left over to sell in the local village markets or to barter for their simple needs. Whole families work together, from the Papa-san, or father, to the smallest child that is capable of walking and doing any work.

We are headed to our assigned duty station, Rach Kein. We have been told in Tan An that this base is twenty miles northwest up Highway Four and ten miles west off the highway. The convoy should arrive there in an hour or so if there are no traffic problems. Other than that, we know nothing of Rach Kein and are quite anxious to get there and see where we will be living and what we will be doing. The paddies stretch on and on, and after an hour we turn right off the highway and pass through a small village and head west on a dirt road. Ah, a dirt road again, the very essence of Viet Nam. Through the open window, the truck driver tells me that he does not know the name of the village, but that they call it checkpoint 69er, and that there are checkpoints every half a dozen miles along the back roads. If convoys get into trouble, they call in on the radio and mention the checkpoint they are close to, so that at the base, they will know where to send help.

We roll on through the choking dust and in fifteen minutes pass into our new base, past a two-story sandbag bunker on the left, manned by two soldiers holding M-16 rifles. Off to the right are wooden frameworks holding barbed wire and rolls of concertina wire, which are obviously moved into the road at night to keep it blocked.

So, this is Rach Kein. My first impression is small and dusty, but that description can be applied to about everything I have seen in this country so far, except Bien Hoa, a large base camp where our flight from the states landed. That could be described as large and dusty. This base is fairly small, laid out at a tee intersection of the road. The straight part of the road passes through the base camp for an eighth of a mile, then out a gate and into the country. The road to the right passes through the camp for another eighth of a mile, then goes through the small town that the base gets its name from, and again passes into the country. There is no gate on this road; the camp merely blends into the town where they intersect, which makes me think this area must be fairly secure. In the coming months, we find that the base is pretty secure, but the outlying roads are not.

The convoy pulls up in a small square to the left of the road, and O'Brian and I jump down, along with four other men that are coming in to join us as replacements. We introduce ourselves all around, and we meet Robby Hernandez, Philip Miller, Bill Howard and Ralph Jacobs. While we are getting acquainted, a sergeant comes by and introduces himself as Sgt. Wainwright, our platoon leader.

"Where are you boys from?" Wainwright asks, and we all tell him where we call home. Our small group is from all over the country. O'Brian is from Chicago, Hernandez is from Texas, Miller is from Pennsylvania, Howard from New York, and I am from Maryland.

At the mention of Maryland, our new platoon leader perks up. "Hey, I'm from Maryland, too, Baltimore to be exact," he volunteers. I am surprised to find someone from close to home halfway around the world, and I explain that I am from Deal Island, which he has never heard of.

I add, "Forty miles south of Ocean City," and that pinpoints it for him. Everybody has heard of Ocean City. He tells me that he lives in a section of Baltimore close to Cherry Hill Park, like the song, and I immediately break into the song about Mary Hill and her wayward life in the park and the sarge chimes right in. There we are, two white guys who cannot carry a tune, singing anyway, and we become fast friends pretty much at that moment.

The sergeant takes us into a stone building with a tile roof, obviously built by the French, as are most of the buildings in this small square. It features solid construction and feels cool, doors missing front and rear, and large open windows with wooden shutters tied back away from the windows. I admire the way the French built their buildings, mostly of stone and always with tile roofs. They built as if they planned to stay much longer than they did. He assigns us cots, and I note they all have mosquito netting over them, as we stow our duffel bags. I am glad we have a good, solid building to bunk in; it is more than I expected.

We talk for several hours, and Wainwright explains that our jobs will be to go out on road clearing trips every morning at 0730 hours. The VC builds roadblocks at night in various places and then booby-traps them, holding up traffic on the roads between bases. We will also escort convoys back and forth between bases. He points out the four jeeps and the three-quarter ton truck parked in the square and tells us they belong to the Falcon platoon, of which we will be members. He further adds that our platoon also pulls bunker guard at night, and that we have one assigned bunker on the perimeter. A final job is listening posts, three men teams sent out in four directions each night, setting up in different places to be the eyes and ears of the base, an early warning system for Rach Kein.

I can see this last bit of information bothers O'Brian, and I do not blame him. While we were in advanced infantry training at Fort Polk, Louisiana, he had to get permission to fly home one weekend to attend the funeral of a close friend. That friend was in Viet Nam and out on a listening post, and the VC threw a grenade in and killed all three men. The information that we will be on listening posts pretty much upsets me too, but I know there is nothing I can do about it.

We inspect our new surroundings. Just outside the back door is a sandbag bunker all of four feet high, so you have to crawl into it. The sergeant says the base occasionally has a mortar attack at night, so to expect it and head for the bunker when we hear the warning siren. He does not mention that three or four rounds have to drop in before the siren is set off, or that sometimes Charley will quit shelling, wait until the siren shuts off, and commence firing just as we start moving around again. This is something we will learn shortly.

The sergeant continues with, "Rumor is this town was once a VC supply base and recuperation area, and then the Ninth Division came in a couple of years ago and ran Charley out. They then took over the area and built this base, and the enemy is still teed off about the situation." He also tells us that we are replacing men that were injured or killed several weeks ago in an ambush of the Falcon Platoon while they were out on a road-clearing mission.

He himself replaced Sgt. Marsh, who was hit five times by thirty caliber bullets, but survived, and is now in Japan recuperating before going home. More unsettling information and it helps to drive home the fact that we are now caught up in a deadly serious occupation, and we have almost a year to go before that flight home.

About this time, a young Vietnamese boy comes through the doorway, dressed in army fatigues way too big for him with a big smile on his face.

"This is Lon, our Tiger Scout," Sgt. Wainwright says, and introduces all of us. I am not impressed with this person. He looks no older than fifteen or sixteen, maybe one hundred pounds with a rifle, and I wonder what use he will be in the platoon. I notice Lon is missing his left arm above the elbow, and the stump is bandaged. After he passes though, the sarge says he lost that arm in the ambush. The VC shot a B-40 rocket at the quarter-ton truck and it hit a bracket holding a fifty-caliber machine gun and exploded.

After the ambush, they found Lon in a ditch, unconscious, with his mangled arm bleeding badly. The medics stabilized him and they flew him to Tan An hospital, where his arm was removed.

"Lon spent two weeks there, then checked himself out and hopped a convoy back here, so he is a tough little character," Sergeant Wainwright informs us. "He might not be much to look at, but he really helps the platoon." Maybe the sarge saw the look on my face, but after hearing the story and having my new-found Baltimore friend vouch for him, I decided that maybe Lon was okay, after all. As time went by, we were to find that Lon was more than okay. He was fiercely protective of his platoon mates, and made sure we got the best prices when we buy anything from the Vietnamese. I soon become a good friend of his, and came to consider him a younger brother, albeit with a funny accent.

The sergeant inspects our M-16 rifles and is satisfied with their degree of cleanliness. Training has taught us to keep them clean at all times.

"Keep them that way all the time, you might need them to save your life some day," he councils, and then we head over to the chow hall, built at one side of the square. Once again, the food is great. Its seems that the army goes out of their way to see that the troops, at least in the base camps, get good food; maybe to pay us back for the job we have to perform. The building is clean and airy, built of unpainted clapboards, with screening from waist height on up to the ceiling, and with screened doors for access, in stark contrast to the heavier built French buildings.

Inside, long tables are built of one-by-four boards with integral seats, like large picnic tables. It looks like the room will seat about one hundred men at a time. The building is a carbon copy of the other mess halls we have seen here in Viet Nam.

We go back to the barracks after chow, and meet our fellow platoon members. The Falcon Platoon consists of approximately twenty men to operate the four jeeps and the truck. Two of the jeeps have 106mm recoilless rifles mounted on them, two jeeps are equipped with thirty caliber machine guns, and the truck mounts a big fifty caliber machine gun. Each vehicle also has a strange vertical piece of angle iron mounted to the front bumper, about five feet tall with the edge facing forward sharpened. I am at a loss to figure out what this is, and one of our new platoon members explains that this is to cut fine wires that are sometimes strung across the road at about neck height when you are sitting down. Damn! This is yet another piece of information that I could do without hearing. How about some happy news for a change!

We six new guys sit on the bunker behind our building, digesting what we have learned today. The platoon certainly has the firepower available, but that mention of the prior ambush, just two weeks ago, sure puts the damper on our spirits. I fire up my pipe and take a few deep pulls that calm my nerves. My friends light cigarettes and medicate themselves in their own way. Tomorrow is a new day, and we have to turn in early because we have to be up at six to eat and go out on the jeeps. Our training is all in the past, tomorrow we go out and use that training in this most serious game of cat and mouse with our enemy. *Let me see, tomorrow will be 356 days left in our one-year tour of duty, and that is a damned long time!*

The morning arrives, and the sarge awakens us. We sleep in our clothes, and there is no place to wash up, so we are out of our bunks quickly and outside. It is a beautiful, warm late February morning, the sun just rising above the horizon. No dust in the air, the base is just starting to stir, and the temperature is already in the eighties. Back home, it would be pretty nippy this time of year, but the air here is great. We go off to the mess hall for a hearty, but quick breakfast, because the road awaits us. Back in the square, the sergeant assigns us new guys to our vehicles. O'Brian draws shotgun on a machine gun jeep, handling the radio, and the sarge assigns me to the back of the same jeep, standing behind the thirty-caliber machine gun. Laughingly, I point out to our platoon leader that O'Brian would be a better choice here.

"He is a smaller target," I point out to Wainwright, but he is not about to change his mind. My good friend is not amused. I climb up into my new office, and note that the floor is covered with the old, familiar sandbags. Charley likes to bury mines in the road, too. We receive an area of operations map, or AO map, which each vehicle carries. On the map is marked each checkpoint on the road, and as we travel, the sergeant will call back to the base when we clear each checkpoint. That lets TAC, or Tactical Area Command, know that everything is going okay, and our location at any given moment.

The maps are extremely detailed and are small scale, covering only about twenty square miles. They are made of hundreds of aerial photos, pieced together by mapmakers, cut and glued together on a backing. The roads, buildings, and other features are then hand inked in, and a high definition picture of the whole thing taken. This picture is then laminated with a thin layer of plastic on each side to protect it, and the finished product is a totally life-like rendition of the area, much better than simple drawn maps. I am awed at the complicated process needed to produce these maps, but I know that in the states a hard to read map can get you lost, but over here, a bad map can get us killed.

We start the engines, and out of the main gate we roll. Our jeep is third in line, behind the truck and the platoon leader's jeep. As we clear the gate, I feed ammo into the machine gun, chamber a round, and then slip it onto safe. I also do the same thing to my rifle, and, up and down the vehicles, everyone does the same. We roll along about twenty miles an hour to keep the dust down, spaced about fifty yards apart. Still, the dust cuts down on vision badly, and we resort to the goggles hanging from clips on the dashboard.

We clear the ten miles of road to checkpoint 69er first, as it is the main convoy route, then we will go back and clear the road to Can Guioc. The road to this town turns off the main road and heads north about three miles outside of Rach Kein. The morning goes smoothly for a while, but I feel very nervous and I keep a death grip on the machine gun. As we turn a dusty corner three quarters of the way up the road, there it is, our first roadblock.

It is an unsubstantial jumble of chunks of dried paddy mud, and chopped up pieces of a small tree trunk. We could drive right over it if not for Charley's nasty habit of booby-trapping some of his obstacles. We halt, and walk forward carefully to examine the junk on the road. No sign of any explosives or trip wires, but we know our enemy is not that sloppy. One of the platoon members, Schultz, comes forward and places a couple of half-pound charges of C-4 on the

road, and calls out a warning. He then lights the fuses and we all take cover behind the vehicles. A couple of booms later, most of the stuff is off the road, and
we do another careful check of the area, then mount up and roll west toward
checkpoint 69er.

We arrive at that checkpoint, the little town at the intersection of our
dirt road and Highway Four. There is a small store there run by a Mama-San
and her two daughters, and our platoon members tell us they always stop there
and take a short break. They wash down the road's dust with soft drinks all
around. Sgt. Wainwright introduces us new guys to the Mama-San and her two
daughters, the oldest one named Anh.

She is small, a teen-ager, with flashing dark eyes and an enticing smile.
I see right away that she is the main attraction here, much more so than the
drinks. It appears half the platoon is quite taken by her, and you can see she
enjoys the attention, but she does not intend to be a soldier's plaything. Mama-
San knows what brings the platoon to her humble store and she hovers nearby,
keeping a close eye on her daughter and the soldiers. Many of the Vietnamese
women are overly friendly with soldiers, but I can tell Anh is not one of those,
which seems to make her more desirable in the soldier's eyes.

We all purchase Cokes in very old, well-used bottles, the glass quite
abraded from the bottling equipment. It looks like they have been recycled for
the last hundred years. Surprisingly, there must be a bottling company somewhere in the area, probably Saigon. The drinks are warm but the woman cures
this by giving us none too clean glasses, and reaches into a crude wooden box
with a block of ice in it surrounded with rice chaff for insulation. She chips
off ice with an ancient ice pick, puts some in each glass, and then performs an
amusing little ceremony I have never seen before. I will see it countless times
over the coming year, all across the country. Since the rumor is that Charley occasionally puts ground glass or battery acid in some bottles, and the proprietor
knows this, she opens each bottle, pours a tiny amount into the glass, and takes
a small sip. She then wipes the rim of the glass with a dirty towel she carries at
her waist, and with the safety of her product thus proven, she smiles and hands
the soldier his glass and bottle. She repeats this with each man. The drinks cost
us ten piasters each, or around ten cents.

The family speaks good simple English, using some French and Vietnamese words and phrases that the platoon understands and that we new guys will
soon pick up. Lon is there as an interpreter, so we can carry on a good conver-

sation with them. Break time over, we load up, and as we pull out, Anh stands by the side of the road as she wishes us a good day and to please come back and see them again.

Then, show time over, she shuts off the smile and returns to the store. I have the feeling that before too long, she will make some unsuspecting young Vietnamese boy's life very miserable.

As we leave, our driver tells us that the rumor is that the family's father was a VC, who was killed about five years ago, so Mama-San opened the store to feed the family. I do not know if that rumor is true, but no one in the platoon seems to hold it against the family. Of course, it is quite possible that the mother is VC also, and is reporting our movements to the enemy. Over here, you never know who the enemy is. In the daylight, they are all innocent Vietnamese, but after dark, it can be another story.

We head back in the direction of Rach Kein, and turn left at the road going to Can Guioc. Up the road a quarter mile is the spot where the ambush happened several weeks ago, and the driver points it out as we stop short, and with rifles ready, walk carefully into a grove of trees surrounding a Vietnam-ese hooch. The VC had been hiding behind the hooch when they sprang the ambush, so now the platoon dismounts every day, leaving several men to guard the weapons, and checks out the area cautiously before proceeding on down the road. The only trouble is, there are hundreds of places where they can hide on this road, giving them an effective ambush. If we stop and check every one we will be out here until dark. We go by that area every day for months, and I shudder every time.

We continue up the road, everyone swiveling their head around and try-ing to see three hundred and sixty degrees at one time, and come across two more roadblocks constructed exactly the same way as the last one. What the hell! Does Charley have one guy that does all the roadblocks? Is there a yellow pages over here, and if you need a roadblock, do you look under "R" and send a message to his village? I ask the sergeant if I can blow them, and after assuring him I received demo training, he tells me okay.

I keep the charges to a half pound, but use three of them. More than a half pound damages the road surface, but the three charges give me more bang for the buck, and since the real reason for the explosive is to set off any hidden booby traps, I reason that multiple small charges are more efficient. Sgt. Wainwright keeps a careful eye on me as I prepare the charges, but I notice he stays a prudent distance away as I lay the charges and erase the roadblock.

Evidently he is satisfied I can handle explosives without killing myself, and I become his go-to man for the next several months when we encounter a roadblock. It sucks to be drafted and sent over here, so I am determined to use up as much of the army's C-4 as I can. I do not worry, I know they will make more, and it is really the only fun this job offers.

We reach the outskirts of Can Guioc, and turn around at an unoccupied base just outside the town. It appears to be freshly built, little used, and I wonder what the story is. Little do I know that, several months hence, we will be sent here, along with the rest of the unit, and find it a poor substitute for Rach Kein.

We head back to base, getting there just in time for a late lunch, which is great as usual. I have never been much for meat loaf, but the cooks here seem to have it mastered. The mashed potatoes and gravy also go down great, and we even have biscuits and apple pie. To any Viet Nam era cook who might be reading this, my hat is off to you. You people did a great job and made the war livable for us grunts!

Our platoon has the afternoon off, once we get back in off the road. We have done our jobs for the day. Now, we have several choices of relaxation. One of our favorites is to stretch out on the sandbag bunker behind our barracks where it is shady in the afternoon and talk of the real world we left behind. We brag about our wives or girlfriends, and everyone thinks their woman is the best in the world. Today, though, the conversation makes us homesick and the talk dies out quickly.

I go into our quarters and pull out several dog-eared letters from my wife, and reread them four or five times, but this is no comfort today, so O'Brian and I go over to the EM club, or enlisted men's club, and order up cold beers. We talk about everything but home now, carefully avoiding that subject.

I want to mention one thing now that really irked me while I was in Viet Nam, something that had nothing to do with combat. To a soldier in such a situation, the letters from home are the most important thing in his life, and he eagerly awaits them. Every soldier saves them, reading them repeatedly, until they are wrinkled and creased, especially if they are from his girlfriend or wife. They are a soldier's anchor, and something to hold onto when the going gets tough or dangerous. Unfortunately, some girlfriends, and even some wives, found the year of separation too much, so some men received Dear John letters. Such letters were devastating to the recipient, causing them to fail to pay close attention to what they were doing and I have something to say on this subject.

The woman that sends a Dear John letter to a man in a combat zone is the lowest form of human being on this earth. Okay, you are lonely and confused, I can understand that, but for God's sake do not send such a letter. Keep your big mouth shut and keep sending him letters of hope and love. It may be hard to do, but is infinitely better than the letter. Tell him when he is home, and out of danger. Sure, it will hurt, but not nearly as much as telling him when he is ten thousand miles away doing dangerous work.

I thank God that my own wife, Wanda, stayed true to me and kept up a barrage of letters the whole year. Her letters gave me hope and buoyed me up, when I was feeling down and sick of the damn war. Please, if you read this, women, keep this in mind.

The EM club is cool and quiet and you can hear current music from the states on their record player. The club is located to the right of our barracks, beside the square where we park our vehicles. We have a really great location, cold beer on one side, and the mess hall on the other. The club has electricity so the beer is cold, and there are fans, with big wooden blades, to keep it relatively cool inside. It also employs a few Vietnamese women dressed in miniskirts to work as waitresses. They serve the beer and various packaged snacks like potato chips, crackers and peanuts. We soldiers keep up a good-natured banter with the women, as happens everywhere in bars, but we know they are off-limits. The army frowns on relationships with the local women, but of course, that does not stop them from happening.

If you insist, the LT will have a talk with you about the transgression. I have only been married a few months, so the women hold little attraction for me. I am much more interested in the cold beer, and you get to sample different brands all the time. The army buys beer in bulk on this side of the world to lessen shipping problems, so one day you may get Australian Victoria Bitter in a distinctive green and gold can, the next day Japanese Suntory. They never serve the local Vietnamese swill, Biere Larue or Biere 33. At times, they also have beer from the states, usually Pabst Blue Ribbon or Schlitz. All the beer is in cans of course, and I feel that the cans alter the taste, so I try to remember, unsuccessfully, the taste of beer in bottles. It is interesting to note, that since I came home, over forty years ago, that I cannot remember ever purchasing beer in cans.

A word about the military monetary system is probably in order here. Soldiers receive pay once a month, and in this country it is always in MPC or military payment certificates. This is all paper money, even what would be coins in the states, and is cheaply made and smaller than U.S. bills. The main reason for this is to keep American greenbacks from getting into the local economy, and then winding up in the enemy's hands. American money is in much higher demand on the arms market, is accepted much more readily, and buys more than Vietnamese money.

The army also changes the design of the script occasionally without warning, so the old money will be worthless overnight. This keeps the Vietnamese from hoarding too much MPC for long, as they could be rich one day and bankrupt the next. I witnessed one changing of the script, and the consternation it caused the locals was immense. Changing the script also made it hard on the hustlers in the American ranks, because they could lose out overnight, and the money was worthless in the states.

The army also kept a very close control on American money you brought from home, or had sent to you. One of the first things you had to do when you got into the country was to show all your money, turn out your pockets, and have your duffel bag inspected by a sergeant. Then they exchanged all your money for MPC. You received warnings that any money received from home had to be turned in and exchanged for the army money. If they caught you with U.S. currency during the year, it was a court-martial offense. In addition, the last thing you did before you climbed on the freedom bird at Bien Hoa, was to have your MPC converted back to U.S. currency. If you had too much MPC to convert, you had a lot of explaining to do. Any Vietnamese money you had, you were stuck with, as they would not accept it, but that fact has filtered back down to us soldiers, so we made sure to spend or convert it to MPC before flying to Bien Hoa to process out of the country.

Only idiots turned in greenbacks they received. U.S. currency was in great demand, so you could go to any roadside stand or small town and convert it. If we accepted Vietnamese currency, we could almost double the money, or if we wanted MPC, we could get up to a third over face value. The exchange rate varied of course, from month to month, and town to town.

A good bargainer really helped in this situation, so we always took Lon and let him do the talking. He never failed to get us a good deal. We always gave him a small percentage, which he carefully squirreled away to give to his family. We usually requested MPC when converting money, because that was all we could spend on base, but the Vietnamese would accept anything, though greenbacks were their first choice.

To make handling script simpler in the EM club, you purchased a book of tickets, or "chits", as they were called, each one being worth five cents with the books costing five or ten dollars. You paid for beer or snacks by tearing out and handing over the appropriate amount of chits to the waitress. The army kept the price of beer and snacks low, and I think we paid around a quarter for a beer and ten cents for snacks. The army made sure that liquid refreshment was available both in the states and abroad, and with the on-base clubs open all day, I think this policy created quite a few drunks.

For three months, the Falcon platoon cleared the roads every morning, and luckily, we never had any more ambushes. However, getting shot at from a wood line a quarter mile away happened almost every day, and it was quite frustrating, because most of the time we could not shoot back. Charley would take a couple of shots, and we would hear the bang and hear the bullets pass overhead, or strike a vehicle. We just kept on rolling, because we knew that at the area we were in, return fire might wind up in that ARVN camp a half mile in one direction, or maybe the village, or ville, as we called it, just through the trees. Most of the area we operated in had either army bases, villages, or Vietnamese bases in close proximity. We could not just open up any time we wanted, especially with the larger weapons.

The 106 recoilless rifle round, for instance, could easily travel for several miles if nothing hard stopped it. Therefore, it was necessary to call in for permission to fire back before you let loose. Back at base, they would check the map, the approximate location of the offending fire and your location to see if it was safe to fire back. Most of the time the answer would be no, so we did not bother to check. Now, if someone received a wound, or the fire was more than a few potshots, it would make it easier to get permission to retaliate.

I must confess that at times we would have some of the guys a few vehicles down fire their weapons to make it sound as if we were under more intense fire, and then permission would be forthcoming. Evidently, the transmission of M-16 fire through the radio back to base changed the sound enough so that they did not recognize that the shots were coming from American rifles.

We felt it was necessary at times to "buy" respect from Charley. If you never returned fire when he shot at the platoon, he got bolder and the incidents of potshots would increase, as well as the quantity of roadblocks he laid down at night. Therefore, every once in a while when he annoyed us, we would check the map to see if it was at all safe to return fire, and if so, we would obliterate the offending wood line with machine gun fire and a round or two of 106 recoilless. Then, as the jungle smoked, we would turn the guns back to the centerline of the jeeps; mount up, and head on down the line. It really seemed as if the show of force impressed the enemy quite a bit, as the incidents of annoying fire would cease for a few days. The sergeant could really get into trouble for allowing this, but he understood the necessity of showing a little force occasionally, and it likely saved lives in the end.

Along with clearing the roads each day, we also had to escort convoys back to Dong Tam. Most of the time they ran unescorted, but sometimes they received attacks, so we would get escort duty for a while. This really ruined our afternoons off. The extra show of force always helped, because most of the people involved were part time VC who felt the need to harass a convoy, and they seemed to respect those 106 mm recoilless rifles that could reach out and touch them from a long distance!

There was a section of road that was especially troublesome for convoys, the ten mile stretch of dirt road between Tan An and Dong Tam. The jungle came down close to the road in some places, which made it easier for the enemy to operate. It soon received the name of Ambush Alley, and several convoys were attacked with loss of life and several trucks. We would escort the convoys for a while and that really helped. While I was in the Falcon platoon for three months, none of the convoys we escorted were ambushed, though the incidents of harassing fire were numerous.

Several of our other duties at the camp are bunker guard and listening posts. Bunker guard is no problem, and we only have to do it once or twice a week, as it is shared with the whole platoon. Four men spend the night at the bunker, two up top behind the machine gun, and two downstairs sleeping, and we change places every two hours.

Up top, you keep watch through starlight scopes, a marvelous invention. They look something like large binoculars, and they magnify light from the moon or stars. You cannot pick out individual features through the scope, but they allow you to see the outlines of someone moving in black against a light green background.

If you see movement and it is obviously coming closer, you can call in to TAC and request a flare be sent up. If they agree, in a minute or two, we hear a big bang from the mortar section, which is located to the immediate right of our bunker, and a streak of light would ascend. It would culminate in a flare with a parachute, and a blinding light that illuminated one whole side of the perimeter for over a minute. It also illuminated us, so we crouched down behind the sandbag wall in front of us for cover while we scanned the area, looking for the enemy.

The only onerous part of bunker guard was getting the machine gun and a thousand rounds of ammo fifteen feet up to the top of the bunker on a rickety ladder, and then down again in the morning, as you could not leave an unsecured weapon in the bunker all day.

Bunker guard was almost fun at times. You were up there fifteen feet in the air, kicked back with the world in front of you. It was nice and cool after sundown, and we always brought drinks and snacks along, and usually a radio. We could sit there and shoot the breeze, sing along with the music, and enjoy the conversation with our friends. Topics were always girls, fast cars, and what we were going to do when we got back to the real world. No one talked about getting hurt or dying here; you saved that for when you were alone with your own thoughts.

Another job that we had was the most distasteful, the one that everybody hated, and that was listening post, which we had to serve on about once a week. After dark three men would gather their weapons and a radio and meet at the main gate. Once there, one of the gate guards leads us through the serpentine maze of barbed wire and concertina wire that is set up every night to block the road. Out we would go into the dark, down the dirt road several hundred feet, and off into the field on one side or the other. We find a place and set up for the night.

I never felt more naked and alone than I did on those nights. Our job was to detect enemy movement toward the camp from this direction, and there would be posts set up on all four sides of the camp. The only cover we would have, and it is minimal, was the dry side of a rice paddy dike, or perhaps a lone tree. It was important to be able to see all around you. If someone was out there to kill you, you have to spot him first to survive.

One person would stay awake at all times and use a starlight scope to scan often through three hundred and sixty degrees. We had to sit still, be silent, and report in every half hour, talking very quietly into the mike.

"This is Lima Peru, sit rep negative, over," I speak into the mike, letting the base know that we are awake and keeping watch and that we are still alive.

The radio operator back at base comes back with, "TAC, affirmative, out." Sit rep meant situation report, no problems. Our contact with base disappears with a little hiss of static, and it feels so very lonely out here. We keep the radio turned down so low we have to lie down with our ear against the speaker and our mouth against the mike. We sleep only fitfully, awakening often to make sure the person on watch is still awake. It is always an eerie, restless night, and we are always so glad when 0500 hundred hours rolls around and we get back into camp for some real sleep.

We always radio the main gate that we are on the way toward the base. We always come in before sunup in case we are being observed, so the enemy cannot see the area where we are setting up. Any VC with half a brain knows that the listening posts are out in four directions, and usually within a hundred yards of base, so it does not take a lot of figuring to know roughly where we are at night. Just knowing this fact keeps me uneasy all night.

The last job we had was a lot less hard on the nerves, though not entirely without danger, but I enjoyed it. We are called on, after the infrequent mortar attacks to blow up mortar rounds that have landed and do not detonate. Charlie's rounds are often ancient, and spend a lot of time hidden underground, or in water, so a good number of them fail to explode.

Another problem is mud. If a round lands in soft mud, many times the shock is not enough to set off the impact detonator. There is plenty of soft mud between the mess hall and an officer's quarters on the other side, due to a tidal pool that covers several acres. It is near the center of the base, an area where the VC seems to be zeroed in. A round hitting the mud burrows down several feet and leaves a telltale conical bump as the mud is forced upwards.

The size of the funnel tells you the caliber of the round down there, and most of the time the enemy uses 60MM rounds in this area. I warn everyone away from the area, though the red flag marking the crater usually keeps people away. I prepare a half pound charge with a four-foot fuse, then gently push it down the hole, trying to get it right next to the buried round. I then stack three or four sandbags around the funnel because the force from an explosive takes the path of least resistance. When it encounters the sandbags, it is compressed for a split second and puts more force on the shell.

Nothing is worse than trying to set off a buried round, and have only the C-4 detonate. Now you have a round down there that has been shocked twice and did not go off, so do I walk up and repeat the process, or do I wait to make sure there is no delayed blast? I created this situation several times, so I endeavored to have it happen as little as possible. Finally, I scan the area one more time, holler "fire in the hole," light the fuse and take cover. A big boom follows, along with a shower of mud, and the offending round is history.

The sarge also calls on me to blow dud mortar rounds that malfunction and never leave the mortar tube when fired. The crews stockpile these rounds, and every couple of weeks O'Brian and I load them on the back of the jeep to take them out to an open field several hundred yards outside the base's west gate. I am in my element now and thoroughly enjoy the job. We kill many sandbags though, and as the season wears on, the field becomes pockmarked and littered with metal fragments, pieces of sandbags, and clumps of sand. As for the sandbags, the base has an inexhaustible supply of them, and I am proud to say that I kill a lot more sandbags than I do the enemy.

The platoon settles into our daily routine of rising early and clearing the roads. The convoy escort duty appears relatively safe and we do not mind too much when we lose our afternoons off to escort the trucks. We know we are helping to keep our fellow soldiers safe. If not for the listening posts and the ever-present heat, this would be an idyllic or at least a passable job. We have almost a year to serve in this combat job and I can think of no better place to do our time.

Unfortunately, major changes loom on the not-too-distant horizon, and we will look back on this time as the easiest part of our one-year tour in this damn war that we do not wish to fight.

340 days left in country.

Chapter 4
It Does Rain In Hell

Rach Kein-March 1968

Most people would tell you it does not rain in hell. I am standing here in a combat zone in what I consider a good approximation of hell, and I have to tell you that it most definitely does. When the rain stops, the sun will be back on duty and the one hundred degree heat will turn this base into the world's largest sauna.

I stare from the doorway of the old French building we use as a barracks, and the rain is falling vertically in such profusion that the nipa palm fronds on the trees across the street are bending downward. It is the early part of the rainy season; it rains every morning, relents for several hours, and then comes down again. We dig out the vehicles that were stuck in the morning but the afternoon rain will liquefy the drying mud and they will be stuck again in the two-foot deep mess. All of the army's vehicles are four-wheel or six-wheel drive but they cannot triumph over the mud. I have seen a pair of two and a half ton trucks chained together with all ten tires spinning on both trucks. Their differentials are hung up on the slightly firmer ground between the axles.

"Getting a little damp out there," points out Sergeant Vickers, in his usual understated way. "This is nothing. Wait another couple of weeks and the only things that will move will be you sad sacks on foot and helicopters." It is so kind of the sarge to make this observation and I hope he has some other pearls of wisdom to help make my day brighter.

My platoon, the Falcons, will be going out on a medicap operation to the village of Ap Cong as soon as the rain relents and the mud dries up a little. When the sun shines again it will bake the mud into a brick-like consistency in several hours, only to return to mud with the afternoon rain. We plan our ten-mile drive there in the drier part of the day, do our job in the village in the pouring rain and wait until the mud dries up some to return back to base. The rain, like the tide, waits for no man in this country during the rainy season.

We do these medicap operations every month, going to a different village each time. It is part of the army's plan to make the Vietnamese like us. We keep hearing, "Win the hearts and minds of the people and we will win the war." *Oh yeah, and Mickey Mouse is a Rhodes Scholar!*

We go out to the villages with food for the adults and candy for the kids or baby-sans as the Vietnamese call them. We take medics with us and they examine anyone sick and then clean, dress their wounds, and hand out medicine. We also take five-gallon tins of kerosene to the villagers and give one to each family. Those tins are a favorite with the people as they can cook and fill their lanterns for lighting for a month or more on just one of the containers.

We talk to the adults through Lon, our interpreter, looking for information on the whereabouts of the local VC. Lon is good at this; they will often give him information that they would not tell us since he is a fellow citizen. We have discovered that what the villagers do not say is often more important than what they do say.

We also play with the baby-sans as we hand out candy and old magazines we have accumulated. They seem fascinated by the magazines, which they cannot read. They stare at the pictures, pointing and talking excitedly. They must think that the U. S. is a strange place with all those big cars, and the people wearing what must seem to them very strange clothing.

It is now near 1100 hours, and the rain stops as if someone has turned off a giant switch in the heavens. It is our signal to clean our weapons, oil them, and load the vehicles with supplies. Once we accomplish this, we take a smoke break, sitting on the bunker behind our barracks. The sun is doing its job, and the plastic material the sandbags are made of is almost dry. What mud is left is no big deal to us; we have partially dried mud up to our knees and smeared on our uniforms from the earlier job of getting vehicles unstuck. We will be living with mud for the next three months, and if it is less than a foot deep, we barely pay it any mind. Our platoon motto should be, "mud happens."

As the mud dries up, we mount our four vehicles; swing by the infirmary to pick up several doctors and medics, and head out the gates toward the village with the deep-cleated tires slinging hunks of mud through the air.

We head west toward the village, the main command vehicle calling back to TAC (Tactical Area Command) as we pass checkpoints on the road. We are reporting in so they know we have encountered no problems on the road. We drive three jeeps that are on one radio frequency, so we can talk to each other, and the command three-quarter truck is on the frequency the base uses. This prevents idle jeep-to-jeep chatter from clogging the main radio channel. We head down the road at thirty miles an hour, anticipating helping some Vietnamese instead of hunting the VC for a change.

The coming of the rainy season has caused a marked change in the trees and greenery, which had been showing the strain of six months of rainless, heat-searing days. The jungle has taken on an intense green color, while multicolored wild flowers are springing up in the edges of the jungle and along the roadside. As we pass by in our road-clearing operations, we notice the freshly planted rice seems to grow an inch a day.

As we round a dusty corner, we hear rifle fire from ahead. It sounds like intermixed AK-47 and .30-caliber carbine, so we know the fight is between the ARVNs (Army of The Republic of Viet Nam) and VC because our Vietnamese comrades use mostly surplus Korean War-era rifles. The fire is sporadic and sounds half-hearted, so we continue until we sight a half dozen of the ARVNs standing at the roadside, firing into the rice paddy on the south side of the road.

"VC ok, VC ok, you shoot," one of the soldiers tells us in broken English. He points out over the rice paddy, and in the distance we see two enemy soldiers running toward the jungle. They are at least three hundred meters away, which is too far for the ARVN rifles to be effective. Our own M-16s are not going to work very well at that distance either.

I jump up on the hood of the jeep for a better look and a better shot, as the two VC halt, turn around, and fire toward us. Several bullets pass close to us and we hear the angry buzzes of .30 caliber bees traveling at over two thousand feet per second.

Ok now, up to this point, it was just a small fight between the two adversaries but it just became more personal in a hurry. Those little SOBs are now shooting at O'Brian and me! We do not take this kindly and with a quick glance at me, my friend jumps into the jeep and turns it sideways in the road, the barrel of the 106mm recoilless rifle aimed toward the fleeing enemy. He then jumps into the rear seat beside the gun, starts cranking the barrel up, and sighting in on the quarry.

I run to the back of the jeep, yank open the breech of the weapon and load the big projectile. We are working quickly as our training kicks in; the VC are close to the edge of the jungle and taking cover. We have no time to spare and I tap O'Brian on the right shoulder, a sign that the breech is closed and I am against the jeep. This is necessary to keep me from being killed by the back blast out of the rear of the weapon.

The 106 weapon is essentially a big rocket, so the propellant blast out of the rear will kill anyone up to one hundred and fifty feet behind it. I close my eyes and hold onto the back of the jeep, and I hear the tremendous whoomph as the gun goes off and feel the tremendous blast of heat on my neck and the movement of quickly displaced air.

We look out over the rice paddy and watch the black projectile flash toward the running men, faster than our eyes can follow. I have set the timer on the front of the round at two hundred fifty meters as I loaded it into the chamber, and it explodes in a blinding red flash behind the two men. Perfect, my guess on the distance has been right on the money.

The smoke dissipates from the explosion and the men have disappeared. We grab our M-16s and several bandoliers of ammo and head for the spot where the round exploded. The ARVNs follow us, chattering excitedly in their almost musical language filled with odd inflections. They seem happy and I am starting to think that in the span of thirty seconds I have helped kill two human beings.

We reach the spot and find it easily due to the large amount of blood we find on the ground and vegetation. There is one bloody flip-flop lying on the ground but no sign of any bodies. We walk another twenty yards to the edge of the jungle and find the remains of two AK-47s, their receivers missing the stocks. They are blackened, bent, and hardly recognizable as weapons. We keep looking for bodies among the trees, but find nothing.

Something hits me on the back of the neck and I brush it off quickly. There are all kinds of bugs in the trees here. What I encounter looks like strawberry jam and my mind halts for a second. *Strawberry jam, my mind questions?* I suddenly realize what it is and as I look up it is splattered all over the fronds on the palm trees. I realize we will not be finding any bodies here today. We gather the damaged weapons and head back to the road. Some things a human should not have to see. It does not help that I had a hand in this.

We go back to the jeeps, explain what has happened, and turn over the weapons. The sergeant will be writing out a report on this action when we get back to the base camp. All around us, our fellow soldiers congratulate us on the "kill," but we feel no elation. I feel oddly hollow, no real emotion, just a flatness that is hard to describe.

This is the first time that I actually see men die in front of my weapon. We have exchanged fire with VC in the jungle and lobbed a few recoilless rounds into the woods when they harassed a convoy we were escorting. In those instances, you never knew if you hit anyone and it was easy to tell yourself you did no real harm. This was a lot different. This time there was zero doubt.

I tell myself that those two VC have likely killed Americans in the past and would do so in the future. My mind accepted this and let me be. I knew that I had passed an important watershed in my life. I have found out that I can kill if necessary and my mind is uneasy about the whole thing. My old Drill Sergeant would be proud of me but am I pleased with myself? I think I have to answer that with a resounding no.

We proceed on to the village and park at the edge of Ap Cong. This village is fair-sized with about thirty hooches scattered around in haphazard fashion. There are numerous nipa-palm trees and some larger coconut trees with tall, curved trunks with the fruit near the forty-foot high top. I have always wanted to try a fresh coconut, just off the tree. That treat is a long way up in the air, and I know the LT will take a dim view of shooting some down even if we warn him first.

All the hooches have the ever-present big earthenware pots situated below the eaves of the roofs to catch rainwater. They are all full of clean, cool water due to the recent rains. We splash the bugs off the surface, empty our canteens, and fill them from the pots. This water tastes much better than the plastic tasting water we get from the water tanks on base. These tanks have an internal plastic coating and the water absorbs the taste as the tanks sit in the one-hundred degree heat for days on end.

Many of the villagers gather in the center of the village as we unload from our vehicles. The baby-sans fly out of the hooches, laughing and looking forward to candy and romping with the soldiers. I think that kids are the same the world over. The language may be different but if you show them the least kindness, they are all over you. They are non-judgmental, inquisitive, and fun to play with no matter where they live.

The adults line up, talking to us in simple English. They smile widely, because they know we will be curing their ailments and handing out food and necessities. They have seen this drill before. I have too, and I know most of what we give them will wind up on the black market in the nearest town. Gifts of food are good, but they prefer the few piasters they will get from the town merchants.

The baby-sans clamor for candy and we are happy to oblige. Jenks has received a box of peanut brittle from his family at last mail call. It is his favorite, but he saved most of it for the kids. They try the treat they have never seen before and relish it. Thirty pairs of hands reach out, so the brittle does not go far. We came prepared though, as other men have saved candy sent from home and we have brought the tropical chocolate bars out of SPs, or Sunday Packs.

The Red Cross sends out the Sunday Packs, and the name derives from the fact that they are given to us on Sundays. The boxes arrive here monthly, packed with cigarettes in cartons, shaving cream, razors, and various other sundries. Each platoon splits up the articles, and the wheeling and dealing attending the sharing of cigarettes is something to behold.

There are enough cigarettes in the box so that each platoon member receives at least half a carton. Some cigarettes such as Marlboros and Benson and Hedges are in greater demand so men wanting these receive fewer packs. I always waited to choose until I got whatever no one else wanted, and received a full carton.

Very occasionally, there would be pipe tobacco in the box, which I received, as no one wanted it. Later on during the month, I would trade or sell some of my cigarettes when the heavy smokers needed more. When things got really tight, some smokers would go to the clerk's office and borrow writing paper to roll their own. They would borrow some of my pipe tobacco and produce a big stiff joint that tasted putrid, but by that time they would smoke anything. Tobacco calmed our nerves and made the day-to-day routine a little more bearable. If you were not a smoker when you arrived in country, you were when you left.

My friends and I walk around the village, playing with the young Vietnamese, but keeping a close lookout with our rifles slung over our shoulders. The VC do not like us to go into the villages and treat the people nicely, and they sometimes send us harassing gunfire or occasionally minor attacks. The VC treats the villagers badly and it infuriates them to know we treat them much better.

Walking around the village, followed by a swarm of baby-sans, we are in a jovial mood. As a joke, I grab the microphone as I pass by a vehicle, and send out an ill-conceived message. My intent is to send it to the three jeeps stationed around the village with their radios on and the volume turned up.

"Attention, attention all armed forces stationed in the Republic of Viet Nam. This is MACVE HQs in Saigon. We have received notice that the Paris Peace Talks have successfully ended and a peace accord has been signed. Therefore, the war is over. I repeat. The war is over! Stand by for more details, out," I announced. I am puzzled when I do not hear the message over the jeep radios, and am shocked at what I hear coming out of the lone vehicle's speaker, proceeded by a harsh crackle of static.

"This is Rach Kein TAC, over. Repeat last message. Repeat last message, over." I suddenly realize I am standing by the three-quarter command vehicle and have transmitted my bogus message back to our base camp. This is bad, really bad. I have not used proper radio procedure and have transmitted a message that is not true. This is court marshal bad. If they recognized my voice, the First Sergeant will hear about it in five minutes, and they will arrest me as our vehicles come through the main gate.

We continue to hear plaintive requests for a repeat of the message for the next ten minutes. Finally, the First Sergeant comes on the radio and his message is loud and clear. It sounds as if he has his face against the mike and you can hear the pure poison in his comments.

"If I identify the son-of-a-bitch who made that call on the radio a while ago, your ass is mine for the duration of this war. You will not see your home until you are old and grey," he said. I know the depth of his anger because he did not use proper radio procedure, either, and the First Sarge never does that. I utter a short prayer that his voice recognition ability is seriously impaired, and I promise myself that I will never, ever pick up a mike without checking the frequency again.

We continue helping the villagers until late afternoon, but my mind is not in this task. The First Sergeant has the power to do almost anything he wants from a simple Article 15 that would take money out of my munificent monthly salary to several months in the stockade in Dong Tam. The army has another catch 22 in its repertoire, one that is especially reprehensible to me. Army rules state that any time spent in the stockade does not count toward a one-year tour. Even worse, is that it will not count toward my two years in the army. I can only hope that this will work out okay.

Another reason I am worried is that the First Sergeant already has me on his shit list and would welcome the chance to mess with my life. This stemmed from an incident about six weeks ago where I again used poor judgment. I had promised myself that I would challenge authority when I could. Quietly, of course, and that seemed the time to do it.

Since I was a demolition man, the lieutenant often sent me out to blow up mortar rounds that landed inside the base, but hit soft mud and did not explode. He sent O'Brian and me out on one such job. We arrived at a small wooden building that belonged to the First Sergeant, his private sleeping quarters. He met us out front and worriedly pointed to a funnel shaped mound in the mud at the back corner of the building.

This was a classic sign of a mortar round hidden in the mud. I sized up the mound and figured it was probably a sixty millimeter round, what the VC in this area usually shot into our base. The sarge was worried about doing damage to his building since the round was within a foot of the back corner and I was going to have to blow it up with C-4 explosive.

On this base SOP (standard operating procedure) was to blow the round in place, or "Bip" it as we called the operation, since it was deemed too dangerous to dig out a bad round. I always placed a half-pound charge down against the projectile. To keep the shrapnel from coming through the mud, I usually placed two or three sandbags on top of the mound. I would have my friend warn personnel away from the area, light the fuse and take cover. The size of the blast would tell me if the dud round exploded and then we would go on our merry way.

The sarge left after warning us to be careful with his building and I stared at his back after he turned and headed down the street. The man always has a way of getting on my last nerve. Maybe if he had not asked his clerk to put him up for a Purple Heart he might have been easier to stomach. Running into a bunker one night during a mortar attack he struck his bare foot against the doorframe and broke his big toe. Then we had to stand in the hot sun while the clerk pinned the medal on his shirt.

At the time, I only thought about him getting a medal that I felt just line soldiers should receive. In his defense, he was correct in receiving the medal. I forgot to consider that the man was a soldier when I was a mere baby, and probably went through more combat than I will ever see. It is easy to judge someone when you are young and have limited experiences.

"You know, O'Brian, I think that may be a hundred and twenty millimeter mortar round down there and I don't see how I can blow it without causing some damage to the building," I said as I surveyed the hole.

"Nah, that is just a little sixty mm size hole, it won't be any problem," O'Brian says. He notices the look on my face and his mouth opens wide. He knows I have the compulsion to jerk the sergeants around when I can, just as they do to us. I have to be a lot more careful when I do this, but the higher-ranking men just screw with us any time they want. I like to walk that fine line. Have them think you do something on purpose but do it cleanly enough that they have no proof.

"Oh man, no! You cannot be thinking of doing what you plan to do. The first sergeant will have your hide and nail it to the wall," said O'Brian. "Leave me out of this completely." He leaves and hurries down the street. The man is getting out of Dodge City and I wonder if he isn't the smarter of us two.

I decide I will never have so perfect a chance again. If I do it just right, he may suspect but he will have no proof. It is up to me to select just the right amount of explosive and stack six sandbags just right to do some damage, but not too much. I decide a pound and a quarter of C-4 is about right. I will stack six sandbags over the hole but offset them slightly to the right. These bags will channel part of the force away from the building to limit the damage in case my charge is a bit too much.

I prepare the charge and reach into the hole, forcing it down until it touches the mortar round. I check the street and observe no one is in the vicinity. I notice there are men observing from a safe distance, but that always happens. For some reason everyone seems to give me a wide berth when they see explosives in my hands. They probably want to see the First Sergeant's building get some damage and guess what, they are going to see that.

I holler, "Fire in the hole," light the fuse and take cover inside a bunker. From inside the bunker the explosion sounds about right, but when I look out the doorway, the end of the building is obscured by smoke. Way too many pieces of one-by-four pine boards are raining down. As the smoke drifts away, I notice the whole end of the small building has disappeared and the sarge's bed is lying in the street upside-down. His mattress is close by, and a lot of stuffing is missing. The mess has smoke curling up from it and torn sheets of paper are drifting down as the dust settles. All the observers are making quick tracks down the street in both directions.

Oh, oh. This is perhaps a bit more damage than I have envisioned. I know the sarge is not going to take this lying down, so I force my feet down the street to his office. I report that it appears that it was not a small mortar round that just missed his building, but a big one hundred and twenty mm one. There has been some damage after the larger-than-anticipated round exploded. The sergeant orders me to attention and leaves to survey the damage this miscreant has made.

"McCoy, give me one good reason why I should not court-martial you and send you to the Dong Tam stockade?" the sergeant asks me. "It better be a damn good one."

"First Sergeant, there is no way I could have foreseen how big that round was with it buried in the ground," I said. "I am so sorry for the damage and will be glad to repair it for you. I was trying to blow the round and cause as little damage as possible."

He tells me to get out of his office and clean up the mess on the road, but to stay out of his building. He will summon the engineers to repair the building, since he does not want me within one hundred feet of his possessions again.

I use a platoon jeep to pick up the wood, the damaged bed, and carry them to a dump on the east side of the camp. It takes several trips to carry the mess away, and no one volunteers to help me. They all want to stay away from the whole situation until they know the First Sergeant has calmed down. They figure I am now a marked man, and just like the gunslingers of the old west, it is safer to stay away from the vicinity of just such a man.

As I clear away the debris from the explosion, I find the sarge's framed Purple Heart citation. The frame is bent and the glass broken, but the paperwork has survived intact. My first impulse is to take it with me and burn it at the dump but I relent and place it back in the damaged building. I have done enough to the man and I am feeling a little guilty. In addition, I do not know when the sarge might exact retribution, so I hope this small good deed might stop any bad karma from coming my way.

In the days ahead, I become a minor legend among some of the men in camp. Very few men here like the First Sergeant. Though I profess otherwise, they all know the size of the explosion was no accident. I hear the guys at night talking about how McCoy "socked it to the sarge." I spend those same nights worrying about when the shoe will fall. I do not think the "ole sarge" will let it go so easily.

The only good thing to come from the incident is that I no longer worry so much about being hurt or killed as I go about my daily job. Charley can only hurt or kill you whereas the First Sergeant can make you wish you were dead for a long time. If we could just clone a few thousand of the First Sergeants and turn them loose on Charley, he would not stand a chance!

336 days left in country.

Chapter 5
Fun And Games Deep In The Delta

Vinh Long-March 1968.

We are finding our base camp at Rach Kein to be a decent quarters for a soldier. The accommodations in the old French building are fairly cool and the roof does not leak too much. The Falcon platoon members have all become good friends and we mesh well. The daily road clearing operations are going smooth- ly and seem to be less dangerous than a job traipsing around in the jungle, like some of the other platoons. Overall, it is a better job than I expected when I ar- rived here. My fellow platoon mates feel the same way. The fact that the platoon lost some men to an ambush a month ago has faded, but we keep our eyes open. We have not forgotten it entirely.

We are all accustomed to the daily routine and are surprised when the platoon leader, Sgt. Wainwright, comes in that evening and tells us about a new job we will have tomorrow. He explains that the Ninth Infantry Division will be building a new base camp down near Vinh Long. This is deep in the delta, or rice farming area of Viet Nam. It is about one hundred and fifty miles southwest of Saigon and about fifty miles from Rach Kein.

Two companies from the Third of the Thirty-ninth infantry will be help- ing to provide initial security and road clearing duties for the troops building the new base. A few little used roads in this area have more than their share of mines, so we will be working with a group of engineers. They have metal detectors and will be locating and blowing the mines on the roads. Seems that Charley has been an industrious little SOB in this area and mines hidden in the dirt roads are his favorite plaything.

"We have received this job because the Ninth Division is centrally placed in the delta and we have a reputation of being good troubleshooters, so we get the oddball jobs," states Sgt. Wainwright. *Great. I am not so sure I want to be a good troubleshooter and get oddball jobs but I guess Falcon platoon is stuck with it.* He goes on to tell us that we leave at 0700 hours in the morning to meet up with a convoy heading south on Highway Four. We will meet up with the convoy at checkpoint 69er.

The night passes quickly and the platoon is up with the sunrise. We have all been in the army long enough now that we wake early; that is the army way. If you are not an early riser, the noisy bustle of the base starting about 0500 hours will make you one. We all go over to the mess hall and have a big breakfast; with the upcoming operation, we do not know what the schedule is or when we will eat again.

We also have to clear the road the ten miles to checkpoint 69er and we have to allow time in case Charley has been industrious with the roadblocks last night. The enemy must have slept in, because we only have one minor roadblock to clear. We arrive at the checkpoint early and have time to visit the roadside stand for cold drinks. The platoon's favorite vendor of cold drinks is there with a smile on her face.

"You GI early today," Anh greets us. "You have time stay, talk beaucoup, drink many drinks, ok?" She flashes those dark eyes again and winks as she opens a Coke. Her smile and facial expression promises much but we know it is just her patented act; she is the chastest Vietnamese girl we have met here. Half the platoon is infatuated with her and the other, smarter half thinks of her as a beloved little sister. I am in the latter half.

We have little time to drink beaucoup drinks, because the convoy shows up then, winding its way through the foot traffic and three-wheeled pedicabs in the little town. We finish the drinks quickly, say our goodbyes and climb on the vehicles. We will be escorting the convoy so we position our vehicles at the front, center and rear of the line of vehicles.

The convoy heads south down the old familiar Highway Four deeper into the delta. O'Brian checks the map, because we have an unfamiliar turnoff to the south in about twenty miles. It will take us into unknown territory and we are all interested in seeing a new area, wondering what adventures it might bring. The mention of mined roads hangs in our minds, a worrisome part of the day's proceedings.

We reach the turn and head almost south on the road heading toward My Tho. This is unknown territory here and we roll along at thirty miles an hour, each vehicle trailing a long dust cloud behind it. I would hate to be tail-end charley back there in all that dust. Another intersection brings us to the road that runs southwest to Vinh Long. This is where the danger begins. You can see the road itself is out of use, but foot traffic and bicycles have made paths off the road and into the dry rice paddies. Ahead we can see several holes in the road in the distance where mines have exploded. No wonder the traffic has taken to the paddies to remain safe.

We brake to a halt and call to the Engineers to dismount and start their sweep of the road. Two men appear with metal detectors and earphones on their heads. They take up a staggered position on the road and move forward, carefully sweeping their machines across the road in overlapping patterns. This is going to take forever, as we will be moving at the pace of men walking slowly. It would be great if the two and a half ton trucks could take to the paddy too, but they are heavily loaded with supplies. This road will lead to the new base camp and therefore it must be useable and reliable, which is where our platoon and the engineers come into play.

Our jeep slowly moves forward about twenty yards behind the men, which we consider a safe distance. We do not know if we are dealing with only anti-vehicle mines or also anti-personnel mines as well. The engineers are not going to set off a vehicle mine, but they could very well trigger a smaller mine meant to stop a single pedestrian. Jenks is driving the jeep and my friend O'Brian is riding shotgun, operating the map and radio. I am standing in the rear of the jeep behind a .30 caliber machine gun with a thousand round can of ammo attached. I am standing on two layers of sandbags to help stop shrapnel from a mine, but I know that some of the bigger ones can split this jeep in half, and ten or twelve sandbags are not going to be much help. If we hit one of those, well, this is one reason soldiers wear metal dog tags.

I ask my friend how long this road is, and he tells me that we have about twelve to fifteen miles to cover. I look back down the road and it looks like we have only covered a mile. The last of the convoy is just turning off the old road and onto this new one. At this pace, we will never get to the location of the new base camp before dark, and this is not the place to be after dark. After a radio call to the main command vehicle, O'Brian walks forward to see if he can speed up the engineers. They protest that this is not a job that can be hurried, but when we tell them we are going to be out on this road until after dark, they find some added speed.

Everything goes fine for the next several miles. The engineers have found two mines, which they dig up, something our platoon does not do. We blow everything in place, because removing them is a dangerous undertaking. Anti-vehicle mines usually have two anti-tampering devices on them. One is a pressure pin that is locked into place on the bottom of the mine by a cotter pin. This pin is placed against a small hard surface such as a small piece of wood that is buried under the mine. Once the mine is buried just below the surface, the installer digs a small hole beside it to pull the cotter pin out and then fills the hole. The weight of the mine holds the pin in place, but if someone lifts the mine, the pin pops out and detonates the mine.

The second device prevents you from moving the mine horizontally during removal. This pressure pin works differently. It is spring loaded in the in position and the pin has a hole that you tie a string to and then tie to a small peg driven into the ground. This string and peg are buried slightly below ground level also, and you remove the cotter pin before you cover the mine. Should someone move the mine sideways a little while digging, the string and peg pull the pin outward and the result is a big bang.

It takes a cool, careful person to plant a mine without killing himself and an even more careful or crazy person to dig it up. We have to essentially reverse the procedure to dig it up. We have to dig down and reinstall those cotter pins while working by touch. Once this is done, you can safely remove the mine. This is the reason why our platoon BIPs everything. (Blows in place)

The air is suddenly shattered by a tremendous kaboom from behind us and I tumble out of the jeep onto the roadway. Half the movement is from sheer fright and the other half is from the pressure wave that washes over the jeep. I hear things hammering into the dry rice paddy all around us. I decide I am still alive and have all my appendages. I look back to see the lead truck on fire and the front end mangled. I also hear an unearthly screaming from inside the smoking cab of the truck.

Our whole jeep crew rushes to the truck to help the wounded man. I do not want to look inside, but I have no choice. I am amazed to find the driver in better shape than I could ever imagine. He has some minor shrapnel wounds, but the main problem is the mangled floorboard, which sprung upwards into the cab and trapped both his legs. Jenks hollers for a hammer, but try as we might we cannot force the metal forward and down off his lower legs. The medic is here by this time and he is squeezing the driver's hand and telling him he will be OK. I can see the pain in the wounded man's eyes and I know he will not be okay until we get his legs free.

I am thankful that several drivers have put out the flames with some fire extinguishers. The metal was starting to get hot from the transferred heat. We have two hammers thrust at us and we go to work on the floorboards, working as fast as we can in the limited space we have. The medic puts his feet against the metal and his back against the cab and pushes with all his might. His neck muscles pop out, he utters a primal scream, and the damaged metal gives. The driver's legs come free and we lift him out of the truck cab and lay him on the ground. I am glad to see no major blood loss and only some bad cuts on his lower legs.

He is in a lot of pain, however, and the medic examines him. The driver is quiet now since he is out of the hot cab and we have assured him his legs are okay. He will not be walking for a while, but he will have a Purple Heart to wear home on his uniform.

The sarge tells us a dust-off chopper is on the way. My fellow soldiers and I head back to the jeep. I find that I can hardly walk and have to grab on to the jeep for support. It has been a very narrow escape for that driver. The right front wheel set off the mine and the truck construction is very sturdy. If not for these two factors, I feel that the soldier would be dead. I am still amazed that the man has survived and it takes me a little while before I remember that our jeep passed directly over that area earlier.

When I finally gain control of my legs, I walk the thirty yards back to the truck. It is hard to tell exactly where the jeep tires passed because of the hole in the road, but it looks like our tires passed right over the mine or very close to it. It has been a narrow escape for our crew also. Either our tires missed the mine by inches, or the much lighter weight of the jeep did not set it off. Such is the margin between life and death in Viet Nam. Had our jeep set the mine off, the much smaller and lighter jeep could not have protected us. There would be three KIAs now instead of one wounded soldier.

My legs abandon me again temporarily and I wobble back to the jeep and sit down on the sandbags in the rear compartment.

"Whatcha looking at, McCoy?" O'Brian calls to me from the right front seat.

I answer simply, "Hey, trust me, you don't want to know."

The engineers are hanging around the jeep, looking very crestfallen. We call them over and tell them we have changed our minds. We want them to take all the time they need with their sweep of the road. In fact, they can sweep it twice if they want. The map shows a small village several miles away and we figure we can set up a night defensive perimeter there. This is much better than risking another mine explosion.

The chopper arrives and the wounded soldier will be in Tan An hospital in twenty minutes. We give him a good sendoff and kid him about his million-dollar wound. He brightens up considerably at that and smiles through the pain. The last I see of him is a wave through the open side door of the chopper. He is off to start a new phase of his military career, and I hope it entails enough convalescing that he will not see this damned little country again. I did not know the man, and I do not even know his name. I find myself wishing I had asked his name before they flew him away to Dong Tam Hospital.

A truck has managed to squeeze past the damaged one on the narrow road and pulled it over to the side, so it will not create a bottleneck. Men are busy transferring its load onto several other trucks, so we get in the jeep and follow the engineers down the road. This time I have made a slight change in my method of carrying the machine gun. I have unlatched it from the post on the jeep and am carrying it down the road with the ammo wrapped around my chest. I stay about thirty feet behind the jeep and put up with the other soldiers calling me some very descriptive names. That is fine with me; at least I will be a live …….. if we encounter another mine. The name of the game is cover your butt in combat, and that is what I intend to do.

A nagging thought flits around in my mind, one that I have asked myself before. I have never been able to answer it to my satisfaction. This is not the first time I have come reasonably close to dying and I wonder. *Am I just very lucky or is someone watching over me?* I have heard the old saying about there being no agnostics in a foxhole. This is one saying that I agree with heartily.

We reach the little village long before dark and set up a defensive position. There is not enough room to park the whole convoy in the village, so it trails off down the road. This is not an ideal setup for defense during the coming night, but it will have to do. Many of the truck drivers have never spent a night outside base camp so they are quite nervous, but the platoon tells them not to worry. *This is no sweat man, a ville (village) is much better than setting up in the jungle overnight.*

We make an inventory of their weapons and find that several have brought only two magazines of ammo and a few idiots have no weapons at all. The two companies will have no problem guarding the convoy and the truck drivers tonight, but the truck drivers are out of their element and worried. A scared truck driver can make an effective fighter if he knows his life depends on his fighting, and we tell them that, hey, if the VC visits us in the dark, the drivers will earn a CIB. (Combat Infantryman's Badge). None of them seems interested in this piece of information or the medal.

None of us men has brought any provisions with us, but a search of the trucks turns up a full load of C-rations, so we all have a good meal and find a halfway comfortable place to spend the night. Some tobacco would be nice but we are outside a base camp and decide that could be dangerous. We forego the cigarettes and explore the village as the sun goes down, then sit and talk, watching the sun disappear behind the jungle trees in the distance. The mosquitoes come on duty and we all oil ourselves up for the coming night.

"No bic GI," says the grizzled old villager as we question him about the likelihood of VC being in the area. He is telling us he does not understand the question, but I have an idea he knows perfectly well what we are asking. The term VC is universal; it needs no translation here. The villager has fallen back on their standard ploy they use if they do not want to tell you anything. This means either he is a VC sympathizer or scared of the local enemy, so we have learned nothing. I give him two of the little four-cigarette boxes that come with the C-rations and he smiles and bows slightly before he walks away. I have either aided and abetted the enemy or made a new friend but I will never know. I do know that treating the villagers decently cannot hurt, and may make the difference in who they side with in this never-ending, dreary war.

Thankfully, the night passes without drama, and we all rise to meet the promise of a new day. We yawn, stretch, and prepare some food. It is daylight so we can heat the C-rations and follow them with cigarettes. With the disappearance of the night, the heat starts to assail us again. It is going to be another hot, humid day, one of a continuing succession here in Charley-land.

It is after 0700 hours and time to get this operation moving if we are to make it to Vinh Long today. Sgt. Wainwright sends a platoon of men back to the damaged truck to await the arrival of a tow vehicle. This is new territory and it is best to be careful even during daylight hours.

We load the jeep and take our position at the head of the convoy. The engineers start their sweep of the road and slowly walk southwest through the dust. With yesterday's adventures fresh on my mind, I again take up my position about thirty yards behind the jeep and shoulder my machine gun. It is going to be a long, hot walk with the sun beating down. I figure that if we do not find any mines in the road, I may climb back aboard the jeep later. It would certainly be easier on the body, but more dangerous.

My mind flashes back about seven years to a movie I saw in school. Occasionally we would see a movie in the high school gym and one I really enjoyed was a black and white one about a platoon on a recon in Italy during World War II. The movie was entitled *A Walk In The Sun.* Sitting there in that gym, I could never have imagined that before too long I would be taking my own walks in the sun. While watching the movie, I tried to imagine what it would be like to be in actual combat, and I wondered if I could handle it. Well, now I know. Be careful what you wish for in your life.

The hot, dusty morning turns into the same in the afternoon. The only difference is the position of the sun in the sky. The engineers find several more mines and to speed things up, we start blowing them in place. This saves the twenty minutes of waiting while a mine is carefully dug up, and I am sure it took a big load off the men. I could not imagine having to dig up something that could easily kill you while the sweat poured off your forehead. I am willing to bet not all of that sweat came from the effects of the sun.

The search uncovers five mines, before we get to the new base camp outside Vinh Long. Right now, it is merely a perimeter made of sand bulldozed into a wall. The wall is four feet tall and inside the wall are numerous truckloads of material spread around in a haphazard manner. I see many piles of heavy timbers to build the framework for new bunkers and I see pallets of the hated plastic sandbags. The sarge said that we are going to provide security for the camp as the engineers build it, but I am sure we are going to be introduced to some shovels and those bags any time now.

This is the first time we have seen a new base built from the ground up and it would be interesting, if not for the fact that we will be providing a lot of the labor. It looks like bunker guard at night, minus the bunkers, and a lot of manual labor during the day. We talk among ourselves and console each other with one important fact. We may be facing many sandbags, but at least we are not facing Charley. As far as our platoon knows, a sandbag has never killed anyone over here; this is one more way of peaceably running out our time. We have plenty of practice in putting sand in bags, and even more experience in appearing to do that while loafing as much as possible.

Our guess about the sandbags proves to be on the money. There is no mess hall here yet, and no cooks, just the people building the base. Lunch is C-rations again and then the sarge points to the dirt wall around the base and tells us to grab a case of sandbags and get to work. We protest that we do not want to use up the wall to put in the bags, as we will need it tonight for cover and security.

"Men, you see that big yellow dozer over on the perimeter? The guy who operates it claims he can build a new wall faster than you can put it in bags, so don't you worry about that," explains Sgt. Wainwright. We are in trouble now and I wonder if I can figure a way to make the dozer inoperative tonight in the dark. I have never worked on a diesel engine, but I do like mechanical challenges. *Lets see now, a diesel has to have a high pressure pump to force the fuel in. If the fuel feed line had a vibration-induced failure occur, the motor would shut down ... ...*

I keep this information to myself and file it for future reference. If the sandbag job gets too onerous, I could work that fuel line back and forth until it cracked putting the dozer out of operation for a while. Sometimes it is handy to be mechanically inclined! I think it best not to share this information with the rest of the platoon. Should the situation call for it later, I think this should be a one-man operation.

In the afternoon, the engineers and our company bonds and we get to work. Our first, most important job is to build a large sandbag bunker, so we start building the framework of large rough sawn timbers. Sandbags are very heavy so the frame must be exceedingly heavy and bolted together firmly. Once this bunker is built, we can use it for protection if we are mortared at night, and then it will become the main building housing TAC. (Tactical area Command)

TAC is the brains of the base, houses the radios connecting the various parts of the base together, and receives radio calls from units operating nearby. It has a complete set of maps for the area and someone is on duty there twenty-four hours a day. It meshes all unit movements and calls in artillery, mortars, or choppers as needed. It controls everything that happens on the base and in the areas nearby.

Our company starts filling sandbags and lugging them over to the new bunker under construction. I think it would speed things up if we had dirt to fill the bags next to the new bunker, but of course, that is not the army way. That would be much too easy. We point out to the engineers that at the speed they are proceeding, we will have enough bags filled to do two bunkers before they are finished with the framework.

The banter goes back and forth and before we know it, we are filling sandbags like crazy and stacking them at high speed. We pass them along as if we are building up the levee somewhere down south as the river rises. Before long, we have a very impressive wall of sandbags ready and waiting.

The engineers do not want to be shown up, so they counter with a burst of speed in their construction. Their chain saws roar, and the men hustle around lifting heavy beams and tightening bolts. The afternoon passes quickly in a burst of one-up-man-ship. Before we know it, suppertime arrives and we all stagger to the center of camp and sit down, too tired to open our C-ration boxes.

"Well, I guess we showed them engineers how a real soldier can work," Sgt. Wainwright pipes up from his position flat on the ground.

His counterpart in the engineers, Sgt. Weir, answers with, "We showed those grunts how to work smart with power tools, no shovels for an engineer."

Someone starts laughing and it is contagious. It passes all around the circle of men and we all start talking to each other as friends instead of competitors. *Hey, these engineers are all right. We are all just biding our time, trying to survive, serving our one-year sentences.*

I lay there trying to recover from the three hours of heavy exertion, wondering why I am having the time of my life. The answer comes to me immediately. These men and I have spent an entire afternoon working hard and have completely forgotten that we are in the middle of a war zone. We have forgotten the danger and misery and the daily mental countdown of days left over here. We have experienced a rare gift, complete release from our mental and physical turmoil, and it is as refreshing as a three-day stand-down. I think most of us understand, as we sit there in the dirt, that we can build their damned base a little at a time with cooperation from all.

Our two companies spend the rest of the week here working on the base. With mutual cooperation, we build a dozen bunkers, square off the perimeter dirt walls, and string hundreds of yards of barbed and concertina wire. It is actually starting to look like a small army base, albeit a little rough at the moment.

In the evenings after chow, we start playing baseball games. We bill the games Grunts versus Engineers. We have no ball or bat and no gloves. One of the engineers showed his skill with a chainsaw and knife and carved a ball out of a short piece of four-by-four lumber. It was not totally round and weighed a ton. Other men attacked two-by-fours with knives and we soon had some rough bats. The new bats could not hit that heavy ball very far, so we found we did not need gloves. The games had little rules, and these were mostly ignored; we always forgot the score halfway through the game, so we judged most games a tie. We were all friends enjoying each other's company after a long day of work; the score was not the important part.

At the end of the week, the officer in charge of overseeing the construction declared that the base defenses were far enough along that it could survive an attack from the enemy so we would be going back to Rach Kein. In truth, the only defending we have done is against the numerous mosquitoes in the area after dark. They seem to be especially big and virulent and we all have the welts to prove this.

The next morning we loaded up the trucks and formed the convoy. We pulled out of camp and headed back up that dusty road northeast to our base. Fun time was over, we were now back to our very serious game with Charley, but the clock is ticking. We are all eight days closer to that big freedom bird flight back home.

I turn around and glance back at that base camp one more time as it disappears into the dust behind us. I leave a lot of my sweat and a little of my blood here, and it suddenly occurs to me I do not even know the name of the base. I hope the base I helped to build is not named after another dead soldier.

324 Days left in country.

Chapter 6
A Horrifying Plane Crash

Rach Kein Base-April 1968.

Falcon platoon is on convoy escort this afternoon. We are guarding a convoy that has dropped off supplies this morning in Rach Kein, and are returning it back to Dong Tam base in the delta area of southern Viet Nam. On the way, we will also stop at Tan An since the convoy has to drop some supplies there too.

We get to Tan An without problems, as there are no VC around with nothing better to do than shoot at our procession along Highway Four. We take a right off the paved highway onto the dusty road leading to Tan An base and follow it alongside the airstrip in front of the base.

Our arrival is well timed since a light aircraft is just taking off, coming down the strip just to our right. Standing behind the machine gun on back of the jeep, I swivel around to watch it ascend. Any type of aircraft, especially the small reconnaissance ones, fascinates me. It appears to be a perfect takeoff. I follow its flight into the air, wishing I was aboard it, but the flight suddenly goes horribly wrong about three hundred feet in the air. The plane's engine suddenly races and it tilts almost straight up and climbs rapidly. I figure the pilot is giving us earth-bound soldiers a show, but I discard this idea when I see the plane stall, drop a left wing and roll over onto its back.

It then plummets downward in an arc and disappears into the trees beyond the end of the runway, falling so fast I can barely follow it with my eyes. I hear a heart-rending thump and call to the jeep driver, but he has seen it happen and pulls onto the airfield and heads toward the crash site about a quarter-mile away.

We have been taught to respond to any crash site immediately; both to render any aid we can to the passengers, and then to secure all weapons and ammunition. If there is any enemy around, they may kill the survivors and strip the plane of any useable weapons in a very short time. They will then head to the woods and disappear.

The jeep bumps over a small ditch and into the front yard of a small thatched-roof Vietnamese house. We dismount, run up to the house, and see the entire roof torn off, with the crumpled remains of the wing lying next to the roof. The fuselage is missing and we run toward a small stand of trees, but I stop as I see some smoke curling out of a six-foot deep ditch. I look into it and see the engine of the plane lying on the bottom in about a foot of water, and the smoke is actually from the hot motor. Papa-San is standing at the edge of the ditch looking down. He turns to me with the most horrible look I have ever seen on a human being's face, a stunned, beseeching look that makes my heart grow cold.

I look into the ditch again, seeing only the smoking motor and the twisted propeller. Strangely, there is a long, white snake curled around the prop. I have never seen a snake this long here, and certainly not white. I take a closer look. I am sure my face shows the same look of horror that the Vietnamese man has on his face.

My mind and my eyes finally work together, as I see half the torso of a child of about ten on one side of the engine, and the rest of his body on the other side of the engine. What I took to be a snake is actually his intestines. My mind shuts down for a few seconds. I try to take my eyes from the horrible sight, but my mind will not respond and my eyes will not move. For what seems like forever, my mind refuses to work. Finally, my mind comes back on line and I realize there is absolutely nothing I can do about this, as horrible as it is.

The fuselage needs locating and the pilots helped. This is now my top priority. A shout from the trees tells me the rest of the plane is located. I hurry over there, and it is only about a hundred feet from the building it damaged. The firewall is lying against the ground with the tail resting in a small tree, which tilts the fuselage at a thirty-degree angle. When the wing came off, it pulled the top of the cockpit and the windows off, but otherwise there is little damage around the pilot and co-pilot.

Both pilots are unconscious, strapped securely with their belts. I see no obvious wounds and absolutely no blood. I have little first aid training, but do see they are both still breathing. As I try to decide what to do, I hear the ambulance siren coming across the field and dying out as it reaches the building. I do not have to do anything that might make their condition worse. I am so thankful for that.

Okay, my next priority is to secure weapons. I reach in and remove both pilot's .45 caliber pistols, glancing quickly at the hammers to make sure they are not cocked. The pilot does not move, but as I remove the co-pilot's weapon, he regains consciousness and turns toward me, trying to say something. A quick rush of blood from his mouth muffles his words and I know this is a bad sign. It indicates internal damage. Two medics rush up and I thankfully turn the scene over to them.

I hear someone barking orders, and I turn and see a wild-eyed second lieutenant, with a .45 pistol held high over his head. He is hollering that all six rockets are missing from the wing tubes and we must immediately secure them. That really worries me, those five-foot long rockets have just taken a hell of a bang, and I know absolutely nothing about them. They are totally outside any of my training. All I know is that they will kill us if they go off. If the fins have popped out into the released position, then they are armed. The rockets fit the launch tubes snugly, and the tubes hold the fins in the closed position until the rockets are fired, then the fins pop out, thus arming the rocket as it leaves the tube. Wherever they are, they are now armed and I do not know how dangerous that makes them. I do know, however, that the quickest way to kill myself is to screw with something that I do not fully understand.

I try to explain this to the officer and ask him to let us wait until someone with a little more knowledge of the rockets gets here. The rockets were loaded on the plane here in Tan An, so someone has knowledge of the system. I am sure that he is on the way, but the idiot officer will not even consider my point. Sometimes the stress of a situation will make an officer act strangely. This is not the first time I have received what I consider a foolhardy order from an officer. A common saying among men on the line is that there is nothing dumber or more dangerous than a second lieutenant fresh out of OCS, or officer candidate school. They have plenty of book learning, but no experience in the field. By the time they become a first lieutenant they have some actual combat experience, and they then know what they are doing.

Under orders, we go searching for the missing rockets, finding them five minutes later about another hundred feet into the woods. What we find is not pretty, and it is worrying. All six rockets are in a thirty-foot circle. They are buried nose first, about a foot and a half deep in the earth. Two of them have broken in half, and of course, the dammed fins stick out. It is almost as if they are saying, "Mess with me if you dare."

The lieutenant stays a wary fifty feet back as we gingerly remove the rockets, freeing them from their new home. We save the broken two for last.

The sweat is really pouring down our faces now. I wonder if this is our last day on earth, and I note with satisfaction that the officer is close enough to be killed too, if one of these babies goes off. He has evidently failed to take into account the fact that if one goes off, the other five will, too, and half this grove of trees will disappear.

God is good to us and I make a mental note to thank him later, but right now all our attention is concentrated on getting those six rockets back to the jeep; and then a half mile to the munitions dump where they store bad explosives, damaged vehicles and such. The three of us make two trips, carrying one rocket at a time. We treat them with loving care, handling them like a newborn infant. It is hard to explain the terror of carrying what I guessed to be three or four pounds of explosive that might blow up at any time. I remember thinking that if this kills me, I hope the lieutenant and I wind up the same place after death, and that there are no rules to stop me from having a very serious discussion with him.

The jeep driver covers the half mile so slowly that I almost want to scream at him to speed up. The seconds tick by and we are still alive, and then we arrive safely at the ammo dump. We transfer the rockets to a revetment, an area dug out on the ground with thick walls of dirt piled high. The army stores malfunctioning ammo this way so that if something blows up it does not set the whole works off. The VC like to fire mortar rounds into ammo dumps, too. They probably stay up late at night, gathered around a campfire, planning things to plague the Americans. They want us to wish we had never seen this God-forsaken little country, and that is pretty much what I feel right now.

I often feel sorry for the poor French people who ran this country for over a hundred years, treating it as their own personal little fiefdom. They built extensive rubber plantations and infrastructure, and then fought the Viet Minh, the forerunners of the VC. The French fought for eight years and were finally decisively defeated at Dien Bien Phu, in North Vietnam, and left the country for good. I often wondered if the defeat really finished them off militarily, or did they finally reach the conclusion that they could never win, and that the war would drag on forever if they did not leave the country.

The Asians are like water flowing over hard rock, and slowly wearing it down. I figured this out within several months of coming to Viet Nam, and I searched in vain for signs that others realized this also. I felt that the army had violated the first, most important rule of warfare; know thine enemy.

After depositing the rockets, we cleared out of the dump quickly and returned to the main part of the base. We had to form up the convoy and finish the trip to Dong Tam. As the convoy lined up, our jeep crew sat in the shadow of a sandbag bunker and reviewed what we had just been through today. Our heart rates had returned to normal and the day had turned into just another one to be endured, one day of our sentence of three hundred and sixty five days.

As I sat in the shade, my mind returned to the horror I had seen in the ditch. I had looked at it; my mind had accepted it, I had written it off as nothing I could do anything about, and I had gone on to do my job. I blotted it out of my memory long enough to get my job done. Then, as I thought about it, I was not bothered too much by the memory. The scene did not weigh heavily on my mind, as it should have done. Any normal person would have had it burned into his brain. I think that was a sad reflection on the condition of my mind. I had seen so much and endured so much that I just could not feel the horror. This is one of the hidden consequences of combat. It strips away the essential parts of human emotion that make you human, and leaves behind a shell that looks human; still allowing you to function, but that is far from what our creator intended.

I often thought of the ditch scene in the coming months, when things were quiet, and you could mull things over in your mind. The scene is not readily available as I keep it hidden far back in my mind where it can do little harm. I can usually keep it at bay, but such things do not easily stay hidden, and stubbornly pop out at the most inopportune times. It bothered me little while I was still in the country, but it has most assuredly bothered me down through these intervening years. Late at night when my resistance is low, or when I feel bad, and cannot force the scene to stay hidden, out it jumps. I can see that ditch and the anguished look on the father's face. I can smell the hot oil, the steam rising off the engine, and I smell the deep, pungent smell of the mud at the bottom of the ditch. I hear the ticking of the metal as the engine cools, and it plays repeatedly in my mind, a tape that has no end.

Think carefully, young man, before you let your mind be swayed by the recruiter. It may all sound exciting, adventurous, or even downright romantic, but war is none of these things. Even if you avoid serious injury or death, you will change in ways you can never guess, let alone imagine. You will not be the man you were when you return, and the worst part is, you will not even realize it for years. The people who love you will notice, but you will not. You will have lost the essential humanness that is vital to your makeup, and that gift, my friend, will never return. It is a one-time gift from God, and you will not find it on the shelf at the local K-Mart. I was a soldier, and this I know.

309 days left in country.

Chapter 7
O'Brian And I Become Carpenters

Rach Kein-April 1968.

Falcon platoon receives orders to move out of our old French quarters near the center of the base to a Vietnamese house about a hundred yards up the road. We see no sense in this as our former lodgings have plenty of room for the twenty-two men in the platoon. The new accommodations are half the size and a tight fit for the Falcons. We hear that the reason for the move is that the officers who live here are having too many mortar rounds land in and around their quarters during the attacks, so they figure Charley has this area zeroed in. Therefore, they move and since we are mere grunts and not important in the grand scheme of things, we inherit their quarters and their problems.

Once we set up our cots with mosquito netting attached, there is practically no room left to walk around in the one-room house. The problem is that a four-foot high bunker takes up half the floor space, but we have to keep it for protection from mortar attacks. The house has a thick, thatched roof and walls made of thin boards nailed vertically to the framework. It is upscale for a Vietnamese house, since it has a wood floor and walls, but the construction will offer no protection from a mortar round.

It does have a rear patio made of bricks set into the dirt and a wooden roof to keep the sun off of our bodies. It is obviously a new addition to the house, probably added by the previous inhabitants, the group of officers. On the plus side, the house is set on a quarter-acre of land planted with nipa-palm and banana trees. This grove of trees shades the property well and keeps the house airy and almost cool even in the heat of day.

An added attraction is a tidal inlet that flows on the left of the land. This inlet almost splits the camp in half. The water is a cul-de-sac about three feet deep at high tide but is much too muddy and contaminated to swim in or bathe. It is however, real waterfront, which is a scarce commodity in this camp.

After O'Brian and I move our cots and possessions to the new quarters, we go out on the patio to clean up what appears to be several years' accumulation of assorted junk, dirt, and beer bottles. I notice a dusty old full-size refrigerator lying on its back beside the patio. When I open the door, it is fairly clean inside, so I decide it will be a good container to store some of our personal belongings. The rubber seal around the door will keep out the weather and allow us to store our stuff out on the patio, since there is no room in the house.

We pull the fridge onto the patio and start cleaning it and I notice it has a large shrapnel hole through the back cover where the compressor and refrigerant lines are located. Out of curiosity, I find a screwdriver and take the rear cover off. My mechanic's natural curiosity has kicked in; I want to see what was damaged to put it out of commission. Imagine my surprise when I find the power line has been cut neatly in two by the shrapnel. It then lodged in the insulation and did no more damage. Some idiot has discarded what may be a perfectly good fridge because he did not take the time to see what damage occurred under the rear cover.

"O'Brian," I say, "I think we may have a fixable fridge here." I point out the damage as I trim and splice the wires together. I then borrow a roll of tape from the medic to insulate the joint and we set the unit upright. We rub our hands in glee because this is a find worth its weight in gold in an area where the only refrigeration is in the mess hall kitchen. Their cooling system works via ice in an insulated walk-in freezer with daily deliveries of ice from the big plant in Saigon.

The only drawback to making it work is the matter of having no electricity to plug into so I scout the area around the house and find that electric wires do run here from a pole out on the street. Glancing up I can see the wires are cut where they enter the house.

This is likely because the previous occupants, who were officers, had access to electricity, but when they moved they had it disconnected. Someone made sure that we mere grunts would not be able to access electricity from the main generator that powers everything in camp. Certain facilities and personnel in camp have access to electricity. The first sergeant, yes, officers, yes, grunts, no. This rankles O'Brian and I and to make our new fridge operable, I will have to do something about it tonight when no one is watching.

I will have to hook up to the pole in a way that is not easily detectable. The big generator has a crew that runs and maintains it twenty-four hours a day. A meter that measures current draw from the whole camp is installed in the generator building and the operators keep a close eye on the meter. Their job is to make certain that current being used does not exceed the output of the generator, plus a small margin for safety. Around the camp soldiers hook up to power illicitly and this shows on the meter.

If extra draw is noted, the crew in the generator room sends out men during the day to find and unhook these extra wires. There is normally no punishment to the men as the current they borrow is usually minimal. When one of the crew notices an illegal hookup, they just unhook it, pull down the wires, and throw them away. We wind up facing punishment only if we continue to make a nuisance of ourselves with repeated hookups.

My problem, as I see it, is to make that illegal hookup in a way that will be hard to detect. If we use it only to power the fridge, no one will be the wiser. If we also use it to power lights, as some men do, this will be a dead giveaway at night. Those generator crewmembers also roam the camp at night, and they know who has the right to electricity, and who does not. We expose ourselves if we hook up one single light bulb.

I could see that if I hooked a wire to the connection at the house there was no way I could hide this. Something more devious is called for here. Fortunately another, better opportunity presented itself. There is a small officer's billet to the right front of our house, and it has an electric wire running to the back corner of the building, then down the wall. It then disappeared under the building and obviously ran through the floor and inside the building. All I had to do was bury about sixty feet of electric wire out to the building and have it exit slightly under the officer's building, then hook it to that power wire under the edge of the building. This way there was no sign that another line is hooked to that building's power line. This will likely be undetectable to the generator crew.

I have no trouble getting electric cord for my nocturnal wiring. Every claymore mine has a hundred feet of brown wire on it, so I just borrow from them. The cord is a two-strand wire covered with brown insulation. It looks exactly like the cord stateside lamps have attached to them, and is probably the same type of wire.

I thought this was an elegant and almost undetectable way to get power to our refrigerator so we could do a test run.

The only problem with my plan is that I must do this after dark on a night the officer is not there, and the little matter of hooking to the wire while it is live. There is no way I can see to unhook it temporarily without someone noticing and asking what I am doing. I have experience working on live circuits from my civilian days and I know that if I hook up only one wire at a time and do not touch the other one, I will not be shocked.

We bury the wire that night about a foot below ground level, working by the light of the moon. My army career has given me plenty of experience doing things at night by touch and what moonlight that is available.

We keep a watch on the officer in the evenings and we receive an opportunity to hook up the wires several nights later after he left and headed up the street. His destination was the Officer's Club, so I knew it would be a late night for him. I headed back to our new quarters and hooked up the wires while holding a flashlight in my mouth and reaching under the building. O'Brian stationed himself out by the road to warn me of anybody approaching. Things go fine and I do the hook-up without shocking myself. Even better, no one shows up asking questions.

My friend and I hurry back to the patio and turn the switch on the refrigerator. Now is the decisive moment. Would it run, or was the work all in vain?

When I turn the switch, we are rewarded with a hum, so we sit there in the dark smoking and talking about our girls back home to pass the time. I talk about my wife Wanda and O'Brian patiently listens although he has heard it a hundred times before from me. It is now my friend's turn and he talks of his girl Cindy and their plans. It is all part of being friends in a combat zone. We listen to each other's inane chatter about home and make the appropriate comments at the correct time.

"Does it feel cooler in here?" O'Brian asks me. After an hour, he can wait no longer and opens the freezer door. I have a moment of panic; it does not feel any cooler to me and this baby has been humming quietly for an hour.

I tell him I think it is a little cooler in the top compartment, but we need to let it run all night as a true test. It was at least eighty-five degrees when we turned it on and I am hoping that it is just taking longer than we expect to cool down. Hell, I will even settle for just a little cooler than ambient. I already have big plans for the future that include a lot of cold beer and sodas at night and renting out some space to cool other soldier's libations. My sense of entrepreneurship has not been totally erased by the army interfering with my life.

We sit a while longer on the patio and contemplate the darkness and our forced involvement in someone else's war. As always, my pipe consoles me and makes the situation we are both involved in a little easier to accept. I puff on the pipe and my good friend burns through a couple of cigarettes. We decide it is time to retire for the night. Since we have no bunker guard or listening post tonight, we will be rewarded with a good night's sleep.

That good night's sleep proves elusive. Too much is riding on the success of our refrigerator and I get up and check it several times through the night. I get my reward in the wee hours of the morning. It is definitely chilly in the lower compartment, and the freezer is downright cold. I stand there in the dark, feeling that beautiful, heavenly cold. It has been three months since I have had my hand in a freezer and it feels great. I mentally kick myself now; why did I not have the foresight to purchase some Cokes and beer at the EM (Enlisted Men's) club today? An ice-cold coke in the morning would be manna from heaven.

We rise at 0600 hours and I tell O'Brian the happy news. He rushes out to the patio, opens the freezer door, and is as enthralled as I am about the cold. He just will not leave that freezer alone and finally sticks his head into it to feel the cold first hand. I finally tear him away from our refrigerator and we head over to the mess hall for breakfast. We have to eat fast, because we have a busy morning of road clearing ahead for the platoon.

As we eat, I tumble something around in my always fertile mind. O'Brien gave me an idea when he stuck his head in the freezer. I am sure the bottom compartment is big enough to hold a soldier if the shelves are all removed. We should be able to sell ten-minute cool down stints in that compartment if I can modify the latch so the door can be opened from the inside. I put that on my mental list to do today as soon as we get in from clearing the roads, after I stock up on Cokes and beer and put them in the fridge for tonight. My buddy and I are going to have ice-cold drinks as we sit and watch the sun go down this evening. I can think of nothing more I could want, except to get out of this damned country.

The day clearing roads goes fine, only three roadblocks to blow off the road and a bit of tenseness as we pass the hooch where the platoon was ambushed just before we became members. We still park the vehicles and walk the area thoroughly before we pass it, but this is only a safety measure at this one location. How many more places the enemy could be lurking, waiting for us to pass by is anyone's guess.

Once we park the gun jeeps, O'Brian and I make a beeline to the EM Club and buy several six-packs of soda and beer. It is all we can afford now as our funds are running low, but payday is coming up soon. We both send money back home, so we are left with less than fifty dollars a month to spend. Even with our extra fifty a month hazardous-duty pay, our pay envelopes are slim. The army is paying us over a dollar a day extra for serving in a combat zone! What a deal, at least for the government.

Back at the house, we check the fridge and both compartments are cold. I examine the door latch and find no problem making it operable from the inside. It involves only trimming some plastic away from the inside liner of the door and punching a small hole in the outside metal panel of the door. I do this with a nail and a borrowed hammer. Then I run a piece of wire through from the inside, inserting it into the hole and wrap it around the lever of the outside door handle. I finish the modification by making a big loop in the wire on the inside where a man sitting in the compartment can find it in the dark. I climb in, close the door, and experience the sweet coolness. I pull the loop and the door pops open instantly.

Perfect, this fridge is going to be a moneymaker and augment our meager salaries. Now, how much do we charge to cool drinks and to take a cool siesta in our cold room?

We want to make a little money, but we do not want to gouge our less-fortunate friends in the platoon. This is a time-honored army tradition; men finding ways to make money on the side. The army considers the practice harmless and pays no attention to us as long as we do not exceed certain boundaries.

The next business is to cool drinks for tonight, so we put our purchases in the freezer to start with and take turns sitting in the main compartment until we have to evacuate, teeth chattering. It is a snug fit for me, and I am a medium build, so some of the larger men are not going to fit. I reflect that there are plenty of men my size in the platoon and the sky is the limit. There are hundreds of soldiers in this base camp, and two-thirds of them are potential customers.

The word gets around camp and we soon have men coming to our house with beer and soft drinks to cool. In lieu of money, we soon establish a charge of one Coke or beer per six-pack to cool a customer's drinks. This part of the business goes well and we soon find we have no need to buy any more drinks at all. In fact, we take in more than we can drink and stockpile them in the corner. The cool-down-in-our-fridge part of the business does not do as well, mostly because the patrons find out that it is a double-edged sword. They love the cold part, but find that facing the heat after sitting in the fridge is worse after cooling down forty degrees. We have to charge ten cents MPC to get any customers and business is spotty. Oh well, any money coming in is better than none and we have more drinks than we can handle. We chill these extra drinks in the freezer until they are almost frozen and sell them for twenty-five cents each.

With our mini-business going well, I mention something to O'Brian that has been on my mind for several weeks. I have been thinking about this and checking out the camp for supplies that are not well guarded. I explain to him that with the small house being crowded, we need a small shack of ours and the perfect place would be that unused piece of ground to the left of the building where we sleep. That land fronts on the tidal pool. A small single-room building with a porch overlooking the water will be perfect to catch the sundown each evening and to consume our stock of cold drinks.

I pitch the idea to my friend, and he loves it except for one big hitch. We do not have wood for a foundation, or two-by-fours for framing and nothing for siding. Even if we procure these, we do not have nails and there is no friendly hardware store on the corner to buy these.

I point out that the engineers just down the road have all these supplies, and do we not escort convoys every few days loaded with just such goodies? I do not think a few two-by-fours and some pine planking liberated from the occasional truck will be noticed. We control where the trucks are parked at night, usually in the small square right in front of our old barracks. They do not always get unloaded by sundown, and a couple of men willing to carry some wood in small batches for an hour or two each night could accumulate enough supplies in a month or so.

A time-honored tradition is carried on in the army. If you need something to make your life a little more livable, and the army has it stockpiled, you can borrow it if you do it quietly enough and do not raise any attention. Sergeants and officers know this goes on continuously and they overlook it for the most part. Men that borrow things are termed hustlers and are often looked upon favorably by others. It may even bring a little admiration for showing some original thinking, of which the army sees little.

Considering this and the fact that we have almost ten months left in our tour, it makes the idea seem more feasible. We start immediately to collect whatever we think is useable in our new building and conceal it in the trees behind our Vietnamese house. A visit to the engineer's compound late one night produces about fifteen pieces of framing and pine planking. They left a partially unloaded truck outside their compound fence and we removed about half of what was left in the bed. We figure we are actually helping them since they now have less to unload in the hot sun tomorrow.

What we actually need first are some large timbers for the foundation. We want to cantilever about a quarter of the building out over the water and this part will be unsupported, so we need some healthy timbers to accomplish this. We want something on the order of rough-sawn twelve-by-twelve inch bunker building material, but are having no luck locating such large pieces of wood. They will be heavy, which means we have to move them with the jeep at night, further complicating the job. We refuse to give up on this and scour the camp for something that fits our specifications.

Our search takes us to the west side of the base camp. This camp has a tank stationed here, and it is occasionally used to shoot out into the jungle at VC who are mortaring us from the surrounding jungle. This perimeter was low and muddy so the crew had installed some long pieces of wood of the size we sought. They allowed the tank to traverse the mud with no danger of being stuck. Since they were set at an angle with one end against the dirt bunker wall, they also allowed the tank to fire at a higher angle than the turret normally allowed.

They are muddy and chewed up by the tank's metal treads but are still solid and useable. Once the building is built, they will not be visible so they will serve our purpose perfectly. They are about eighteen feet long and exceedingly heavy, which presents a problem. That night we borrowed the jeep and about ten platoon members and headed out to retrieve our foundation beams. It takes all of us to wrestle one on the jeep, and it hangs over each end.

We made three trips that night, because we took three of the beams. Since they would take some work to cut through, and we had only a borrowed dull handsaw, I decided that two of the beams placed parallel would be the length of our new building and one cut in half would be the width. The next afternoon we sawed that one beam in half. It took O'Brian and me over an hour, taking turns with the old saw to make the cut.

We also did a little digging to level the beams by eye as we do not have a level and eyesight will have to do the job. I tell myself that we are building something that only needs to last ten months at the most. We now had the foundation laid and the beams set so the last five feet are over the water. Nails are a problem we have not solved yet and those beams needed big bolts, not nails.

We don't have any big bolts and no way to drill the holes for them but I located a roll of rusty strapping. I knew the strapping, applied with enough nails, would hold the beams together.

We solved the lack of nails problem by walking around the camp for a couple of hours after dark pulling out every nail we could find that was sticking up a little. The mess hall, the EM Club, and assorted other buildings all gave some of their nails, so that we might continue our project. During the afternoons, after our road clearing duties were over, we roamed the camp looking for nails that we could borrow. We would make a mental note of them and then come back after dark with a hammer. We named this-*going out on nail patrol.*

We continued to abscond with every piece of wood we could get off the convoy trucks and platoon members often helped us; they had heard of our project and were duly impressed with our brazen idea. We heard some men had started a pool on how long we would get away with this, and that annoyed me. We were trying to fly under the radar and this pool could not help matters.

We hit the jackpot several days later on one of the convoy trucks. A soldier riding on one informed us that they had some wooden barrels of nails aboard, and after inspecting the load we removed a container of ten-penny nails that must have weighed at least forty pounds. Our nail problems were over for good, and so were our midnight nail patrols. It looked like our project was a forgone deal; every time we needed something, it showed up with a little looking.

The only negative point was that the building was taking up all our spare time in the afternoon and evenings. Bunker guard and the occasional listening post also cut into our building time, but the joy of doing something like this made time in a combat zone pass faster. We had much less time to worry about what could happen to us down the road.

We had only been working on the building a little over a week and we had the foundation in and the floor nailed down. We also had the framework for two walls up and braced, but we ran out of two-by-fours for framing. None of these has shown up recently on the trucks. I told my friend we would have to make a late-night foray over to the engineer's compound as I had spotted a big stack of the needed framing material just inside their fence. The fence was tall, but could be scaled if we parked the jeep beside it and stood on the hood. We would need the jeep anyway, because I figured we needed another fifty pieces of framing stock for our humble abode. We were not able to come up with any wood for rafters, so we would have to nail them up with lighter wood forming a truss to support the roof.

I was not a carpenter by any means and I had never heard of roof trusses, but I invented them in my mind that day. I turned the problem over in my mind and that was the only way I could come up with the needed rafters for the roof. This building would never pass an inspection from a contractor, but then it did not need to. This is the one beauty of a combat zone; there were not a million little niggling rules to follow. The big rule over here was; see Charley, shoot Charley.

In another week of afternoon and evening work, we finished the walls and planked them with one-by-four pine planking. I nail these on with a slight gap to let air flow through, a feature I noticed most of the army buildings employed. The top foot of the walls we leave open and we plan to cover that with screen when we find some. The roof trusses work out okay and we started looking for some corrugated steel roofing panels to keep us dry. I want to sandbag the roof against mortar rounds but know my lightweight roof construction will not handle this. We solve this problem by starting work on a small two-man bunker just outside the rear door of our new abode.

I build two doors for the building and we start looking for hinges. Another search of the camp turns up a couple of unused army buildings we have paid little attention to in our foraging walks. One is semi-completed; it looked like the builders just stopped work one day and left it to the elements. Plans must have changed somehow since they did not finish it.

It has a couple of hinged doors, so I removed the hinges and screws and just nail the doors back in place. There is a good chance this will never be noticed. With hinges in my inventory, I install the doors along with a railing on the front porch.

The porch is small, the width of the building and four feet wide so it will not take up too much of the interior volume of the building. The width was carefully figured. It gave us room for the chairs, which we would have to find, and room to rest our feet on the porch railing. We could sit there with our feet up and survey the world beyond the porch, while we smoked and drank cold drinks out of our fridge. We were quite sure that no soldier, in any combat area in any war, had as nice a setup as we do. Sure, there are some unexplained things floating in that little inlet, and the mud sometimes smells pretty bad.

These were small prices to pay for our idyllic waterfront getaway, and we are as proud of it as if we had a mansion in an exclusive part of Long Island.

We were roofless, but we moved in anyway. We finished off the interior by building a wooden framework for bunk beds. Next, we cut the canvas off the cots we used and nailed it to the framework, which made a quite comfortable bed, at least by our standards. We finished by building a small desk by the front door with just enough room to write letters home, and nailed some wooden 106mm recoilless rifle ammo boxes to the wall to hold various possessions. Another cot we scrounged up gave its life for the hinges for the boxes. We cut the canvas into strips and used small doubled over pieces for hinges.

We needed only metal roofing to finish our roofless chalet, and this is where we almost blew the whole deal. On another expedition past our home improvement store, aka the engineer's compound, we notice a fresh stack of galvanized roofing just sitting there asking to be borrowed.

Borrow it we did. We returned that night about 0100 hours and commenced loading the sheeting. Every light was off in the compound and no one has been about for an hour because we have been watching. The army training in stealth is paying off in ways our old Drill Sergeants could never have imagined.

"What in the hell is going on here?" asked a voice in the darkness behind us. I jumped and froze, then turned around to face a Second Lieutenant. There was just enough moonlight to see the officer's bar and a stern, unforgiving face.

"Sir, we are just delivering this roofing that was unloaded at the wrong place this afternoon. The sarge told us to move it over here, but we forgot. When he came back from the EM Club and found it, he woke us and told us to get it over here right away. We are just following orders," I told him The army experience has taught me to think and improvise on a second's notice, and I did my shining best at that moment.

"I do not give a damn what your sergeant told you to do," the lieutenant replied. "You men get this mess back on the jeep and get the hell out of here. Come back in the morning with the proper paperwork and deliver it correctly. Do you understand me, soldier?"

I understood him perfectly. This second louie was telling us to steal his roofing and leave quickly. We did just that, and when we had loaded what I thought was enough to do our roof we jumped in the jeep to leave. The lieutenant was having none of that; he insisted we take the whole pile. We finished loading, hardly able to keep a straight face, and drove off into the darkness. We are very thankful he did not ask us our names, and it was too dark to read our blackout names on our fatigue shirts.

The next afternoon and evening, we finished the roof. The large metal sheets went on quickly and we have some fellow platoon members help us move our prized possession, the refrigerator, into our new abode. The platoon members are only too happy to oblige, since they have a vested interest in seeing that the fridge receives good care. We finish the evening with an impromptu party and invite the whole platoon as they have helped us in our month long endeavor to build our new house.

In the next week, we liberated enough screen to finish the upper wall openings and our building is finally totally finished. It is just as well, because we are spending all our off duty hours out on that front porch on several chairs that happened to turn up when we needed them. We use kerosene lanterns we have purchased in the village to light the place, that way the generator patrol does not know we are stealing electricity for the fridge.

O'Brian and I sit on the porch that night and consider our blessings. We have a snug little shack with the latest amenities and the total cost to us is around five Vietnamese dollars for the two lanterns. Life has indeed been good to us and we figure that the next months will pass soon enough, so we can get out of here. We admit we will almost be sorry to bid farewell to our little abode on the glorious day of our departure.

We finish that evening watching the sun set behind the jungle to the west of the base. It is a beautiful sundown as usual, and we toast the disappearance with cold beers and our tobacco friends. Life is indeed pretty good.

We continue to go out every day and clear the roads and risk our lives. We come back to the base every evening, have supper in the mess hall, and retire to our little shack by the water. The platoon assembles in our shack just before sundown, ten or twelve soldiers jam themselves onto the porch to say good-bye to today's sun, we toast the nightfall, and the fact that one more day has been expended.

On a recent stopover in Dong Tam, O'Brian and I pool our money and buy a record changer and a few albums. We now have entertainment above what the local radio station offers, and we borrow other soldier's albums so we have a wide range of music. We decorate the front of our little desk with album covers carefully nailed on with small nails, so we will not damage the covers too much.

We have a roof over our heads, a refrigerator, cold drinks and music, so the shack balances out the heat and danger of the day. The platoon gathers almost nightly, except for men on bunker guard and listening posts, and it seems almost like parties back in the real world. Only one more essential ingredient is missing, and that is our girlfriends and wives. This makes the gatherings bittersweet for most of the men, but that is one thing we cannot change.

I have become an excellent scrounger in the last month, but I cannot furnish female companionship that is ten thousand miles away, so we surround ourselves with what amenities we can and try to forget how much we miss our women.

Life goes on in this combat zone and we continue to look for diversions. The village attached to Rach Kein is safe, so O'Brian and I often walk down to it and have a cold beer or two at one of several roadside shacks. We talk to the Vietnamese proprietors and practice our poor Vietnamese on them. They laugh and correct us, and they ask us about our country and what it is like. They hear much about our country from the hundreds of soldiers they serve, and they seem continually surprised that no one carries a weapon on the streets in the U.S.

They find it hard to visualize that for the most part, our country is peaceful and a land of opportunity for someone willing to work hard. I see the wistful look in their eyes as we describe it, and I try to imagine how hard it must be for them to begin to understand our country. These people are born into a life of poverty and strife and are used to danger and scrambling to make a living, as were their parents before them.

I try to put into words the fact that this country could be a little heaven on earth if not for the continuing wars it faces and the fact that the ruling class takes everything they can for themselves and leaves little for the common man. I try but my words fail me. I do not know enough Vietnamese, and they do not know enough English. I think I see some understanding in their faces, however. I think they understand that I do not view this country through the eyes of someone who thinks he is a conquering hero, or of a superior race, but someone who cares for their country and would really like to help with their problems. That is a tall order, and one that I cannot fulfill, though I will often wish that I could.

291 days left in country.

Chapter 8

Combat Isn't Enough So I Get Malaria

Rach Kein-April 1968.

It is a morning like any other on the base. I wake up around 0630 hours and proceed to get out of bed. I have trouble getting out of the top bunk in the building O'Brien and I have recently finished. As I rise and swivel my legs outward, I realize something is wrong. I am feeling weak and a little dizzy and I cannot blame it on beer, because it has been a while since I have even seen one. I wash my face with water out of the canteen and make a beeline for the mess hall as I do every morning.

I expect my body to get with the picture any time, but it refuses to cooperate. I grab a plate of eggs, bacon, and a cup of hot coffee and then sit down. My stomach revolts at the first taste of the eggs and I settle for downing the coffee but even that is hard to drink. A second cup does not rouse me, and I begin to get worried. I am feeling really lousy and disoriented which is not good, because we are leaving camp on the gun jeeps to clear the roads this morning. We have to hustle through this and then get back to escort yesterday's convoy back to Dong Tam.

At the moment I feel like I cannot even escort myself back to the bed, and that is where I long to be. This is another sign that things are not right with my body; I am always eager to go in the morning, always ready to face new adventures. This is because every new morning has a new evening, and those two together represent one more day gone in my tour. I do not even think to report to the aid station for sick call and I will be regretting that omission in several hours.

I still think I can work through this temporary illness in a little while. The jouncing of the jeep and the fresh air in my face will have me feeling better in no time. I am standing in my customary place behind the machine gun, but today I have to hang on much harder. Before long, I have to relinquish my position and sit down on one of the folding seats on the side of the jeep. The dizziness is getting worse and I realize that if I do not sit down, I may fall out of the jeep as we roll down the road. I hate to give up my position behind the gun; we are the second vehicle in the procession and an alert gunner is important, but I cannot do any good lying on the road either.

I am still sitting in the back of the jeep, grimly hanging on when we reach checkpoint 69er. I do not have the energy to get out and buy a cold Coke, so I ask O'Brien to get it for me. A cold drink always tastes good and boy, I do need something to make me feel better. My forehead feels very hot, but I am starting to shiver a little, even though it is a balmy one hundred and five degrees today.

"McCoy look bad, you need cold drink, okay?" I hear the musical voice of Anh and it pulls me out of my stupor. I look over and see two Anhs for a little while, both wavering in the bright sunshine. I take the glass she offers, ice tinkling and full of my favorite drink. It is an effort to raise the glass and drink, and the cold liquid is hard to force down my throat. *Okay guys, you can shoot me now. I cannot even stand to drink this Coke today.*

Anh puts her hand on my forehead and then asks me if I feel cold one minute and hot the next. This is exactly how I feel. She tells me I need to go to the hospital because she thinks I have malaria. I start to argue, but then remember she has been born in this country and spent fifteen years here so she has probably seen more than her share of malaria.

The closest hospital is Tan An but we are heading to Dong Tam and there is a hospital there so I tell myself to hang on and if I do not feel any better when we get to the base I will report for sick call. I do not know just how debilitating this sickness can be, and like an idiot, I feel I will be better by the evening.

The one-hour ride to the base feels like four hours, and when we get to the Ninth Division barracks, I stumble off the jeep and fall into the closest bunk in the closest barracks. I now have a very painful headache and what feels like the world's biggest bowling ball in my stomach. These, added to my other woes, makes me feel like I am dying, and at the moment I do not really care if I do.

I spend the rest of the evening in a haze, awake for a while and then sleeping. When some of the jeep crew tries to rouse me to go to the aid station, I tell them I am too sick to go and since I am dying, it does not matter. This is my second mistake, but I cannot even sit up and want only to be left alone.

That night is the most terrible one of my life. I am alternately lucid and then totally out of my mind. I fight VC in the jungle and I scream, mutter, and generally keep everyone in the barracks awake most of the night. By daylight half the men in the barracks volunteer to take me to the aid station in the jeep; they just want me out of their barracks. They pick me up like a rag doll and carry me to the jeep and then to the aid station.

A sleepy-eyed medic hears their tale of woe and examines me. I am quite unable to coherently explain my symptoms. He decides I have food poisoning and gives me some medicine and an ice bag for my head. The medicine puts me to sleep and I know nothing until early afternoon. O'Brien comes by to see if I am okay and if I want to make the trip back to Rach Kein on the gun jeeps, as the convoy will soon be leaving. Still hopped-up from the medicine, I make my third mistake and go with him. I am woozy and weak, but I feel so much better. It looks like I am not going to die after all.

My euphoria lasts all of fifteen minutes, just long enough to clear the gates of the base camp, and my symptoms reoccur with a vengeance. It is too late to go back now so the only thing I can do is lie down in the cramped quarters in the back of the jeep. My body is contorted in a half circle around the tube that supports the machine gun. This puts my head and feet near the back edge of the floor, which is a good thing, because the way my stomach feels I am going to evacuate at any time.

All I can think of is my wife and my mom. My wife Wanda is a nurse, and my mother Pauline was one in her younger life. It would be so great to have one of them here to help me through this terrible sickness. I hate to admit it to myself, but this rough and tough combat soldier sure could use his wife or his mommy right now! Like last night I am pretty much out of it and do not even realize what is happening until they unload me at the sick bay in Rach Kein.

Medics evaluate me again and the diagnosis this time is malaria. All they needed to do was talk to Anh; she knew what it was after looking me over for ten seconds. The girl could possibly have a bright future ahead as a doctor, if only she had not been born into the poverty and bedlam that is currently afflicting this country.

They keep me in sickbay for the rest of the day and night, giving me more medicine and another ice bag. I do not believe it possible, but I feel even worse than last night. The drugs finally put me in a twilight world. I am half-conscious and hurting, but not awake enough to feel the true brunt of this horrible sickness.

I spend another terrible night wrestling with demons and the VC, and hoping someone will just come in, shoot me, and make this pain end. No one does me the favor and after a night that seems to stretch twenty-four hours long, I greet the new day feeling slightly better, but unable to do much more than crawl to the toilet. I did not know that any sickness could make me feel this bad; could I be sick enough to be sent home?

I abandon this thought, since it hurts too much to even think. I try cursing this misbegotten country and its damn illnesses, but I cannot concentrate enough to do more than attempt to talk and I just give up. I lie there in the greatest misery I have ever been in and pray for sleep.

It does not come, but the medic comes in and tells me something, but his voice is far off in the distance and I cannot understand what he is saying. I can see his face hovering above me, but it is fading in and out. He is trying to take my rifle away from me. He does not understand but the VC are coming and I have to defend myself, so we fight over my non-existent rifle. This idiot medic does not understand that we have scheduled a big battle sometime today and, and ......

I wake up as they are loading me aboard the truck. I cannot sit up, so they stretch me out on the dirty floor. Someone tells me I am going to Tan An Hospital, but his face starts melting and the words stretch out until I cannot understand them and trail off into the abyss.

I lie there on the floor, bouncing around with every bump in the road, but I am so far out of it that at times I feel like I am floating above the bed of the truck. People try to speak to me, but they are talking some foreign language I do not understand and their faces keep changing shape. I see an American face floating above me and then it morphs into a horrible yellow-toothed Charley and he has come to kill me. This is not going to happen because I have lived this long and I am going back home to see my family. I reach for Charley's throat and then a heavy weight settles on me and I cannot move. I try to throw it off, but I cannot move and it is crushing me down.

I wake up again as they are lifting me onto the table at Tan An hospital. A nurse has her face close next to mine and she tells me I am going to be okay; to just relax, but they are trying to take my rifle away again and I cannot let it happen. I hear someone scream in the background, something bangs against the floor, and something is holding me down again. I struggle but I cannot overcome the weight, it is just too much, and I lose consciousness.

I remember only tiny snatches of the next several days. I hear pieces of disjointed conversations and metal banging on the bed and arms moving me. It is just too much trouble to concentrate and I drift, sometimes feeling pain and sometimes feeling that I am floating above my bed and looking down at a soldier I do not recognize.

"Welcome back soldier," says the nurse with her face close to mine. I look up and focus and the face stays the same. It does not change, as they have been doing. The nurse is very pretty and smells so good and I realize I am alive and feeling ok, but I am very weak as I try to move. The terrible headache is gone and that lack of pain is a great feeling.

"You gave us quite a time the last couple of days. My name is Carol and I am from Chicago back in the real world," the nurse says to me. "How about you? Where do you hail from?" My mouth is fuzzy and I try to tell her but the connection from mouth to brain is not quite there yet, so I mumble a bit and give it up. *Good job, McCoy, you are staring at a goddess and you sound like some tongue-tied teenager at his first sock-hop!*

They keep me another day in the hospital and then turn me out with admonishments to take the pills they have given me and the malaria pills from the medics. I have been taking the big yellow pills we call horse pills every time the medic hands them out, but that has been infrequently.

I shuffle slowly out into the bright sunlight and head toward the mess hall. I am familiar with the layout of the camp since I spent one night here months ago when I first came in country. That night seems like years ago. I went through my first mortar attack here and I think this is the barracks I was in when it happened. Man, I was so green then! My stomach is rumbling and I think some food will really feel good so I must be a lot better.

After eating enough for three men, I walk back outside to check the convoy forming up on the road to see if I can get a ride back to my base camp. Walking is still a chore, but I am feeling so much better that I am almost high with relief. A driver tells me the convoy is on the way to Dong Tam. This is in the wrong direction, but it will be loading up there this afternoon for a trip to Rach Kein tomorrow afternoon. This is perfect, as I will get back to Dong Tam for one night and then get back to my base camp. I am not sure how long I was sick, but I figure with this extra day, I might have used up another week altogether. Another week gone in this country is a great feeling, but it is not worth all the pain I endured. That medic better produce one malaria pill a week from now on or he will have some explaining to do.

Once I get to Dong Tam, I climb over the tailgate and seek the cool shelter of the transient barracks. It is early afternoon and no one is here, so I pick a cot close to the door and the breeze and get some rest. This base camp has a large inflatable swimming pool that I have taken advantage of several times and I put it on my to-do list this evening. When that time comes, I try to summon enough energy to walk the mile to the pool. My mind is willing, but my body does not want to cooperate, so I stay on the bunk instead, making plans to visit the mess hall later. *Let us see, I want two plates of whatever they are serving, and at least two one-quart containers of the chocolate milk they usually have.*

Plans made, I fall asleep and when I wake up it is late. I go outside and check and I see only a few lights burning in the mess hall, so I have missed supper. Breakfast is only six hours away and my body still craves rest, so I retire again.

I have a hearty breakfast in the morning as I am feeling somewhat like my old self, then kill time until the convoy leaves for my base camp of Rach Kein. I climb up over the tailgate and find a spot to sit on the pine ammo boxes and it feels like I have come full circle. I remember a long ago ride in the back of a truck to my first duty base of Rach Kein, and I was sitting on the same type of boxes. I have learned a lot since that time, and have been through a lot.

One thing is different, though. At that time I had a freshly issued M-16, serial no. 918409, and that weapon is back at the base camp. I am feeling decidedly naked with no weapon in my hand, and Ambush Alley is ahead of us. If anything happens, all I can do is duck and wish for the best. The Alley is as dusty as ever, but it is also quiet today.

The quiet holds for the trip up Highway Four and back to camp. I hop off the truck when it brakes to a halt in the small square on the base. I have only a fifty-yard walk to our shack by the water. It feels like I have been gone a month, though I know it is no more than a week. The platoon is not around; they are still out on road-clearing duties, so I have the little building to myself.

I help myself to a cold Coke out of the fridge, grab a chair, and retire to my favorite place, the front porch. The tide is down and the inlet stinks, but the view of water is calming and peaceful. I have nothing to do, as I probably will not go back on duty until tomorrow. I just sit there and savor the day with my temporary respite from labor. I remember my pipe, go in, and get it. I tamp tobacco into the bowl and light up, and this afternoon is complete. No worries until tomorrow, but I will not think about that today.

I get an attack of malaria later that year in December. It is less vicious and keeps me bed-ridden for only two days. Even a mild attack of malaria is very painful, however, and I am careful to take those big yellow pills every time they are dispensed. Some men seem less conscientious about taking them, and I warn them of the roulette they are playing.

***

The disease continues to plague me when I get home. Within a year, I get another very bad case and am flat on my back again. At least I have my wife Wanda to take care of me. On the second day, I am delirious and back in combat. They are trying to take my rifle again and I struggle to hold on to my possession. Like my previous attacks, my mind is returning to Viet Nam and Wanda does not know what to do for me. Her nurse's training has certainly not prepared her for a case of malaria. She gets worried and calls her father for re-inforcement. He takes one look at me and suggests the emergency room. They half carry and half drag me to the car with me protesting all the way. Wanda hands me a small plastic trashcan I can use, just in case. My mind is so foggy I do not understand what she means so I drop it and lay flat on the back seat in agony. The motion of the car soon necessitates the use of the receptacle, and I manage to reach it in time.

I am in a wheel chair in the waiting room at Peninsula General and I have an agonizingly long wait to see a doctor. Wanda is frantic at the wait and I tell her not to worry. I feel so bad that I plan to die shortly, so the wait is not impor-tant. She tells me that she waited for me a year while I was in Viet Nam, and I am not going to die. Not on her watch, anyway.

I finally get to see a doctor and Wanda explains my symptoms and the fact that I have contracted malaria in Viet Nam and this was how I felt with prior attacks. The nurse draws blood, they run tests, and the doctor mercifully gives me something. I enter that old familiar half-conscious state. I know I feel bad and things are happening around me, but they hardly register on my brain.

I wake up the next day feeling like the victim of a hit-and run acc'
in the street. I am weak and so sore, but I am over the hurdle and just

after all. The doctor releases me that afternoon and when I get home, the discharge papers say I was the victim of an upper respiratory infection. What? *This is malaria, doc. I have way too much experience with this particular disease.*

The experience continues with recurrences every several years and the diagnosis is always the same, an upper respiratory infection. Sometimes it is a full-blown three or four-day attack and I wish I were dead and other times there is a milder two-day one. There seems to be no rhyme or reason for the appearance of the disease, so every time I get a cold I worry that it is malaria again, and I am so relieved when it is not. No doctor seems to be able to help. They give me medicine that only helps when I am in the middle of an attack; it does not ward off the next occurrence.

Wanda and I separate and finally divorce. She tried her best to help me get over my hidden injuries and recapture the person I was when I left for the army. I know it was hard on her being married to a man she hardly recognized. My experiences changed me too much and I just could not make the transition back to my former self.

My care when I have another attack passes on to various girlfriends. Most are scared out of their wits when I get really sick, so I continue the bi-annual visits to the emergency room to get a diagnosis of upper respiratory infection. I am so tired of hearing this term that I press the doctors to declare my illness as malaria. Not one doctor will do this and I finally decide there must be some kind of collusion between doctors and the army. The army must be worried about a class action suit from malaria sufferers, so they tell doctors not to make the diagnosis. I begin to believe this; it is the only thing that makes sense to me.

I want nothing from the army. Now that I am out of their clutches, I hope never to be involved with the armed forces in any way. I am still on inactive reserve for the next couple of years, but I have decided that the army will never have me in their power again. They just do not have a man big and mean enough to come and drag me back.

***

et and later marry my second wife, Lori Ann Wanex. She
re are very happy for fourteen years until she passes away
e five years to get over her death at age thirty-eight and I
rain. I cannot expose myself to that kind of pain any more.

Before she dies, she becomes my unsuspecting caretaker when I have my malaria attacks. Like others before her, she takes good care of me when I get sick, but when I get delirious and start calling for my rifle she gets very concerned. Therefore, we do the old emergency room routine again with help from her father or my brother. As usual, I get the same old lame non-specific diagnosis I have come to hate. The only good thing is that as I age the malaria attacks seem to lessen in quantity and severity and I am very thankful. Still, no one can offer me a cure for my malady, just temporary respite.

***

In 1999, I have a milder attack that I weather without going to the hospital and I hope it is the harbinger of fewer problems from this persistent sickness. I caught it ten thousand miles from home and no one seems to be able to cure it in this country. I have an appointment scheduled for a physical with a Dr. Weaver in several weeks and decide to mention the malaria to him in the hopes that he knows of a cure or can suggest someone who is knowledgeable about this particular disease.

Imagine my surprise when I find that Dr. Weaver is female and this will be a comprehensive physical. It is a little embarrassing, but I figure I am old enough to handle this so I keep the appointment. The doctor is very nice and thorough and at the end I mention the malaria and my fight with it through the years. The doctor looks electrified when I mention malaria and questions me closely.

She explains that she has training overseas in tropical diseases and malaria in particular. She saw many cases while out of the U.S., but has not encountered any once she came back home. I am her first malaria case in the states and she is intrigued. She goes on to mention new medicines that are available and new methods of treating malaria. Before I leave the office I have a prescription that she feels will finally cure me of this disease or at least prevent me from having any more re-occurrences. She explains that once you catch malaria it stays in your bloodstream the rest of your life, always ready to bring you misery again.

This turns out to be the doctor I have been searching for over a twenty-year span. Fate or dumb luck has finally brought us together. I have a final question for Dr. Weaver before I go. I explain the many trips to the emergency room

I have endured and the refusal of any doctors to diagnose malaria. I tell her that I feel that it is some kind of cover-up instigated by the army.

She smiles and explains my twenty-year-old mystery. She says that doctors in the U.S. are not trained about malaria, since it is so rare here. The doctors do not have the training so they will not diagnose any illness as malaria; hence, my illnesses are lumped under a general upper respiratory infection. I am glad to find there is no great cover-up, but still mystified that I could suffer from something so long and receive no cure.

I took all the medicine prescribed for me, and I have had absolutely no malaria attacks since that last one in 1999. I do not know if the medicine cured the problem or if my body finally learned to fight it off on its own. Whatever the reason, I am just glad that the terrible affliction that has bothered me for twenty years or more seems to be at an end.

Through the years, I have met hundreds of Viet Nam vets and talked with them but I can find no one that also contracted malaria. I can only conclude that I was one of the few very unlucky men to meet the wrong mosquito.

I have spent the last thirty years trying to forget the war and the lack of support and respect that we received when we got back. It is very ironic that Viet Nam gave me one more final gift that would make it even harder to forget the whole sordid, long-running experience. Combat resolutely hangs far back in the innermost reaches of my mind and refuses to be expunged. I think I am repressing it successfully when days pass with never a thought of the country or the things I went through. A war experience is devious, however, no matter how strong you think you are.

With no other way to attack me, it will force in happy memories. I will remember good friends and happy times. It will not force in the dark shadows, the men who are no longer alive and the situations that led to their death. Instead, it will replay the camaraderie and the good experiences I had in that movie screen in my mind. It toys with me, and feeds me happy pabulum until I am suffused with joy and nostalgia for those long ago, happier times.

Then it will sense that opening, that dropping of my defenses, and it will shoot a pain-filled arrow directly into my heart. The bad times return to engulf me, the pain repeated over and over. In addition, just for good measure, let us throw in a nice three-day bout of malaria to make this old soldier really feel his war experiences.

I am so glad that I managed to shrug off the worst of the feelings and be-come a productive member of society, as I had been when I received those draft papers. Many soldiers did not manage to do so. One of my own friends relayed to me of how he spent fifteen years on the street as a drunk and drug addict be-fore he ran into a nurse that cared enough for him to get him the help he needed. Not all the returnees from war made out as well as I did, so I consider myself lucky and very blessed. Not a lot of soldiers can fight post-traumatic stress and malaria for years and still call themselves blessed, but I am one. Two good wives and a loving family over the years have aided me greatly, and to an old soldier in the autumn of his life, that is all that is important.

284 days left in country.

Chapter 9
Big Operation In Three Corps

Can Guioc-May 1968.

The country of Viet Nam is long, narrow, and curved. The curved ends face west and in this direction are its three bordering countries, Laos, Thailand, and Cambodia. It is bordered on the north by Communist Red China and on the east by the South China Sea. This area has been a hotbed of political unrest and fighting throughout recorded history. Viet Nam lost its freedom many times to stronger countries, most notably the Chinese, then the Portuguese, and finally the French in the 1860s. The country rarely saw peace and the struggle to survive created a race of physically small but mentally tough people who often dreamed of a free country in the future. This was a dream that many other people across the area embraced.

Our country in its great misplaced wisdom saw only that Viet Nam was a country on its way to Communist domination. In the thinking of the 1960's era, this was a very bad thing and had to be halted at all possible costs. The U.S.A. did not stop to think that most of the people in the area wanted only to be left alone to farm their little piece of land and make their living as best they could.

After the United States entered the war, they divided the country into four zones which they called "Corps." One Corps started at the border between North and South Viet Nam and stretched southward. This area boasted a larger population whereas Two Corps to the south was less populated and mostly mountainous areas interspersed with plains. Three Corps, which was further toward the south was also heavily populated and the start of the country's farming area, since it was much closer to sea level. It also had many rivers to keep the land well watered. Four Corps was the most southern and most populated and much of the land was devoted to millions of acres of rice production, which kept the country fed.

This Corps was almost at sea level and had many rivers to deliver water to the fields. Much of the area not farmed was marsh and tidal estuaries, where much fighting took place.

Fate delivered me to Four Corps and to the area where fighting was especially hard on the soldier. You fought the waist deep mud in the Delta area as much as you did the enemy. In addition, if you were not pleased with mud, all you had to do was wait several days and a chopper would deliver your platoon to a jungled area. There you could fight the heavy brush, the snakes, and the heat and if you had any energy left over, the enemy.

My company's base camp at this time is Can Guioc. It is a small forward base with few amenities and a lot of dust. Then the three-month rainy season came along and replaced the dust with a sea of mud. Can Guioc had one more distinct disadvantage; it was right in the middle of what we called "Indian Territory." This meant an inordinate amount of VC roamed the area, and they had the temerity to think the area was theirs. We were locked in a quiet struggle with them, but we owned the whole territory during the day. At night the VC owned select areas because it was too large an area to cover completely. The army's policy of taking an area, and running the VC out, then promptly leaving the area did not help. Charley just melted into the jungle if we pushed him too hard. Then, he would wait until the choppers carried us away and he would come back, and it was business as usual.

My company has been locked into the daily patrols and nighttime ambushes for over a month now, and it is getting tiring and disheartening. Every few days a man loses his life or receives a wound and we have had just about enough. We always kill more enemy than they kill of us, but that is little consolation for men on the line. I am beginning to think that the enemy does not think we are serious about owning this area.

The daily rains also add to our general misery. Almost everyone is having trouble with immersion foot, the malady that affected soldiers when their feet stayed wet for too long. The skin on your feet would turn white and wrinkled and then the friction of the sock starts abrading the skin. This leaves us with bloody, painful feet, making walking very difficult. On our last overnight patrol, I removed my shoes and socks and walked in my bare feet for most of the day. It is painful, but not as painful as wearing boots. The only redeeming feature to this affliction is that you can show your feet to the LT and get a few days off to recover.

In the midst of all this, the LT calls the platoon together and tells us we are going on a company-sized operation up to the central highlands in Two Corps. We have never been there, but have heard that the higher elevation means the absence of mud even in the rainy season. We have also heard about the rugged mountains and flat plateaus in this area. Men that serve there also tell us there are fewer people, and more importantly, fewer VC in this area.

They also warn us that you are more likely to come across hard-core NVA soldiers from North Vietnam. These men have a reputation of being professional soldiers that tend to stick around and fight when located, unlike the local VC.

The platoon talks it over and decides this sounds pretty good to us. We are sick of the area we are in now and the absence of mud is a definite plus. Maybe we are exchanging more VC for less NVA, but with the reputation the NVA has, it is a wash. In addition, it might be better to face an enemy that sticks around and fights rather than a hit and run enemy. We all agree the change of scenery will do us all good and it starts sounding like a great adventure. Only a platoon of grunts could possibly think that meeting experienced fighters can be an adventure. Of course, we are all experienced soldiers ourselves now, and just maybe we want to fight our equals. I have no doubt that the new adversary will not find us wanting in battle.

The LT told us we had two days to get our feet straight and to pack as if we will be away several weeks. He is still awaiting final information on the operation along with the necessary maps. He is not sure exactly how long we will be gone. I decide to treat the whole thing as a vacation, so I do not let it bother me too much. Soon the whole platoon adopts my outlook and we sit on the bunkers at night and smoke, talking about our upcoming vacation. As far as I am concerned, our destination could not be any worse than where we are now, and maybe has a chance of being better. Optimism is a good thing to cultivate when you are a grunt; it helps to keep you farther from insanity.

We pack as if we will be gone a long time, because we do not know how long that is. The platoon gets together and decides who will carry personal items, no use in every one of us carrying a camera or small pocket radio. We actually wash some of our uniforms in a big puddle of water that is forming in a low area near our barracks due to the rainy season. We usually wade into it when we come in from operations to get the mud rinsed off our uniforms. We have no laundry powder, so we use hand soap vigorously scrubbed into the material. At least when we hit the highlands we will smell a little better.

We all walk around barefooted for the next several days, and coupled with some salve the medic gives us our feet improve considerably. A soldier moves on his feet, so when the feet are hurting, we are in a world of trouble, to use the old army saying.

That night we hold a private platoon meeting, and do not mention it to two of our members. We manage to make ourselves scarce for a short while, and discuss a mutual problem, one that has been building. We want to solve this before we head out on the new mission.

Somers, our medic, is a druggie and Lawson is a slacker. Somers seems always slightly high and claims it is the Darvon pills he takes for headaches. We have been keeping a close eye on him, but never catch him with drugs or pot. Either one is widely available over here. Five dollars and a word to practically any street urchin hanging around the front gate will fix you up with enough "herb" to get an elephant high.

Lawson, though an agreeable person, is very untrustworthy. I have personally caught him sleeping while he should be on guard when we are out on listening post. This can get all three men killed. Other men have reported that the same thing is happening to them. Our platoon has been drug free all the time; it is something we all agree we must do. We occasionally go to the platoon leader and ask him to transfer someone because of this problem, and now we feel it is time to do it again.

We hate to point accusing fingers, because some men just cannot take the strain of combat and find that pot eases the pressure. We all know that someday, that could be us. However, we cannot put up with a medic, of all things, being high while on patrol with us. Lawson we just cannot trust anytime, so the two men must go. We just hope the LT can get us two replacements in the short time before the upcoming operation.

Bouncing men out of a platoon and replacing them is a crapshoot, because you never know whom you will get. Some sergeants get rid of undesirables this way so we may get someone worse. In fact, that is how we came by Lawson. If we get new men we will not know their worth until we are on the operation, but all agree it is worth the risk. I have already told Medic Somers that if I receive a wound and see him crawling toward me to bandage it, that if I can still use the machine gun I might shoot him. I am almost serious, but he thinks I am kidding and laughs it off.

Several of us went to the LT's quarters that night to tell him of the no confidence vote on the two men, but he is already ahead of us. He tells us he is wondering how long it would be before he heard our complaints about the men, and that he will do his best to trade off those two for better replacements. Lt. Sharp is a "righteous" officer, the term we grunts use for a man that keeps the safety of his men foremost in his mind. We are happy to have him. Many of the officers in charge of our company during the year I was there were much less capable, and some were downright dangerous. Classroom training is important, but when Charley has you in his sights and the bullets are kicking up dirt all around you, it takes a cool head to command correctly. Coolness under fire is not teachable in a classroom. This takes OTJ training and even then, some officers came up wanting.

The whole platoon gets up at 0600 hours the morning of the operation, even though the trucks will not be here until 0900 hours. We want to get a good hot meal in us before we leave. Word has come down that we will be issued LRP (Long Range Patrol-pronounced "lerp") rations. This is a good sign that the mission is going to be long and that a lot of walking will be required. Smith and Lawson are in the mess hall eating but they do not come back to our barracks afterwards and I notice their gear is gone.

It looks like the LT did a quick and quiet transfer, no goodbyes and no arguing. This is good because we are already wired up over the upcoming mission; we do not need any more pressure. We only hope that any replacements we receive will fit in and be capable.

"Recon, meet your new men, Zucharella and McMasters. Zucharella is a medic and his friend knows which end of the rifle points forward," said the LT. We shake hands with the new men and carry on a conversation about where they are from and where we call home. We go over our gear for the fourth or fifth time, making sure we are ready to roll before the trucks arrive.

I get ready for the trip with my flak jacket going on first, then seven hundred rounds of ammo draped around my shoulders and waist. I follow up with two grenades clipped to the jacket and my big knife and sheath at my waist, angled so I can pull it out quickly. Next are the .45 caliber pistol and six magazines. The armorer has finally issued me the sidearm and now I will not have to worry about running out of machine gun ammo and being defenseless except for the knife. That knife is a last ditch effort for a soldier. I never want to have to use it, which would be much too personal; however, I know I can use it if I have too. I am in my kick-butt persona now, and I know I look much meaner than I am.

This is what combat in the delta is all about. When we go out on operations, we want the whole platoon to look badass. Charley is always watching and the meaner we look, the less he wants to invite us to play. Every day Charley leaves you alone is one more day off that three hundred and sixty-five day tour, and one day closer to going home.

Every one has his equipment on now and we are ready to head out to the road where the trucks are forming in line. I hear the last minute clinks of pieces of equipment being discarded, the soldier hoping to lighten his load for the coming operation. We try to take everything we think we will need, but a man can only carry so much, especially when the going gets rough. We have all been in a situation where we had to discard personal belongings to lighten the load and when we drop them, they are gone for good. We will never see that little piece of real estate again.

I think one more time, one canteen or two? Some men are carrying three canteens, which is extra weight. I prefer to carry that weight in ammo. I find that I can usually exist on one canteen a day if I carry a few small, rounded stones. These I pop into my mouth one at a time and they tend to make you salivate and keep your mouth wet. This is an old tried and true Boy Scout trick and it always helped on those long Scout marches we occasionally did. These long marches came about when too many of us Scouts caused problems at Camp Rodney back in the real world. I think our scoutmaster figured that a worn out Boy Scout was a good Boy Scout.

We head out to the road to wait for the trucks and congregate, jostling for the limited amount of shade. There are at least two hundred men here and shade is at a premium. Everybody finds places to lean on or lies flat, conserving their energy. We are all carrying between forty and fifty pounds and we know the road ahead is going to be long. Everyone pulls out the soldier's friend; a cigarette, or in my case, a pipe, and we light up and talk about everything except the coming operation.

I look around the assembled soldiers. I am a student of human nature and I love to study the men and their actions. I can spot the newbys right away. They are the ones too dumb to find some shade, and they are standing or squatting down, thus wasting energy. The scared look in their eyes pretty much clinches it. We long-timers have a carefully practiced air of indifference and we oc-casionally throw in a bored yawn. We are not scared! Well, maybe not much.

The way we act, we could be waiting on the corner back home to meet the bus, which is late. The newbys though, have one leg up on us in this respect. They are scared of something coming that they know nothing of, something that their limited experience does not allow them to see. We vets already know what could be coming and what might happen, and let me tell you, knowing is no comfort.

The platoon is getting comfortable with the two new men already. They know what they are doing because they have that almost indefinable look and walk of seasoned fighting men. It is an air of calm competence with an added hint of cockiness thrown in. Only the seasoned vet's radar notices this and tells them that these men can be trusted. It is great to get two replacements that know what they are doing, especially on such short notice. The platoon leaders always hoard their good men, so I know the LT called in a big favor somewhere, and I wonder how he is going to repay the deed.

They use trucks to transport us because we have over three hundred miles to travel, which takes the choppers too far out of their operating range. It also takes way too many of them. This clues us in to the fact that this is a carefully planned operation with a flexible time schedule. It is not one of their normal "fly them out and jam them in there" operations. The army never gives you any information and we have learned to read between the lines whenever possible.

The trucks roll up, slinging mud off their tires, and screech to a halt. The drivers have erected the canvas roofs over the beds of the trucks, so we will have protection from the sun and rain on the trip. *Nice gesture, drivers, we never expected to get deluxe accommodations on the road.* We climb up and load the trucks, jamming in until the seats on each side are full, and then filling the floor space. Each man has just enough room that he can lean back against the bed or against a friend on the floor. Snug, but if someone has to go to the toilet over the tailgate, it is going to be a real pain. Army convoys do not stop for toilet breaks, and you sometimes have to see more anatomy of a fellow soldier than you really desire.

We roll northward on Highway Four in high spirits. Someone brings out a small transistor radio and we sing along to the latest offering from Radio Sai-gon. The singer is admonishing a girl to "come back when you grow up girl," and the song reminds me of soft summer evenings spent cruising in the GTO with Wanda sitting on the console on a pillow. I would shove in the clutch; she would shift the car to the next gear. I thought those evenings would never end. A small tear escapes my eyes, and I wonder what I am missing most. Is it Wanda or the sound those three deuces made when the throttle was wide open and I was working that floor shift? Gone, all gone now, I realize. Wanda and I are married, she is waiting for me, and I am damned sure I will get back home to her. However, that moment in time, that glorious teen-aged innocence is gone forever, and I will never, ever regain that.

I watch the countryside roll backwards behind the tailgate and listen to my fellow soldiers playing cards. They manage to get a game going regardless of the cramped quarters. A third of the platoon are avid card players and I never cease to marvel about their infatuation with the game. I have run to a bunker during a mortar attack and observed the fools calmly playing cards, barely ducking when a round goes off close by the building. They are always trying to teach me the game, but I know better than to mess with card players that dedicated. What little money I have will disappear quickly from me under the guise of teaching me to play.

We pass by the giant base at Long Binh now and it stretches for several miles along the road. We all entered the country here and received several days of training on the various booby traps Charley makes, and his method of fighting. This is the farthest north I have been in Viet Nam and I am eager to see what lies around the next corner. Will it be as beautiful as the simple elegance of the delta area? The U. S. is pretty in my memory, but this country has its own loveliness in a simple, backwater sort of way. Maybe the danger adds to that, adding a little extra spice like an extra thick layer of icing adds to a cake. Man, what I would not give for a good ole'American cake right now!

After a while, the road starts climbing and the vegetation gets thinner. No mud is visible and my old nemesis, that damned yellow dust starts enveloping the truck. A third of the soldiers are asleep, sitting upright or leaning against a friend. I know I should try to get some rest too, but I am too excited as I look for new sights. This may be my one and only chance to see the central highlands, which the army has named them. The army has given me a crap job, but at least they are giving me a tour of the country, and that is worth staying awake to see.

The scenery is getting a little strange, certainly not what I am used to seeing. We ride through rolling hills that slowly get larger and steeper, and perched on top of these hills are small ARVN outposts built just like the ones in the delta except for the steep hills. They have concertina and barbed wire running across the hillsides and in places the approaches are near vertical. I would certainly not want to try to take one of these little hilltop fortresses, they appear quite formidable. I suddenly realize the fighting here is going to be quite different, and not at all to my liking. If Charley has installed himself on some of these hillsides further along the area, the fighting could be quite bloody.

As we roll along I see larger and larger foothills and in the distance the high unmistakable dark blue of mountains. These mountains have heavy forests and all of a sudden I realize not only is this serious jungle, but almost vertical jungle to boot. I did not sign up for this, just stop and let me leave. I will walk back south and the little matter of several hundred miles will not matter. I can see on the face of those that are still awake that they do not love the area either. From a pure looks standpoint, the terrain is great. If you factor in trying to fight or take some of these hills, I believe I would rather have the delta.

The trucks slow and make a sharp turn to the right up a hill; the road is so steep that it looks like if the driver had to stop the emergency brake would not hold the truck on the grade. The truck grinds slowly up the hill and I am almost holding my breath. We finally level out and pull up into a base camp, much like the base camps in the delta. There is one big difference, though; this camp is perched on the top of a fifteen hundred foot high hill. It looks like the top five hundred feet have been bulldozed off the hill and the resulting material shoved over the side. This makes the approach to the top of the hill near vertical. It is also covered with loose, shifting raw dirt that is packed against wooden walls anchored on the steep hillsides, forming vertical ledges. There is some concertina wire at the edge, which is all that is needed, the ledges forming enough of a barrier to keep out all but the most determined enemy. That most determined enemy would have to climb that steep terraced edge while weapons were being fired at him, and grenades tossed over the edge to roll down to meet him.

This base camp is named Fire Base Houston. Since camps receive the name of an illustrious past leader or a person who died in combat, I wonder if this Houston is back in the real world prospering or if he occupies a small piece of real estate in a shady field somewhere. I guess it is nice to have a base camp with your name on it. I prefer to be one of the nameless, quickly forgotten men who rotate through this country and return home safely.

This camp has little extra accommodations, so we follow the sarge to an area near the north perimeter where some twelve by twenty wall tents are arraigned in rows. We receive inflatable sleeping mattresses and the nearest bunkers are shown to us. I pick an area near the entrance, drop the mattress and flop down. It has been a long trip and we are all tired. A little small talk ensues, and then most of us try to get some rest before we head over to the mess hall for supper. Alone with my thoughts, I reflect on the day that has almost passed. I have seen some new sights and a different kind of beauty in this country. I have not heard one rifle shot today, and in this country, that is a rare thing.

I lie there, luxuriating in the feeling of having to do absolutely nothing for this moment. As usual, my mind drifts to the time I have left in country, something I calculate every day in my mind. We are all obsessed with this and some of us even have little calendars of the months and days inked on the canvas cover of our steel pots. Every night those men solemnly ink out that day on the map just before it gets dark, and that day will be one less. I prefer to do my calculations in my mind. Having it written out for everyone to see is somewhat like asking for it. I am not superstitious, but my mind calendar is better.

Let us see. Um, I have been in this beautiful hellhole for ninety-two days. Subtract that from three hundred and sixty five, and that leaves two hundred and seventy three. Two hundred and seventy three! That is a lifetime, that is forever the way time moves over here.

We rouse and go to supper and meet some of the locals and exchange information. They warn us that Charley has outposts on the tops of some surrounding hills and he will be monitoring what we do. They knock them out with artillery or patrols but old Charley just keeps coming back. They have named their nightly artillery barrages of the hilltops "whack-a-gook." These men are just like us, they endure and they use laughter to mask the frustration of fighting an enemy that never seems to sleep.

The warning we receive is correct. We are sitting on a bunker at the perimeter smoking, when we hear the telltale whoosh of a mortar round dropping down on us. We jump into the bunker and hear the explosion several hundred feet away. As we peek out the doorway, we hear dirt and little pieces of wood patter down on the bunker. These are small and falling vertically, so we pay them no mind. Other rounds follow as the warning siren comes on. In the darkness, I see the movement of men a few yards away. They are taking the canvas covers off large artillery weapons and others are stacking rounds. Someone will be on the radio to TAC, waiting to get the coordinates for a fire mission.

If the mortars are not over several miles away, the men in the observation tower in the middle of the camp will sight them. They will figure where to fire and in several minutes, the artillery will be sending Charley some late night greetings. Charley counters this by sending off a few rounds, then moving quickly to a new position and starting the barrage again. We counter by refiguring, and sometimes this goes on half the night. It is more like a game than actual combat.

The night passes quickly after the mortar attack. We awake at 0600 hours with the sarge hollering to wake up. It is time to get up, clean up and head to the mess hall. Today is the start of the new operation and we feed ourselves good in preparation for a week of LRP rations for food. We discuss what is coming up amongst ourselves and too soon, it is time to go back over to Headquarters Company for the mission briefing. Over three hundred men are gathered and the briefing starts outside because they do not have enough room inside.

"Good morning men, I am Colonel Amherst. Today we will cover an outline of the coming week's operations," says the tall, tanned speaker. I listen because this dude looks like he has been around the block a few times. He exudes that competent manner that some professional soldiers manage to carry, and it is easy to tell this man is not just talk. *He has also walked the walk, as we say in the bush, so he can talk the talk.* I relax a little because we have a solid man in charge.

The colonel continued his speech. "As you have probably heard from the local men, Charley is getting a little too big for his britches, with the help from the NVA. Last night as you slept, we sent out elements from Able and Charley Company and they are now in a blocking position. They are in a line between Hill 217 and Hill 222. They command the heights and the valley between the two. Your job is to go out and walk the enemy into Able and Charley Company. You are the hammer and the two hidden companies out there are the anvil. If we do this right, we might get numerous body counts. Good luck men and give 'em hell'."

Amherst stepped down off his wooden ammo box podium and the sarge revolves his arm in the air, the signal to roll. We pick up weapons and march out the gate single file, a long line of men stretching down the road a half mile. As usual, I get that little lump in my throat and that feeling of a great adventure ahead. I just hoped it was a little adventure and not too much.

About a mile down the road, we peel off into the sparse vegetation and form a long line reaching from one side of the valley to the other. The operation appears well planned since the hills on each side of the valley are very steep with dense bushes and trees on them. The enemy will know we are coming and it will be natural to retreat through the sparse vegetation on the valley floor, rather than climb those formidable hills. If the two hidden companies have done their job well, and set up without being seen by Charley last night, the enemy is going to be in a squeeze in several hours.

"You think we gonna get in any heavy shit today?" I looked over to my right and the question comes from Atwell, one of the new men. He is already sweating heavily and dragging his feet, though we have not been walking over a half hour.

"Don't worry man. We have point men out ahead, they will have problems first and that will warn us. Get flat quickly if you hear gunfire. Keep an eye out to the front and scan any dense bushes ahead of you," I say. I am trying to condense a lot of soldiering into a few sentences but it is just to show him someone has his back. Often that is all a newbie needs before his first combat, some words of advice from someone he views as an old hand at this.

We continue northwest down the valley. Occasionally a short burst of gunfire breaks out and we halt while that is corrected. So far, Charley is backing up as planned and is shooting just enough to show his displeasure at us intruding into his domain. I reflect that we are walking roughly in the direction of the Cambodian border and I wonder just how far away the border is located. The border of Viet Nam is bad karma anywhere you are in the country.

Charley's supply route runs south down the border of Viet Nam and Cambodia from North Viet Nam. It is inside Cambodia far enough that we cannot stop the resupply without infringing on a supposedly neutral country's border. This is pure crap, because we bomb the hell out of the route. I cannot see any difference between bombing the route or going in and fighting. Whether it is bombs or men, they both wind up inside Cambodia. This is one of the crazy constrictions of the war. We cannot touch his supply routes directly, but if we could, we would cripple his ability to fight the war. I always thought we should forget Cambodia's border as it is all dense jungle there with little or no people around. If we can fight this war, we can convince a tenth-rate country to let us operate in the area, one way or the other.

Heavier gunfire is now erupting in the valley ahead of us and we hear multiple explosions to our front. Our radios blare out and we hear reports of heavy contact up ahead. Charley has walked into the trap and is now pinned down and fighting back. This presents a problem for which we are not adequately prepared. The bullets shot by the anvil force ahead of us at the VC are now flying over us and becoming a danger. We must stop our advance and cannot move forward any further to help the two companies that are engaged in the firefight.

We drop to the ground, our bodies hugging the terrain as tightly as we can. There are few trees for cover, and over two hundred men looking for cover. I hear the bullets snapping overhead and leaves and small branches rain down on our position. The only redeeming feature is one of topography. The enemy has halted on a rise ahead of us and as the anvil men fire slightly upwards at them, the angle of fire puts most of the bullets well over our head. That is little consolation to us in the crossfire, however. I wish I had an entrenching tool to dig me a burrow and I could probably get down five feet quickly, even digging from a prone position.

I do not have that tool and even if I did, it would take far too long to get everybody dug in. We must make a decision, and do it quickly. The platoon is strung out along the valley and no one can stand up and move quickly to pass orders along. I do not see the sarge anywhere so he is probably pinned down somewhere out of sight. We have to make a decision without his input and hope that the rest of the platoon observes our movement and follows suit.

There is too much gunfire to hear any orders or the radio, so we must make our own decisions as to what to do. The decision is very simple. Bullets are slowly cutting down any cover, no matter how minor and the only trees are on the steep hillsides to each side of us. I judge the left hillside to be much closer to my position, maybe a quarter mile away. A long crawl to be sure, but that is better than staying here. If we vacate this area, we will not be able to stop the enemy from coming back in this direction but we have to get out of here due to the crossfire.

I give the problem only a quick thought. It is imperative that we vacate the premises. I roll the machine gun up on my shoulder with the strap around my neck. This faces the barrel back over my butt so it will not jam into the ground and fill the barrel with dirt. I plan to set the world record for the quarter-mile low crawl and I cannot be worried about the barrel right now.

Off I go at a fast clip and as I pass men prone on the ground, I holler for them to head for the high ground and cover. Some are in a little world of their own, afraid to move and I do not have time to hold anyone's hand. The more astute ones follow me and before long, we are trying to see who will get there first. That machine gun is slowing me down, jamming me into the ground, but I cannot abandon it. I may need it very badly before long.

My breath becomes ragged, my shoulder joints are burning, and I cannot go any further but I keep reaching my arms forward and pushing with my feet. About the time I am ready to give up, only halfway to my goal, I realize that if we can make it partway up the hill, we will be in an even better position to stop Charley should he retreat in our direction.

Up there we will have cover in the trees, and the height will give us command of the valley floor. The vegetation is sparse on the valley floor, and we will be able to spot him fleeing even better. Damn Charley, this is his entire fault! If it were not for him, I would not be here; breathing like a man in cardiac arrest, and all my joints would not be hurting. My knees feel like they are on fire and I have worked myself up into quite a furor over those bastards wearing black pajamas. It will be so fine to be up on that hill so Mr. Machine Gun can do his thing. Thinking about being up on that hillside with Charley in my sights on the valley floor reinvigorates me and gives me the extra energy I need.

All of a sudden, I feel like I am good for at least another mile and I crawl with renewed energy. I even pass some of my fellow soldiers. We finally reach the edges of the hill and then the work really starts. It is very steep and the trees and underbrush almost impenetrable. I do not hear bullets over my head now so I can stand up, but I am so tired I sink back to the ground almost immediately. I figure I need at least twenty feet of elevation to get to a good firing position, so I crawl and bull my way through the underbrush. *Come on McCoy, you can make it. You only need another ten feet.* A fine big tree is up ahead and it will make great cover. I notice the firing is dying down to sporadic shots and I realize I am screaming at myself about that last ten feet.

With my last ounce of strength, I attain that tree and flop down behind it. I rest a little while before I pull the machine gun off my back and unclip the ammo from around my chest. The ammo is filthy from all the dirt I crawled through, so I brush it off as best I can. I check the weapon for dirt and it has stayed clean riding on my back. I fold down the legs and position the muzzle out toward the valley floor and I wait. I pull the .45 caliber pistol out of its holster and lay it close by, situating the magazines carefully. All around me, my friends have taken up firing positions and we lie on that hillside in the afternoon sunshine. We wipe the sweat out of our eyes and keep a close watch. We draw beads on that valley floor and we wait.

272 days left in country.

Chapter 10
Chasing Charley In The Highlands

Near Gia Ngia-May 1968.

We lie on that steep hillside in the hot sun for fifteen minutes, sweat pouring off our faces. We finally recover from our exertion, and we wait in vain for Charley to appear in front of our weapons. Where is he this time?

The firing has died off to an occasional shot at the head of the valley. It looks like the battle is over and we have missed the main show. I do not know if I am pleased or annoyed. My friends and I head back down the steep slope and see the sarge at the bottom, flushed and relieved to see us.

"Juliet Recon, assemble on my voice," he says. "We have work to do at the end of the valley. We have to reinforce the anvil company and clean up the mess. Beaucoup bodies are on the ground."

We head northwest up the valley, counting heads as we go. We are all relieved to find that not one of us has suffered an injury. We all know that the topography has saved our bacon. We cannot rest or lose focus. There is a lot of ground to cover between here and the ambush site, and we will likely find some enemy hiding in the sparse cover. We could also find some injured, and Charley is just as dangerous when he is wounded as he is whole.

We stay spread out across the narrow valley, trying to cover all the area that could hide a man. We make our way slowly onwards, but pause to call ahead on the radio. Everyone is going to be trigger-happy right now and we want to let them know we will be joining the anvil platoons shortly. We come upon men from the two ambush companies searching the bodies lying on the ground. The battle has been fruitful because more than a dozen men are prone on the ground, their faces frozen in death masks. Some show surprise, and some show last-minute pain.

We join in with the distasteful task. As we come to each body, we tie a line to a foot, retreating a safe distance, and pull the body about five feet before doing a search. This is to make sure the body is not booby-trapped. Fleeing soldiers could have done this, and it possible that a wounded man might pull the cotter pin from a grenade then wedge it under his body as a nasty surprise. When the body is flipped over, the handle pops loose to arm the grenade, and boom! Charley will try to kill you even when he is dying.

We have a bonus in the bodies. Most of them are wearing the uniforms of the NVA instead of the black pajamas the VC wear. This is the first NVA that I have seen this close, and they look more soldierly than the VC, even in death. We also recover some rifles, AK-47s and several SKSs. The enemy has fled the battleground quickly and has not had time to carry off bodies and weapons. I wonder if the ambush got them all, or if some managed to climb the steep hillsides and disappear.

After the bodies go through a thorough search, we leave them side by side in a clearing. Several men take pictures to document the body count, and we walk off to climb the steep flanks of hill 222 to get to the rendezvous point on the summit. I take a final look at the dead men, lying there in neat rows on the bloody ground, and turn to face the disheartening climb. We leave them there, so their friends can find them and perform the final duties for their fallen comrades.

Climbing the hill is long and arduous. It is steep and as heavily forested as the earlier hill we partially climbed, but we have to get to the top of this one. The sarge tells us that we will make camp on the summit. We will then form a defensive perimeter and spend the night there. I am convinced this is merely a taunt at the local enemy. In essence, we are saying, *we have your hill and we are staying here tonight. Do you want to do anything about it? The army makes us expendable. We give our youth and our lives to purchase small pieces of ground a hundred miles from nowhere, then we leave.*

With relief, I find that the summit is almost bare on the top. There are many artillery holes in the soft ground and fallen trees have been stacked and burned. Some one has been here before, probably many times. The holes will make good defensive positions and we will not need our entrenching tools, which no one brought with them.

Once we set up simple defensive positions and leave some men on guard, we pick an area and clean off the little undergrowth, so a chopper can land. It will soon be on the way, dropping off ammo, water and C-rations. It is starting to rain, not as hard as the delta rain, but still enough to soak us quickly. We can tell it is going to be a miserable night on that hill, but as far as our army career is concerned, *what else is new? I am glad I had the foresight to bring my poncho; I almost left it back at the hillside base.*

The chopper arrives in late afternoon, blades blowing the wet afternoon rain in our eyes as we quickly unload the supplies at the far side of the hill. I think about the earlier dust-off flights before we climbed this hill. Able and Charley Company were not as lucky as our company was; they lost three men KIA and five wounded, some seriously. Battle always extracts its toll and today was no different. At least three families are going to receive crushing news in the next twenty-four hours, and my heart goes out to them. The chopper rises into the air, banks and heads back toward civilization. I wish I were on it and not on this damn barren hilltop in the middle of NVA territory.

I figure the enemy is going to be annoyed about today's proceedings. After all, we waltzed into their territory, killed some of their men, and now we are claiming what they probably consider their hilltop. Considering this, I grab two one-thousand round boxes of machine gun ammo and a half dozen grenades and head toward my position on the perimeter. I am loaded down and puffing for air by the time I reach the bomb crater. I set the ammo down and flop into the hole, badly winded. The chopper brought a very large quantity of ammo so the higher ups must think we may need it tonight. This is not a good sign.

My friend Jenks has borrowed an entrenching tool from a man in Able Company. He is engaged in squaring off the crater, putting the resulting dirt around the edge of the hole and packing it down. This will help to stop bullets should the enemy come calling tonight. I use the tool for a while, my wet clothes binding against my skin as I shovel the dirt to make the sides of the hole vertical. We are hoping the rain will quit and allow us to dry out before dark. We have spent many wet, cool nights in the jungle, and we do not want to do it tonight.

Thinking about the coming night, I chamber a round in the .45 and put it on safe. I walk over to the edge of the hill and select some bamboo plants, cutting down and stripping a half dozen of them. I wind up with six slender but sturdy three-quarter inch diameter poles and take them back to the hole. We bury the first several feet of the bamboo in the dirt in a square pattern, and then lash our two ponchos to the resulting framework. This will keep the majority of rain off us tonight, thus making the night pass more comfortably. We then retire to our hole and pack the dirt down, spreading nipa-palm fronds on the bare dirt to keep the mud at bay.

Ok, our little castle is squared away, time for some supper. We heat some water in our canteen cups with some C-4 and pour it into the LRP rations plastic bags. Once it soaks in for several minutes, we have a decent supper. I have selected beef stew from my pack, and Jenks has gone with his favorite, spaghetti. No one would mistake these rations for restaurant food, but on the top of a wet hill in the middle of enemy territory, it tastes quite fine. We follow up with a few swallows of warm water from our canteens. Again, not exactly our beverage of choice, but it will have to do.

The day slips into evening and the sun follows its path across the sky and slowly dips behind a hill on the horizon. It has cooled down, becoming my favorite time of the day. We have no bunker to sit on, and we cannot risk lighting any tobacco in the gathering twilight. We know the enemy is out there somewhere and that he is calculating and considering his actions for the coming night. Likely, he knows there are almost two hundred men on this hill. He knows the hill is steep and we have had time to dig in. He also knows we are deadly serious for we have proven that to him earlier. Now he just has to decide if he feels lucky. Me, I am feeling that there is not a gook bad-assed enough down there to come up this hill and hurt my friends or me.

The sarge comes by the hole and tells us to be on the watch. He wants four men to a hole and two awake at all times tonight. He also informs us that the colonel expects the NVA will mortar us tonight.

As he heads for the next hole, he gives us one more piece of advice, "Once it is completely dark, the enemy will have a hard time zeroing in on us in these hills, so he will probably try a probe of our defenses, and then use our return fire to locate us exactly." He tell us to not return fire if we do not want to have to dodge mortars. He also informs us that the old man (the Colonel) is sending some of the men over to the far side of the hill to flash a few cigarette lighters occasionally after dark. He thinks Charley may try to zero in on the flashes, if so, the rounds will land way over to our right.

We discuss the information and decide he is correct. I tell my three holemates that I could see this colonel knew his shit from the start. Fighting sucks, but if the person in charge knows what he is doing it becomes much more palatable. We lie there in the dark, almost dry now, drawing strength from each other, talking about the real world back home.

Jenks asks, "You think Charley will mess with us tonight?" He leans back against the side of the hole. All I can see is his silhouette, but his voice sounds strong and secure. He sounds the way I feel, solid.

"Not unless he wants his ass kicked all over this hillside," O'Brian replies. "Whatta ya think, McCoy?"

"I think we have those NVA pretty pissed off and I know they will try something tonight. We just have to make it too painful for them to get up this hill and we will be all right," I reply. There, I have expounded my thoughts from the writings of Saint McCoy, and I expect the night to go the way I say it will. Down deep, I just hope it will be easy to make it too hard on them.

Everything is quiet until 2300 hours, and then we hear a metallic click from the bottom of the hill and an amplified voice. I cannot believe "ole" Charley has a bullhorn out here in the bush, but the voice tells me it is so.

"Greetings to the men of the U.S. Ninth Division. We welcome you to our area but we must warn you that you will have to leave." The voice is unmistakably Vietnamese, but with a cultured, educated sound. The English is quite good. The bastard was probably trained in an upper class French school in this country. He is now using that training against us. So many of the upper class Vietnamese men took advantage of French schooling, but came to hate the French colonialism. It was an easy choice to side with the Viet Minh, and later with the VC to rid their country of the oppression they came to hate.

The flawless English slips a little and you can detect the hate in his voice as he says, "We kill you tonight, ok soldier. You will die and your momma will never see you again."

I am wishing that I could locate him exactly in the dark. I would like to use the machine gun to tell him up yours! We know that it is just a ploy to get us to fire and reveal our positions. These men are not your simple VC soldier, but are sophisticated enough to try whatever it takes to locate our positions and use that information against the company.

We sit there and listen as he berates us for a few minutes and then stops talking. If he is trying to scare us, his game does not work. It just renews my hatred of the enemy and makes me vow to myself that he will pay heavily trying to take this hill, and that will be all he does, try. We also realize that if he thought they could handle us, they would already be coming up the hill silently, trying to get over the edge before we hear them.

Before the interruption, we have been in the hole listening to a transistor radio turned real low. O'Brian brought it to the position when the sarge decided he wanted four men per hole tonight. At the first sound of the bullhorn, we turned off the radio. We have now turned it back on at very low volume as we try to listen to it again. We have the volume so low that we have to sit side-by-side in the hole with his ear against the speaker and mine against the back of the radio.

We listen to several nondescript songs on Radio Saigon before we hear the announcer mention a song we want to hear. "Now we have 'Procol Harum' coming up for all you guys out in the bush tonight. Can't figure out the lyrics, but the song is bitching," said the announcer. O'Brian and I are electrified as we have only heard the song a couple of times and have been waiting to hear it again. As the strains of *A Whiter Shade Of Pale* drift from the speaker, we turn it up a little and I will it to never end. I thought, *this is so surreal it could only happen in a combat zone.* We are lying on a hilltop in a combat zone, waiting for an attack, and all we want to do is listen to a song.

About 0100 hours we hear the telltale whoosh of a round overhead, and we know Charley is sending us the expected aerial bombardment. The round disappears over the far right side of the hill and hits the trees with a resounding crash. More fly over and they are either overshooting the hilltop and landing down the far slope, or striking the far right side of the hill. They hit with a tremendous thump and sparks fly everywhere, but they are causing no harm. We realized they are zeroing in on that side of the hill where the old man had soldiers flick cigarette lighters earlier. This was proof that Charley was not invincible after dark. Some rounds finally do land inside our perimeter, but everyone keeps well down in the holes and no one is hurt.

After an hour of sporadic mortar fire with no response from us, the enemy opened up with small arms fire from the southeast base of the hill. He was firing uphill in the dark and our holes were well away from the edge of the hill, so the rounds went over our heads at an angle. He followed this with half a dozen B-40 rockets for good measure, but again they went over our heads and high into the air before arcing gracefully downward and exploding harmlessly in the jungle behind the hill. It is a little startling to hear the boom of the rocket from the valley and then have it appear over the hill, trailing a long line of fire, but we could see they were causing no problem.

It was obvious to us and Charley that the only way he was going to be able to engage us was to climb that hill in the dark. Once he reached the brow of the hill then he could fire directly at us. We did not intend to let that happen. We proceed to hop out of the holes, one man at a time per hole, and run to the edge of the hill with a grenade. We then pulled the cotter pin and flung the device over the edge, trying in the dark to get it near the base of the hill. Occasionally we would be rewarded with a bloodcurdling scream mixed in with the last part of the explosion.

For good measure, the machine gunners would lug their weapons to the edge, and then loose a stream of bullets down the slope. Able Company had a supply of LAWs (Light Antitank Weapons) and they would shoot one down the slope occasionally. By carefully looking over the edge, we could judge how far they had made it up the hill by observing where the tracers left the barrels.

A few hardy souls make it about halfway up the hill so we concentrate on them with grenades and LAWs, and soon stop the advance. In a lull, we hear choppers coming over the hill and we scurry back to our holes. The old man has called in several gun ships and they work over the flanks of the hill really well.

It is mesmerizing to see the solid red line of fire coming from the thirty caliber machine guns on the choppers. Every fifth round is a tracer, but the machine guns fire so fast it looks like one solid line of red. The choppers turn and bank through the night sky and the tracers show graceful arcs on their way to the ground. Ricochets bounced at crazy angles and flew high into the night sky. It was very entertaining and I was bothered little by the fact that men were dying on those slopes. Those same men will attempt to kill us if they are able to gain the summit.

Out of ammo, the choppers leave and with them Charley's ambition to take the hill. All gunfire ceases and we listen to badly wounded men scream and cry in the night. We quit firing down the hill and throwing grenades, a kind of non-verbalized cease-fire to let them tend their wounded and carry the dead away. We do not trust them, though, and we gather by the edge of the hill with weapons ready and ammo piled up just in case.

No one gets any sleep that night. We are too wired and too untrusting of the NVA at the bottom of the hill. We post sentries at the edge of the hill all around with flares, and shoot them off at irregular intervals. This is nerve racking because we have to expose ourselves to look down the hill and the same flare that shows the enemy to us shows us to the enemy. It is actually worse for us, because we are silhouetted against the night sky whereas they can hide in the vegetation on the slopes. We started rolling grenades down the hill occasionally just in case, until we ran out of them around 0400.

Daylight comes early in these climes and we keep a careful watch until daylight. The various platoon leaders formed us into patrols and we carefully went down the slopes searching for bodies and booby-traps. We did not expect to find any bodies or weapons as the enemy had had several hours to police the area, but we did find a lot of blood and discarded equipment. There were no booby-traps either. The enemy had departed to the deep jungle to lick his wounds. We all knew this was temporary. He would rest, resupply, call up some reserves, and come back again. The next time he would be better prepared, because he had seen with his own eyes that we were serious about owning this particular piece of real estate, if only temporarily.

We gathered the discarded equipment and burned it in a clearing. It was nothing anyone wanted, just filthy clothing, web belts and packs. We did find about four hundred rounds of AK-47 ammo that the enemy had missed in their retreat in the early morning half-darkness, and we took it back to the base camp with us. Some of the men at the camp had captured AK's that they used at night on the perimeter and would welcome the extra rounds for firing at the firing range the camp operated.

It was against orders, at least in our company, to use captured AK's out in the bush. Not only was there a lack of captured ammo most of the time, the main problem was that the weapon had a distinct sound when it was fired. It sounded nothing like an M-16, which our troops carried. If we are American and fire the enemy weapon at night, we may find ourselves on the receiving end of friendly fire. In night combat, the sides are mixed up in the darkness and we depend on the sound of the weapons to tell us who are friend or foe. The enemy occasionally used tracers that left a green glow instead of red so that would identify them also.

Back at Fire Base Huston the whole group of men involved in the operation gathered at the mess hall and had lunch. The cooks and helpers had extended mealtime just for us and they had whipped up a bonus for us weary soldiers, apple and cherry pie. We sat together and celebrated the victory over the NVA, but more importantly, each of us celebrated still being alive.

Just before we left the mess hall for some hard-earned rest, the chaplain came in and spoke to several sergeants. We inwardly groan because we know the mock funeral will be coming up shortly, and each man prepares himself for this. My platoon knows none of the dead men, but to some of the men in the mess hall, these soldiers were their friends. We went to honor the men but it was not good to see a reminder of our chances of winding up the same way one day. This reminded me of a favorite bit of verse from the noted English poet John Donne, ... *any man's death diminishes me for I am involved in mankind; therefore, send not to ask for whom the bell tolls, it tolls for thee.* It has been a while since I have read that particular verse, though I really love it. I could not remember it all, but I was sure I remembered the important parts.

After we paid our respects, we headed to the tents to get some rest. We were all dead tired and it was no problem to sleep. I remember wondering what the men in charge were cooking up for us next, but I was so tired I decided just to get some sleep and worry about it tomorrow.

To our annoyance, the sarge was in the tent waking us up about 2200 hours that night. He told us that the same scenario would be happening tonight. The only difference was that our Echo and Delta Company would be the anvil and elements from the base would perform the duty we did yesterday. This meant we had to get up now, suit up and head out into the darkness in an unfamiliar area. A platoon of local men, who knew the area would be guiding us to our positions tonight.

We would be going southwest tonight about three clicks. Seems there was no shortage of little valleys and steep hills in any direction around here so the brass had picked out our own little patch of heaven to carry through the mission. Our whole platoon had serious doubts about running the same game plan two nights in a row; the NVA were not exactly dumb. Here it was though, the brass said go, and we had absolutely no choice.

I was very nervous about leaving the base camp after dark; it would be all too easy to walk into an ambush. The only good point about this operation was that we had a large force, which meant the enemy would think twice about taking us on if they were out here tonight. This very strength was also a weakness; this amount of men could not help but make enough noise to wake the dead trying to move in unfamiliar territory. In addition, the column of men would be long and we would have to move slowly to keep anyone from losing their way in the dark.

The moon was not out tonight, which made movement more difficult. Since we could not see well, however, that meant Charlie had the same problem. I was about three quarters back in the long procession and I was really sweating this move tonight. This was the only plus to carrying a machine gun, you did not have to walk point or tail gunner position. This meant you were much more likely to survive an ambush. Once the ambush happened though, and we fired the gun, then the enemy fired at us. The machine gunner could hurt Charley the worst, so he tried to eliminate the gunner immediately. Combat here was always a good-bad proposition.

It took several hours of walking and flailing around in the valley to reach our objective and by the time we arrived, everyone's nerves were on edge. Since I was a machine gunner, I would be much more useable off the valley floor. A little bit of height would allow me a better field of fire, so I climbed thirty feet up another one of those steep hills. I did not mind this at all since the hillside was safer. If things went bad, the narrow valley floor would be the killing field.

Forming a straight long line of men southeast to southwest was the best we could do in the dark. We settled down for a long night of little sleep and a lot of worry. Even with all the men in the position, I am feeling pretty alone since we are stretched out about ten feet apart to cover the valley floor and around thirty feet up each hill.

We lie there in the dark alert, but each with his own thoughts and worries. One good sign was that the frogs had started croaking again and the assorted little animals in the underbrush had started rustling around again. They were disturbed by our earlier movement and went silent, waiting to see if our moving was a threat to them. After we took up position and quit making noise, they decided we were no longer a threat and resumed their nocturnal stirrings.

This is something you learned early in your combat life. If you are in a position at night, sitting there silently listening to the small creatures move and they suddenly get quiet, then it is time to get worried. We were silent, the little creatures kept up 'their quiet noise, and the dark slowly gave way to the wan light of sunrise. I was never so glad to see the sunrise. This did not mean we were home free, however. The soldiers from Fire Base Houston would be on their way toward us, and any enemy they flushed would be slamming into us any time now. Now was the time to inspect our surroundings to see if we had adequate protection. I exchanged my little tree for a larger one, moving silently now that the light gave me the ability to move quietly.

Minutes later, a message was sent down the line that the soldiers from the base were nearing our vicinity. We are to hold fire unless we can identify the enemy without a doubt. This is a dangerous time, two elements coming together in the early morning, with the chance of enemy trapped between them. Things work out fine, there is no enemy and we meet up in that inhospitable place and smile at each other. We have all dodged the bullet again, we form a line, and head back those long three clicks that are made much shorter by the daylight and promise of hot chow waiting for us.

With chow over, some of us sit on a sandbag bunker and look out over the miles of jungle and hills that are spread out in front of us. The view is quite nice and it is going to be a great day. I look around at my fellow platoon mates, and I am overcome by the feeling of a brotherly connection I have for them. Okay, it is more than that. *I love these men like brothers!* I look up at the sun in the cloudless blue sky and love that too. I am experiencing the euphoria of a man that has survived another night out in the jungle. I have lived through it and we are going to get to sleep all day. I do not know what tomorrow may bring and I will not worry about it. Right now, being alive with my friends by my side is the greatest feeling in the world.

271 days left in country.

Chapter 11
Changes And More Changes

Can Guioc-May1968.

It is early morning at Can Guioc base. We have recently moved here from Rach Kein and have experienced many changes, none of them good. At our former base, our platoon is named the Falcons, and we ran road-clearing operations in the early morning and convoy escort the rest of the day. This was not always a safe activity for us, but it was certainly better than being out in the jungle looking for Charley.

Then our luck changed and the division got orders to move here to Can Guioc. It is a recently completed and poorly designed base. The base has few perimeter bunkers, being surrounded by open fields and the occasional Vietnamese hooch. The buildings are roughly constructed single-story barracks, lightly framed and covered with metal sheeting on the roof and walls, with nothing but dirt floors and, of all things, circular brick ovens on one end. The army never cooks on anything like that, and it leads me to believe that the base was originally built for the ARVNs, or Army of the Republic of Viet Nam, a grandiose name for an underperforming military outfit.

The rumor we hear is that they moved here, did not like it and left and we are the unlucky souls to be here now. I could certainly see why they disliked it. Instead of being a more easily defended rectangle or square, it was shaped like two squares separated by a narrow road a half mile long, so it could easily be cut in half during a half-hearted ground attack, and the lack of perimeter bunkers all around the base made the situation much worse. I wondered who the idiot was that designed a base camp to such strange specifications.

To make matters worse, the new inhabitants of our old base took over the road clearing and convoy escort job we had been doing, so we become a recon platoon. We receive the name Juliet Recon, since our unit already has a Romeo Recon. We take a lot of ribbing for that name until everyone sees that we are up to the new task.

A recon platoon is supposed to walk out or fly out and recon an area and report back on what we see, but there are just enough small units of VC operating locally that our job basically came down to going out, getting shot at, and then we knew where the enemy was. The contact with VC was light and infrequent as the enemy in this area seemed to have little inclination to fight, other than an occasional burst of gunfire to cover a quick retreat when we got a little too close to them. Of course, it could also have had to do with the fact that we could call in artillery, choppers equipped with machine guns and rockets, or planes loaded with bombs on a moment's notice.

The platoon has been out all night on ambush patrol. We get back in just before sunup and we are all asleep on inflatable rubber mattresses to keep us off the muddy dirt floor since the rainy season has just started. I can see that as it progresses, we are going to be spending all our time wet and muddy. Long timers here say the rainy season lasts several months and by the middle of it, nothing moves but soldiers on foot and helicopters in the air. Viet Nam is determined to make my time over here a misery.

Someone rudely kicking the bottom of my boots awakens me, and I jump, about ready to tear someone a new one. I see my attacker is Sgt. Williams. He is our squad leader and a well-liked member of the platoon, and a person who does his best to minimize danger to the platoon while out on operations.

I relax and Williams says, "McCoy, sorry to bother you, know you have not had much sleep, but we got an LT here who needs someone to drive him to Saigon, and you are the only one that I know of who has a license."

This is a strange army quirk. They will send anyone out to fight, but if you want to drive their vehicles, you have to get training and pass the test to get your license. They pick four or five soldiers out of each training class to get driver training and my name came up. For once, having my name come up was a good thing, because it got me out of several days of physical training, and some of the ongoing and ever boring classroom instructions.

I looked up to see a dapper looking, spotlessly clad officer, shiny boots and actual hard creases in his tailored fatigue pants. Where the hell did this person come from, I thought, and how did he get here so clean? His hand came out, and the sergeant introduced us. Now, I have never been one for spit shined officers, or for that matter, any officers, but the prospect of getting to Saigon was tempting. If I had to baby-sit this person and lose some sleep, it will be worth it.

Lt. John Franklin Jones, as he called himself, is ready to roll for Saigon and when I mentioned cleaning up and getting a little dried mud off me, he told me not to worry but to bring full gear. I put on my flak jacket, knife in a sheath strapped to the jacket, and three bandoliers of ammo, pretty much what I carry out in the field. I grabbed my rifle and the slouch hat we wore because they made no noise at night, but the LT insisted I wear a steel pot, so I rounded one up and we headed for his jeep.

"Don't worry about chow, we will stop by the commissary in Saigon and have a good meal," Jones promised. I was more worried about why he thought I needed all that gear for a forty-five minute ride to Saigon than I was about food. Highway One to Saigon is pretty secure with all the military traffic, and the city itself is even more secure with the thousands of rear-echelon types stationed there.

I checked the jeep for fuel, checked the oil level and kicked the tires while the LT waited impatiently, then stowed my M-16 in clips on the left end of the dash that kept it right at hand, and off we roared for Saigon. The pace of combined civilian and military traffic held us to under 30 mph most of the time. It was always fun traveling the crowded main road of Viet Nam, but at least Highway One was paved, courtesy of the U.S. Army. We had to pay close attention to our driving, and the only rules we had to obey were-there are no rules. The biggest vehicles get the right of way, and the smaller fry fight it out with each other. No one with good sense tries to argue with the occasional tank or the much more common tracked APC, or armored personnel carrier.

We reach Saigon, cross the Y Bridge, and roll through Cholon, the Chinese section of the city. Traffic is chaotic, as usual, a mix of military vehicles, hundreds of three wheeled pedicabs spouting noxious two-stroke oil fumes, dozens of garishly painted buses, and foot traffic everywhere. Couple this with Vietnamese women herding pigs in the street, chickens scratching underfoot, and the ever-present street urchins begging for food or money or wanting to shine your boots and the street is a mess.

Lt. Jones has me run him by Sub Sector on Tudo Street, not far from the American Embassy. I wait while he delivers a canvas satchel that he has been carefully handling. This stop, and the satchel, clues me in to his real job, obviously intel. Our platoon has occasionally stopped here before, an innocuous looking building in an affluent section of town, when escorting convoys through town, in our previous job of convoy escort. They always pumped you for local info while you were there, all the while giving you free cold soft drinks and beer. It did not take us long to figure out they were CIA spooks, because Saigon is full of them. It was always a funny scene with them asking for info on the latest operations and the results, from our view. They pretended they were not spooks and we pretended we did not know they were. There were tape decks and headphones everywhere, which was very high-tech in those days.

"Ok, down the street and to the left, let's see what is good in the PX commissary today," said the LT as he bounded into the jeep. After cruising around awhile I found a parking place that was not too illegal, but Jones said not to worry, the local police officers never ticketed military vehicles. Not that I was worried, chances are I would never be in Saigon again. We walked a serpentine pathway between large, circular steel drums full of cement and painted a bright yellow, placed there to prevent VC from driving explosive-laden vehicles through the front doors of the PX. We passed a pair of stern looking MP guards, and though they paid little attention to Lt. Jones, they looked at my disarray and me closely. I did my best imitation of a good guy, but the dried mud, the flak jacket and my weapons did not help my case.

We passed into the interior, an old French building, all stone and high ceilings, with large, slow-turning fans moving the air gently, and American rock issuing from a jukebox in the corner. There were inviting wicker chairs placed around tables with colorful checked tablecloths, and it seemed a lot like home.

All talk ceased around us as we took our seats, and a harried looking noncom rushed over and informed me that no weapons were allowed in here, to go back to the coatroom and check all my equipment. I spent the next five minutes trying not to laugh aloud, as two Vietnamese hostesses, sporting very short miniskirts and flawless English, carefully racked my equipment. They wrote me out a receipt in tiny, delicate writing. I glanced at the paper and listed were, one M-16 rifle serial no. 918409, one knife and sheath, two grenades, one flak jacket, and three bandoliers of magazines. Another surreal Viet Nam moment, to be sure. I thought, *I will never be doing this again in my lifetime.*

Again, the talk totally ceases as I make my way back to the table, and I see some of the spotlessly garbed soldiers stealing glances at me. I am feeling pretty uncomfortable because, to be frank, I stink. The clothes I have on, besides being spotted and clumped with dried mud, have been on my body for at least three weeks. I have forgotten how long it had been since I have shaved and washed up. When you are in a recon platoon at Can Guioc, bodily hygiene usually consists of splashing a steel pot of rainwater over your head, and tooth care is accomplished by breaking off a small twig, chewing up the end a little to make a toothbrush, and then pretending we have toothpaste. I am wondering how far my body odor is carrying, but I notice no disgust on any of the soldier's faces, just naked curiosity. At the table, the LT is positively beaming as he passes an order to the shapely waitress.

I sat down, drinking in this little piece of America, so far away from home and wondered what it would feel like working in Saigon, all the comforts of home, clean clothes, and a bed to sleep in at night. Instead, we had to bed down on soggy ground in the jungle.

Lt. Jones immediately launched into questions about my experiences, asking what I thought about the way the war was going. I soon decided I liked this man, even if he was an officer. His thoughts on the war were pretty much like mine, which was no way could this war be won the way we were attempting it. They send us out one day to secure an area and the VC fight a little or just run away into the jungle, so they call the area secured and then withdraw us from the area and send us to another area to do the same stupid thing, repeatedly! As we leave each area the VC come back again and take over and it is business as usual. Why did the idiots in charge think this was a way to win a war? What the hell were they thinking, or were they even capable of intelligent thoughts? The LT and I discussed how the war was being handled and if there was any way of changing things, any way to wake up the powers that were in charge.

"LT," I said, "there is no way to win a limited guerilla war. The only way to win is to truck us all to the South China Sea, put us all in a line stretching across the country, an arm's length apart, and march us north shooting anything bigger than a dog. That is the only way to be sure to kill all the VC." Of course I knew that could not be done, it was just my way of stating how difficult the job was that the army was trying to do.

More soldiers came in and took tables, and the waitress arrived with delicious-smelling cheeseburgers and French fries. We ordered cold American beer to wash it down with, not the locally available Biere LaRue or Biere 33, products of an old French brewery that was taken over by the Vietnamese after they gave their former masters the boot. I have not had a cheeseburger for four months, so all my attention is focused on that wonderful hunk of meat, but as I finish it and start on the fries, I notice our table is still the center of attention.

I suddenly realize that I am on display. I am the LT's war trophy! He has brought me here, stinking and heavily armed, to show the rear echelon soldiers that he has been out to a war zone and went through a degree of danger, and I am his proof. I start to get riled but realize that it does not feel half-bad. I am looking like a real, down in the mud combat soldier, and half the prissy soldiers in this room are wishing they were I, at least for a little while. Hey, if they only knew how readily I would trade my filthy clothes for their spit-shined appearance, but I immediately wondered how long I could put up with it. Clean and comfortable here meant order and a lot of non-coms and officers keeping close tabs on you. The forced servitude adhered to in the states is undoubtedly SOP here, so it is not all wine and roses.

Lt. Jones picks up the tab, and I am surprised! An officer buying me lunch! Can the day get any stranger? Oh, yeah, I forgot. I am the big combat trophy. We pass through to the cloakroom and the girls quietly return my gear. I slip everything on and we head out into the bright sunshine with a little bit more swagger in my step than when I came in, I do believe. I could get used to playing the dirty, but romantic looking soldier of fortune, I think, but I know there is absolutely nothing romantic about going out at night and setting up an ambush position, hoping to kill a few unlucky VC, all the while endeavoring to keep the same thing from happening to you.

We reach the jeep, passing by the two guards, who look me over closely again. The first thing I notice is that the gas cap is missing, since it is on the left, the gas tank being under the driver's seat. I immediately suspect one of the street urchins and start watching them. It is not unusual for them to steal your cap and then offer to sell it back to you, claiming they found it.

Mr. Combat Soldier is not having any of this crap today, and woe be to the kid who pops up with a gas cap. Lt. Jones calms me down and tells me it is just as likely to be another jeep driver looking to replace his own missing cap. We see several jeeps parked at the side of the street about a mile from the PX and the day gets even stranger.

"Pull over and borrow the cap off one of those jeeps," Lt. Jones orders. What? I cannot believe an officer is ordering me to steal a cap from one of those jeeps. Well, it is an order and I am game, so a quick stop and our jeep is whole again. Wait until I get a chance to tell this to the men in the platoon.

I drive through Cholon, and over the Y Bridge, and the traffic thins out and we hit a dizzying thirty miles per hour. The jeeps, made by Ford and designated an M151A1 in army language, have small four cylinder engines and are geared low for use off road. About forty-five to fifty is max, but with a narrow track, high center of gravity, and a weight of only 1800 lbs. or so, they are quite easy to roll over. This trait is constantly stressed in drivers training.

Up ahead on the right, we see a jeep pulled over to the side of the road, hood up and a driver peering underneath as if he knows what he is doing. The major in the passenger seat is tight-lipped and about ready to explode. I pull over to help, because you do not want these people out here after dark, and besides, I love a mechanical challenge. I ask what happened as the driver turns around and walks to my jeep.

"I don't know, we were riding along and it just cut off. It has plenty of fuel in the tank," the driver says.

I ask, "Does it crank over okay but not start?" He answers in the affirmative, and I am sure I know the cure, because in jeep class I really paid attention. The jeeps are tough, you can beat them to death and they keep on rolling, so I admire them for that. They have one idiosyncrasy, however. The designers, to prevent soldiers from running the vehicle out of oil, soldiers being soldiers, included a low oil pressure ignition cutoff. Low oil means low oil pressure, and that means off goes the engine. I check the oil level with the dipstick, and sure enough, the oil barely touches the end of the dipstick. Got it! I rummage through both jeeps and find a dusty quart of oil under my passenger seat, add it to the stalled engine, and it instantly fires up. The driver grins, the major thanks me, and off they roll. The day just got even stranger. Lunch paid for by an LT and thanks from a major. I am doing well today.

"Pretty slick, McCoy," allows Lt. Jones. "You nailed that diagnosis. Where did you learn that?" I explain to him that I was running my own gas station when the army took me away kicking and screaming, and I have been a mechanic all my life. I am a total gear head and I love working on engines.

Lt. Jones said to me, "Well, I think you can solve a problem for me. My driver left for two weeks R&R in China Beach, so how about being my driver for those two weeks?" I told him I would like nothing better, two weeks of clean clothes, a soft bed, and good food were my idea of heaven. In addition, I silently thought, an officer who treats me like an equal, rather than something to be walked around on the road for fear of soiling his shoes, is a definite plus.

We get back to Can Guioc about 1700 hours, or five o'clock in civilian time, and Lt. Jones talked to Sgt. Williams, and just like that, I am an official temporary jeep driver, and we are in the wind, motoring as fast as I can for Dong Tam. Traffic is light on Highway Four that time of day and I manage to approach 40 mph at times, and by 1830 hours, we are through the gates.

Lt. Jones has me drop him off at his quarters, mentioning that I need to pick him up in two hours and run him by the hospital to pick up a nurse, and then over to the officer's club. After that, I am free until one in the morning. I then have to come back and take them back to quarters.

"Requisition a new set of fatigues at supply, just mention my name and there will be no problem, clean up as good as you can, and grab some chow before you come and get me," Lt. Jones requests. Wow, looks like my new job will force me to drive around a lot while waiting for the LT. What a life, free wheels to use, gas on the government's tab, and great food. Just last week I was walking through mud all the time and trying to kill people. I cannot figure what I have done to get such a great break. I am also feeling guilty that my platoon mates cannot share in my newfound life.

I grab new clothes at supply, borrow a razor and shave, and take a shower in my boots. First shower I have had in months if you do not count the almost daily rain showers we walk through. After the shower, I evaluate my boots. The water removed most of the outer layers of mud, but it was easy to see the leather was too far gone to ever accept a shine, and I did not have enough time to get to the PX for polish, anyway. The army made sure there was always plenty of boot polish and brass polish available at the larger base camps, since most of the people stationed there were what we front line grunts called spit-shiners.

These men had to live and dress as if they were on a base back in the states, complete with standing inspection in the morning. Just thinking about that made me very uneasy. I was going to be what I had ridiculed ever since coming to Nam, and I wondered if I could fit in, if I could handle the very large change. I put those thoughts aside, knowing I would somehow get through it. This assignment certainly increased my chances of surviving Viet Nam and I owed that to my wife and parents.

What followed was mostly two weeks of pure bliss. I was on call to the LT every day, but I had a lot of time to just cruise around and inspect all of Dong Tam. It is a very sizable base, a rectangle probably a mile and a half deep and a mile wide. It is surrounded by sturdy two-story sandbag bunkers, and the jungle is cut back a quarter mile on three sides to allow a clear line of vision. The south side was bordered by the Mekong River, a half mile wide at this point. This was not a base camp that Charley would be likely to try a ground attack at, even with darkness on his side.

The south side of the camp also boasted a channel cut from the river into a rectangular lake, which soldiers call the turning basin. Around it is the headquarters of the Mobile Riverine Forces, who keep a fleet of jet drive, shallow draft steel-hulled boats thirty to forty feet long. They are made in several different configurations, from sharp bowed high-speed interceptors, bristling with .30 and .50 caliber guns, to flat-bowed troop carriers equipped with front ramps that folded down, capable of running up against a mud bank and disgorging twenty heavily armed soldiers very quickly. Some of the boats even have 40mm cannons with tremendous firepower. In short, they have a hull configuration for about every situation likely to be encountered, and they patrol the hundreds of miles of the Mekong and its tributaries day and night, three or four boats in a group to protect each other.

Their main objective is to stop and inspect the hundreds of boats using the local waterways, because Charley uses small boats to carry weapons and war material all through the delta area. What looks like, to the casual observer, a family of Vietnamese carrying a load of rice downriver to sell, is often a boat commandeered by the VC and loaded with war materials, carefully hidden. The VC kept the families aboard to cover the ruse, and warned them they will die if they say anything. The VC kept hidden weapons nearby to enforce their threat, and it is a dangerous undertaking to stop the boats and search them, as gunfire can break out at any time. All weapons are pointed at the people in the boat, and every soldier is on hair trigger alert. The difference between life and death could come down to half a second's head start as the VC reaches for weapons.

During the search, you had to check the ID of each passenger and compare the picture on the plastic laminated card, issued by the army to all civilians, with the person's appearance. This is made harder because by the time they are twenty, the sun and hard life make the people look forty. It was often hard to match photo to face, the brown, seamed faces looking, frankly, the same to us. To top it off, it was hard to determine who were civilians, and who were VC after dark.

If your section chief or village headmaster vouched for you, and he happened to be a closet VC, then you got an ID. If a local VC needed an ID and could not get it otherwise, they simply killed a villager that resembled him, buried the body, and presto, he was legit. This may seem inhuman and cruel to the reader, but such was the reality of Vietnamese life. I observed some of these things first hand, and found that the Asian can be both a friendly, agreeable person one minute and an absolute savage the next, would the situation call for that. They seem to value human life much less than we do, which makes them formidable opponents.

Dong Tam also had a large airstrip on the west side, no pavement but a sturdy landing area made of SP, heavy steel folded and punched full of holes with interlocking plates on each end. Each piece was twelve feet long and several feet wide, sized so that several soldiers could carry it and it stacked well for transport. Once an area is bulldozed flat and compacted by heavy equipment, the steel can be laid down quickly. A work force of twenty or thirty men could easily lay down the steel for a runway in one day, though your back would remember the task for several more days.

The revetments for numerous choppers were also located in this area. These were just recesses scooped out of the ground, angled on each end and flat on the bottom. The dirt that was removed was piled several feet high and thick on each side of the recess, and a chopper, when down in the hole, was fairly well protected from mortar blasts. The whole thing is configured so that when in the recess, the blades of the chopper cleared the dirt piles by about three feet. It took almost a direct hit from a mortar round to total a chopper, but they were cranking them out every day back in the good old U.S.A., and everyone knew the taxpayer's pockets were bottomless, though; as it turned out, their store of patience was less so.

The camp also had a large swimming pool, at least a hundred feet long, of wood and packed dirt located above the ground, with a thick plastic liner. The water was pretty clean, coming from the water purifier supply on base, not the filthy brown water of the Mekong. Charley occasionally put the swimming pool out of action for a few days with a direct mortar strike, and it happened often enough that it was not an accident. VC mixing with the hundreds of Vietnamese who were employed on the base would walk off distances, careful that no one would spot them, of various installations on the base, then plot them on a rude hand drawn map back home, and use them to plan mortar attacks.

I have no doubt that the local VC knew the location of everything on base to within a few feet, and used that knowledge to their advantage. Charlie may have been a backwater little dude with little formal education, or most likely none, but he made up for it easily with cunning and determination. In war, it is poor policy to underestimate your enemy, and I think the powers in charge did that repeatedly and completely.

Add to that numerous showers, EM clubs with cold beer and food for the enlisted men, Officer's clubs with the same for the officers, and a movie theater. There was also a large PX where you could pick up food, electronics, up-to-date music, guitars, watches, and a hundred other things the soldier needed or did not need. It was a little city, most of the comforts of home if you did not mind the incessant dust due to the total lack of pavement, and having to use candles or flashlights at night, unless you were an officer. They usually got electricity, because of all the reports they had to fill out.

In my drives, I often took the jeep down to the Mekong River. Soldiers used a small beach there if they did not mind the muddy water. I would drive the jeep into a foot of water, and then wash it with a rag. There was no soap available, but the wash job and rinsing it with buckets of muddy water made it almost look clean, and the LT commented that he had the cleanest jeep on base. Daily washings were a necessity; the dust was ever present due to the dirt roads. I think the washing made me feel a little more normal, since it reminded me of the times I washed my blue Pontiac GTO and tore up the stateside roads. I sure missed that car, gone now to a new owner, thanks to the intrusion of the U.S. Army into what had been my mostly happy life.

Then the end of my idyllic adventure came. Lt. Jones' regular driver came back, and we made quick friends and spent an evening drinking beer, trashing the army, and discussing the limited chances of the U.S. winning the war. We both felt the army was a large, slow-moving behemoth, incapable of change, hell bent on forging ahead with an unworkable plan and a war impossible to win. The LT shook my hand and we said our goodbyes, and I was sorry to see him go, and not just because of the loss of a great job. He was the only officer I had known that cared about the plight of the common soldier, and he had the foresight to see this war was not heading anywhere good. I hope the LT survived the war, made it home sane, and has a good life. I am not much of a drinker, but occasionally through the years, alone at home, I will hoist a cold one and toast his memory.

Lt. Jones had one final, unexpected gift for me. As he climbed into the jeep, he told me to hang in there and to report to Staff Sergeant Taft in supply at Can Guioc in a couple of days. He had arranged for me to work in supply, which meant I would still be off the line. Sounded like a demotion from a comfortable job to a semi-comfortable job to me, but supply was probably a lot better than going back to combat.

I told him, "Thanks for the job, sir." I whipped off a good, sharp salute, the only one I gave him in the two weeks as the jeep disappeared into the darkness.

I hopped on a truck in the convoy going back to Can Guioc the next morning, because I wanted the supply job to start with no problems. Better to show up early rather than have Sgt. Taft wonder where I was and label me a screw-up in his mind. In my experience, it was better to start out on a good footing with a new sergeant, because some of them could be difficult to work for, once they got a little rank.

To my surprise, Sgt. Taft was a mellow, thirty-something kind of person, not like some of the sergeants I had the misfortune to know. Supply was just several big fifteen-by-thirty foot wall tents, jammed full of various supplies and equipment, and we had a separate wall tent to sleep in. Most of the time we kept the sides of the tents rolled up, trying to catch any vagrant breeze. When it was not raining, it was one hundred degrees and the tents were like saunas. Stifling during the day, but they became pleasantly cool several hours after sundown.

My duties were to help unload the fifteen to twenty trucks that showed up every morning. It was back-breaking work and the temperature and humidity did not help at all. We climbed up on the two and a half ton trucks and handed down endless eighty-pound crates of artillery and mortar shells, cases of C-rations and LRP, or long-range patrol rations.

Supply also had an open-air ammo dump close by, so we also unloaded thousands of rounds of small arms and machine gun ammo, cases of grenades, and cases of C-4 plastic explosive. Once we unloaded everything onto the dirt road in front of the tents, the trucks moved off and then we transferred everything into the tents, or stacked it nearby if we ran out of space. As we moved supplies into the tents people were also picking up supplies for the various units in camp, so that meant space opened up and the outside piles had to be shifted inside as space became available. It seemed like a never-ending task, but it was a most necessary one. It was usually late afternoon before we finished, but then our evenings were free unless we had overnight bunker guard, which came up every other night.

Overall, a fairly decent job, as jobs went in Viet Nam, but my back was always aching from the constant lifting. I found myself missing my former platoon mates, and horror of horrors, my former job on the line! I would sit on the bunker at night and watch the sun slide below the horizon, the inky blackness descending all around me. There were few electrical lights around this small base camp, and electricity was carefully rationed to the few.

The darkness made the night sky so much more vivid, a million pinpricks of light scattered across the sky, shining down on us mere mortals. The constellations above me were unfamiliar, a reminder of just how far I was from home. As I gazed up, I wondered how many of those heavenly bodies I could see were no more. Were they just so much cosmic dust, felled by tremendous explosions a mind-bending amount of time in the distant past? Their light, traveling across millions of miles of cosmos, was just now reaching my eyes, a sad reminder of their former glory. Gazing up into that great void, I wondered if, somewhere up there, are there other races, and do they fight stupid wars like us, or have they evolved far beyond fighting each other?

I did a lot of thinking that month of June, sitting on that bunker and taking in the peaceful darkness. Occasionally the spell would be broken by an incoming mortar round, or outgoing rounds when the mortar platoon down the road had a fire mission, supporting some unlucky platoon out in the jungle somewhere in contact with the enemy. Deep thoughts, mostly, to hide the growing conviction in me that I hated this supply job, safe as it was, and just maybe wanted to return to the line. I wondered what had happened to me; why I could even be thinking of the line again, when I had a job my former platoon members would love to have? Have I become an adrenaline junkie somewhere along the line, and is my body just now telling me? I knew I hated combat, so why was I even thinking about it?

Was it just guilt I was feeling? I wrestled with these thoughts every night and tried to tell myself I was one lucky soldier, but my mind just kept telling me this supply job was mind-numbingly boring. I finally admitted to myself that I wanted a little danger. Danger made you feel so alive, so much in tune with the world around you. Therein lay my problem. In this base camp, you either had boring jobs like supply, or the never boring but often scary life of a man in combat. You normally had no choice in the matter; you just did what they told you to do. I knew I was extremely lucky, so why was I feeling so crappy?

Then, in early July, my life took another sharp turn. Returning from visiting my old platoon, I came across several soldiers clustered around a 106mm recoilless rifle mounted on a jeep. Astride the weapon was a perplexed looking

E-5. They had the breech totally apart and could not figure how to get it back together. Explaining that I had received training in the weapon, I soon had it back together and operating properly.

Talking to the sergeant, I learned the unit had found the need for a vehicle-mounted road-clearing crew again, so they had recalled some vehicles and weapons from Dong Tam. The army, in its great wisdom, had simply assigned twenty men to the crew, none of them having any training on a 106mm weapon, and thus causing the problem I had just confronted. Road clearing and convoy escort, huh? The answer to my problem! This is great; some, but not too much danger and every day something new to do, and new places to see.

Before I realized it, I opened my big mouth and mentioned that I would not mind being on the gun jeeps again, and the sergeant was happy to hear that. He told me to hang around so he could do some horse-trading with supply, and in an hour, I was out of supply and back on the jeeps. He simply sent one of his men to supply in exchange for me, and as the soldier packed up his belongings to head out on the half-mile walk to supply, he could scarcely conceal the look on his face that I was a complete idiot. I was having the same thoughts about myself. To be honest, I probably sealed my fate as soon as I showed the sergeant that I had 106mm experience. It was likely already on his mind to do a transfer when I violated the first rule of a soldier. Never volunteer for anything and never, ever let them know you know how to do something.

I walked back to supply, dragged together my few possessions, and said my goodbyes. My friends commiserated on my transfer, and I heard many comments on my tough luck but I thought it best to keep the true story silent. I returned to my new platoon, who was using our old platoon name, the Falcons. I knew no one on the crew, but soldiers make friends quickly, probably because you leave old friends and meet new ones constantly. Sgt. Franklin assigned me quarters in one of the old familiar mud-floored barracks. They certainly had not gotten any more comfortable, and I settled in and gave my M-16 a good cleaning and oiling, something I had somewhat neglected while in supply. I gave the magazines a good going over too, cleaning them and wiping down each round of ammo. It felt good, somehow, to get back in the routine of cleaning your weapon everyday and making sure your gear was ready to go at a moment's notice.

The next several weeks we went out on the vehicles every morning at about 0700 hours, to clear the road from Can Guioc through checkpoint 69er to Tan An and Dong Tam. The routine was the same as when we were at Rach

Kein. The VC would build simple roadblocks in the night of nipa palm logs and chunks of mud from the nearby rice paddies, and then booby trap some of them so it stopped traffic except for the brave of heart. We had to get out early and remove these roadblocks to keep traffic flowing. You might encounter three or four in thirty miles, or as many as ten or twelve.

They were never big, and you could always drive over them with jeeps or trucks, if not for the occasional booby trap. The VC would put explosives in them in no apparent pattern, so you had to BIP each one, as they were too dangerous to push off the road. BIP meant to blow it in place with C-4.

We turn a jeep sideways in the road to act as a shield about thirty yards from the roadblock. Two people go forward, carefully checking for trip wires and plant two or three half-pound charges on the roadblock. The lit fuse would burn one foot in forty seconds and we always used a three-foot fuse. We holler 'fire in the hole', light it and run back behind the jeep. The blast rocks the road and blows the roadblock into the rice fields. Occasionally we hear a secondary blast, most often a grenade, but sometimes we get a heart-rending ka-boom, the road dancing and the jeep swaying, and we hear pieces of wood, mud and shrapnel fly overhead, smacking the jeep with a loud clang. Debris came down everywhere, and our response was to roll under the jeep. When you hear a big one, you knew the ever-resourceful Charley has included a mortar round or artillery shell along with the grenade, and the result is a large hole in the road. The really aggravating thing is, you know the shell is likely one of our own, something Charley dug out of the mud.

Mortar rounds and artillery rounds often came down in soft, deep mud and did not explode, and the VC always came back to a previously shelled area later to check for free munitions. They were experts at sighting the characteristic funnel-shaped mounds in the mud, and the size often gave clues as to the caliber of the hidden round. They would then get to work, often forcing local villagers to dig down three or four feet to retrieve the round.

It made my blood run cold to think of having to do that, knowing that somewhere down there were eight to ten pounds, or possibly more, of high explosives inside a steel shell designed to fragment easily. They also would remove the fuse and then disassemble the shell to retrieve the explosive. Occasionally captured documents included crudely drawn instructions on recognizing the different American munitions, and instructions on how to take them apart. You had to admire Charley; the little buggers had ice water in their veins.

I was the only one in this platoon that had any demolition training, so I was the one to set all the demo charges. I had started training the crew on firing the 106mm rifle, but since we could not fire live rounds until we ran into trouble, it was hard to prepare the crew for the shock and noise of lighting one of those rounds off, let alone instill in their minds the awful force and size of the back blast. Sgt. Franklin noted I was hogging the setting of the demo charges and told me to train some of the other men, quickly. No one seemed to want to volunteer for the training, so the sergeant did it the army way, and volunteered three men by calling out their names.

Demo was a lot of fun for me, and pretty safe as long as I was careful and followed a few rules. The fuse came in ten-foot rolls, and you always cut off the first foot, lit it and threw it off the road to burn out. You never left fuse that was not burnt for the VC to scavenge and use against you. Moisture intrusion into the end of the fuse could make the first foot hard to light or it might go out, and no one wanted to walk up on a freshly placed demo charge that failed to go off to troubleshoot the problem. The second foot you also cut off, lit, and dropped at your feet to burn, timing the burn to make sure it matched the rated time. Someone could always have a bad day at the fuse factory, hence the test.

The blasting caps were small aluminum cylinders about two inches long, and we carried ten per small wooden box, actually just a wooden block sawn in half, with drilled holes inside for the caps. These we carried in a compartment on the jeep, with a sandbag on the top to protect them from shock and fire. We also separated the explosive, keeping it well away from the caps. Each blasting cap was strong enough to mangle a person's hand, sort of like an M-80 firecracker, so you were careful to keep them protected. Ten going off at one time could be quite a hazard, to say the least.

The C-4 explosive itself was a marvelous invention, a semi-hard, white block of material, one pound in weight, about a foot long and several inches thick. It was enclosed in a clear, sealed plastic wrapping with a wide strip of double-faced adhesive on one side. Peel the covering off the adhesive and it would stick to almost anything, even under water.

To prepare it, I cut off what I needed, reamed a hole in the material with the handle of a pair of pliers, then inserted the fused blasting cap in the hole and pressed the C-4 around the fuse to seal the hole and hold the cap securely. I have separately prepared the cap by inserting the length of fuse into the cap until it bottomed, twisting gently to feel the friction of fuse against the compound inside, then crimped the cap's aluminum body against the fuse. The crimping sealed the fuse and cap joint together, and I could even set the charge underwater as long as the end of the fuse remained above water to keep moisture out of the inner powder core. C-4 also had the added advantage that it took both heat and shock to make it explode. You could light a chunk of the material on fire and it would burn merrily with no danger of explosion. We often used small pieces of C-4 to heat C-ration cans. You just had to be careful because it burned so hot it could ruin the bottom inch or so of food if you held the can too close or did not stir vigorously.

We could also beat C-4 with a hammer until we were blue in the face with no danger. However, we did not light it on fire and then hammer on it, as that might cause an explosion. My experience was that almost nothing would set it off except a blasting cap with a fuse or an electrically triggered cap. I have even fired twenty rounds of M-16, some of them tracers, at a cautious distance away, and failed to get an explosion. All said and done, a fine invention, and about as idiot proof as it could be made.

The roadblocks, though annoying to deal with each day, had one plus for our platoon. Occasionally our opponents would include a VC flag or a propaganda banner on the roadblock, held up by bamboo poles, and they were considered primo war trophies. Only catch was, Charley occasionally booby-trapped these offerings with a grenade, hoping to bag the incautious or the fools. We were having none of this as we always carried a grappling hook and one hundred feet of small diameter line. We would throw this from behind a jeep, and eventually hook the bamboo poles or the banner and drag it toward us. Once it was pulled away from the roadblock by ten or fifteen feet it was considered almost safe, because Charlie always kept his trip wires short to make sure they functioned correctly.

We took turns as we came across these gifts, and the deal was it was ours, whether we received the offering whole, or in some instances we were rewarded with a big bang, and our prize came fluttering down in pieces through the air all around us.

My turn came one fine July morning, a ten-foot long propaganda banner, red paint applied to an off-white, roughly made piece of cloth supported by two bamboo poles. After repeated throws and much ribbing by my friends, I finally hooked the banner dead center and carefully pulled it toward the jeep. No bang occurred and I was soon the proud owner of a genuine war trophy. I carefully guarded that banner and always kept it close for the remaining eight months of my tour of duty, and carried it home with me.

***

On the plane ride home I displayed it around to the passengers, all soldiers going home like me, and was quickly offered three hundred dollars for it. I was tempted, for that was close to two month's pay, and a soldier is always low on funds. This was especially true with me because I had been sending home over half my pay every month. Even with the princely sum the army was paying me each month, my total take, including fifty a month hazardous duty pay, was less than two hundred. On reflection, I decided to keep the banner. The money would soon be gone but a banner is forever. Besides, I stuck my neck out for it and that was worth more than three hundred dollars.

***

I still have that banner, stored carefully in my closet, and guarded these forty-three years. I lent it to my daughter Christy once, to take to school when they were learning about the Viet Nam war and she came back excited, all of twelve years old.

"Dad, Dad," she said, "I told everyone the red on the banner was blood, and it really grossed everyone out. No one would touch it." She never asked me about my role in the war and I am thankful for that.

I still pull it out occasionally, usually on Veterans' day, and sit there holding it, feeling the rough texture, and smelling the faint otherworldly odor. It talks to me and brings back pictures of a fine summer day half a world away and almost a half-century in the past. I am reminded of a young man hale and hearty, only twenty years old, so happy to be alive, and full of hope for the future. However, it also brings back the darker side of war, remembrances of friends long dead, and some tears trickle down my cheeks, as they do now as I write this. Damn you, Viet Nam, get out of my mind! I did the best I could for my friends and for you, but in the end, it was not enough.

259 days left in country.

Chapter 12
Juliet Recon And Fun On The Mekong River

Can Guioc-June 1968.

We have been here about a month and are finally getting used to not having windows and missing floors on these wood-framed sheet metal buildings. The floors are bare dirt, so we sleep on inflatable rubber mattresses, and there is zero furniture in here. There are no chairs, tables, or any place to sit. We either stand all the time or perch on our mattresses. The metal walls and roof make the building almost unusable during the day due to the one hundred and ten degree heat, as it is the high point of the dry season now. Only after sundown does the building cool down enough for habitation and sleeping, so we spend most of the time outside in whatever shade we can find.

My job has changed again. I really liked being back on the gun jeeps but Juliet Recon has lost a few members and since I am considered experienced I am moved back to my old platoon. The army moves us where it wants us and it does no good to complain.

I am back to my old job of going out on operations during the day searching for Charley, or sometimes at night, and I cannot decide which is worse. It is harder for the enemy to spot you at night, but it is also almost impossible for a platoon of twenty men to move through rice paddies or jungle after dark without making considerable noise. We work on this problem and slowly improve.

To add insult to my injury, since I carried a machine gun as a member of Juliet Recon, the sergeant has made me a machine gunner once again. I just cannot seem to get away from that twenty-two pound M-60 thirty-caliber machinegun. On the first operation I carried both the machine gun and my M-16 but quickly found that this was unworkable, too much weight and too unwieldy in the field. The sarge requested a .45 caliber pistol as backup for me from the armorer and they managed to locate one. These pistols are in short supply all the time. I figured that was because every officer in Dong Tam sported one on his waist, but the army always has trouble coming up with one for a soldier on the line. It feels good to wear that three-pound chunk of steel on my waist again.

A typical day mission would start with a briefing in the morning, usually around 0800 hours, just after breakfast. We would be called together in the shade behind a barracks, and our squad leader would detail the day's mission and what we were to accomplish. Sometimes it would be just a recon, fly out to an area and check it over, looking for signs that Charley was operating in the area. We would walk the forested areas, looking for hidden bunkers or tunnel entrances, and any villages would have to be thoroughly checked. This included entering each hooch; checking for hidden weapons in extra-thick thatching on the walls, noting how much rice was stored and checking for anything hidden in the bunker inside the building.

Almost all village residences have a four-foot high square bunker built on the floor inside. It is built of mud bricks, dried in the sun, and stacked. It is then covered with a thick layer of mud inside and outside. The mud is reinforced with straw, and once the assemblage dried well, it resulted in a foot thick wall that would easily stop small arms fire. The top of the bunker is covered with numerous thick planks, and the family would spread out straw mattresses on these planks and sleep there. If they heard gunfire in the night, it was a simple matter to transfer to the bunker for safety. We made use of this knowledge if we went into a village at night. We would quietly slip into the buildings looking for families who were sleeping in the bunkers, which is a sign that they know there are VC as well as Americans in the area. This usually results in a firefight if Charley wants to come out and play that night.

We would also have to check the pigpens and toilets for hidden weapons and supplies. The enemy figured the Americans would not want to mess with those areas, so it was his favorite hiding place, along with gravesites. We had four-foot metal probes to force into the ground in the pigpens, and no one enjoyed walking around in a foot of stinking mud, probing the ground, while fighting off the squealing pigs, who seemed quite territorial in such situations. The enemy wraps weapons and supplies in plastic sheeting before they bury them several feet down, and we have to play hide and seek. Ditto the toilets, which were even worse to probe than the pens.

In addition, there were the recent graves to check for hidden booty. All Vietnamese villages have small graveyards close by, and we have to check fresh burials to make sure there is nothing hidden inside. We also have to keep an eye out for older gravesites that look as if they may have been disturbed. You had to do this carefully and respectfully to prevent distressing the villagers any more than necessary. Ever present in your mind is the fact that the enemy would sometimes booby-trap the burial sites. Had I known all the fun I would be subjected to in Viet Nam ahead of time, I think I may very well have climbed into my Pontiac GTO and headed due north!

I liked the Vietnamese people and felt very bad when we had to ransack their belongings looking for contraband, but I knew it was necessary. The people were caught between the enemy and us. If the VC determined they wanted to hide equipment in the village or use it as a hideout, the villagers had no choice but to agree. The VC were very cruel and if there was a disagreement, they would often shoot the village chief between the eyes, and sometimes his whole family. Hundreds of villagers perished because of this. Then, we Americans would come along and ask if they knew of any local VC or hidden supplies. They had to say no, knowing if they cooperated with us, they would likely be dead by the end of the day. Talk about being caught in a difficult situation! Our platoon never burned down a village because we found contraband in it, as we knew the villagers had no choice in the matter, but I understand such destruction sometimes happened in other areas. However, if we encountered fire out of a village, we would open up, trying to protect the civilians as much as possible. Usually the villagers would clear out ahead of time, if they suspected the VC would stay and try to ambush us.

Villagers were usually happy to see us, smiling and offering us water out of the big earthenware pot they kept at each corner of their hooch to collect rainwater. We usually had to splash the bugs out of the water before filling our canteens, but that did not dampen our enthusiasm for cool water. We in turn, often carried a bit of candy to hand out to the kids, and sometimes some C-rations to the adults, if we had any to spare.

If our recon was going to encompass more than one night out, as it sometimes did, we often carried LRP rations, pronounced "lerp" rations. They were quite different from the C-rations, taking up less room and weighing much less. The food was freeze-dried, and consisted of a single sealed pouch, which you tore open and added water. If time and location allowed, it could be heated with a small ball of C-4, if you remembered to bring your canteen cup. This was a small pressed metal container that fitted over the bottom of your canteen, thus taking up little room. The food came in several choices, including meat and vegetables and spaghetti and meatballs. It was quite palatable once it soaked up some water. However, you did not get any extras, like cigarettes and toilet paper that came with the C-rations.

Most of the contact in these overnight recons was usually minor, some harassing fire from a few rag-tag closet VC. They tried to wound a few people and then ran away into the jungle, though occasionally it was more serious. This caused us to hunker down and return fire, calling back to base for mortar support, which usually convinced the enemy they would be better off somewhere else. The enemy's tactics were to wound or kill one or two without putting themselves in much danger, and then "diddy-mau" to use the Vietnamese word, which roughly translated meant to "get out of here."

Rarely did the VC actually stay and fight a set-piece battle, it was mostly shoot and run in the delta and elsewhere in Viet Nam. Occasionally, if they thought their numbers and the terrain favored them highly, they would put up a tremendous fight. This resulted in some memorable battles, like the A-Shau Valley, or the battle to take Hamburger Hill. These battles happened in the central highlands, or up near the border between North and South Viet Nam. The contact my platoon ran into rarely lasted over five or ten nervous minutes.

Once we had covered the area we were assigned to cover, searching any villages we came across, we would then call in to get choppers to return us to base. If it was an overnight mission and we had more area to cover tomorrow, we would walk toward the new area, carefully checking the paths for signs of use, as we looked for a place to set up an ambush position for the night. We usually picked an open area near a wood line that had little-used paths, reasoning that Charley would be more likely to favor the less used routes and that there would be less chance for civilians to blunder into our ambush. In the middle of the night, we have to assume that anyone moving in our direction is the enemy; this is the only safe way to think. The Vietnamese all knew that it was hazardous to your health to move after dark and normally refrained from this.

As we walked, we would pick several places to set up a main position and a secondary position. We would continue on awhile trying not to get too far away from the places we picked, waiting for dark. Once it got good and dark we would double back to our secondary position, form a circular defensive perimeter, and set the claymore mines out in a circle in front of our positions, at the end of their one hundred foot wires, trying to make little noise. We would then dose ourselves with mosquito repellent and wait quietly. In case we were under observation, after about an hour we would pull up the claymores, and move to the primary position we had picked earlier. It was twice the work but then, we were playing a dangerous game and moving might just throw the enemy off in knowing exactly where we were located. Then, we set out the claymores again; set up a guard rotation for the night, and the men not on guard duty at the moment tried to get some sleep.

It was eerie, lying there in the rice paddy, rifle over a dike, listening to the night sounds of the area. The frogs croaked loudly and various strange animal noises came from the jungle areas not far away. We could hear the mosquitoes buzzing up to your face and ears. They didn't bite because of the repellent, at least on your face, but flew around, looking for a chink in your repellent armor, usually finding one.

We would spend the night moving as little as possible, waking the men for guard duty and trying to sleep, but the most I ever accomplished was a semi-sleep, bringing my watch up to my eyes often to check the time and eyeballing the men on guard to make sure they were awake. Then, you would hear something moving out past the perimeter, and several starlight scopes would be brought into action. Our eyes strained to see the movement clear enough to determine what it was, sweat rolling off our foreheads and down into our eyes. It usually turned out to be a monkey or a pig rooting around for food, roaming away from his village, never understanding just how close he was to dying.

On one of our patrols, something happened that was not the least bit funny that night, but I can now look back at it and produce a little smile. It was the middle of the night; the moon was shining brightly, so we had set up in a small grove of trees just big enough to hide the platoon, but small enough that we had that all-important three hundred and sixty degrees of visibility. The night sounds had died down some and half the platoon was on guard while the others dozed, or tried to do this.

Suddenly the stillness was split by an ear-shattering explosion, a bright flash of red that lit up the night for a split second, and almost everyone opened up with their weapons. Tracers were flying everywhere, but they were all going outwards. The sergeant was screaming for us to cease fire, trying to be heard above the racket we were making. He finally succeeded in stopping the fire, and then sheepishly admitted that he had set off his claymore by mistake. He had rolled over in his sleep onto the "clicker" and set it off. Well, now, everybody in a least a square mile knew we were out here, and exactly where, so we had no choice but to move our position for the third time tonight. This time we had to pick the new area in the dark, and set up again. Nobody slept the rest of the night since we had managed to alert the countryside to our presence, and we were worried the enemy would find us. We said nothing to the sergeant that night, but when we got back to base camp, it took a long time for him to live that down. For months he heard the question, "how many sergeants does it take to blow up a claymore?"

We spent several months doing the recon by day, ambush position by night, until everyone in the platoon had shaky nerves. Then one afternoon, our mission changed. We all slept late in the mornings if we were out on operations the night before, and as we were waking up in the late morning, getting ready to hit the mess hall for lunch, our claymore-blowing sergeant came into the building and informed us we had been detailed, or attached, to the Mobile Riverine Force for a week. I perked right up; having lived on an island, I loved boats and the water, and slogging through the rice paddies and jungle was getting to be a real hassle. He further informed us that we would be going out on operations with them during the day and setting up defensive positions on the riverbank to protect them at night. Well, that sounded like more of the same, but at least we would not be humping all day, the boats would be carrying us part of the time.

The town of Can Guioc was just on the north edge of our base, nestled on the banks of the Mekong River, the largest one in this delta area. We had to meet the boats that afternoon just to the east of town. The AO map showed it to be about three kilometers away, just a short walk for a platoon that had been covering as much as fifteen "clicks" a day, the army shorthand for kilometers. We gathered the equipment we would need, keeping in mind we would not see the base for at least a week. Along with weapons and combat gear, we carried our ponchos and the liners, which could be used as a blanket. We also carried personal gear like small transistor radios, cigarettes, and in my case, a pipe and plastic bag of tobacco. Thus loaded down, we slipped out of the east side of the perimeter, and made a beeline for the riverbank. Once through a small area of scrub brush, we picked up the ever-present paddy dike with the soldier on point carefully checking for booby traps. It was unlikely there were any this close to the camp, but it was dangerous to make that assumption. Besides, we were used to checking our path for danger, and did this almost automatically.

We reached the riverbank with no problems, and sitting there in the sun with heat waves radiating off them were three magnificent steel-hulled boats, each about forty feet long, painted a dark, dull green like all army equipment. These were our chariots of fire for the next week, and I inspected them all closely. The men operating them were proud of their equipment and gave us a complete tour from the conning tower and fifty caliber machine guns, to the enclosed spaces and the motors that propelled them. There was little space below decks since almost all areas were taken up by equipment with the crew's bunks fitted in wherever they could be fitted.

The boats had huge marine diesels powering water jets that exited below the water line that could be turned for steering, so there was no need for propellers or rudders. These would have caused continuing problems due to the shallow water, frequent shoals that continually shifted, and deep mud. In all, a perfect design for this area, allowing them to slide over shoals and power through muddy, shallow areas with no damage.

They also had another adaptation to help protect the hulls from the enemy's rockets. Since a rocket does not blow a hole in steel, but burns a hole through it due to the five thousand degree heat generated when the explosive goes off, it has been found that if something sets off the round before it hits the hull, there is less chance of the heat burning a hole through the hull. Through trial and error, and plenty of damaged boats to inspect, the engineers found that welding common steel rebar to the hulls helped reduce the damage. The rebar was welded to vertical pieces of angle iron spaced several feet apart, and this angle material spaced the rebar out two or three inches. The rebar was welded in horizontal strips; about two inches apart, down both sides of the hull, and across the transom, from the waterline to the joint between the hull and deck. This gave the hulls a strange appearance, but when the rocket hits, the rebar sets it off several inches from the hull, providing protection. It was not a perfect solution, because a rocket hitting straight against the hull might still burn through, but if it hit at any angle, which was the most likely scenario, the hull was only scarred rather than penetrated. The real problem was not the hole, but the jet of heat that went through the hole, destroying engines and blowing up fuel tanks.

It was love at first sight when I saw those three boats and examined them closely. The first one had a normal pointed bow, and was designed as a high speed, highly agile vehicle, with speed and handling designed to carry it out of trouble. It had one fifty-caliber machine gun mounted at the front, and two thirty-caliber machine guns mounted port and starboard about two thirds of the waterline length toward the rear. This armament helped to suppress enemy fire while it escaped problems with its speed, and could be used to engage enemy forces as it patrolled the waterways.

The second was similar in hull design and weapons, but had the bonus of a twin-barreled forty-millimeter cannon mounted on the stern. If the conditions warranted something stronger than a machine gun, this weapon could hurl explosive shells several miles and each shell was like a grenade when it went off, as it fired a stream of them at the target. Reaching out and touching someone was quite easy with this weapon.

The third boat was quite different in design. It had a flat, angled bow with an open hold to transport troops, and a ramp on the front could be released so it fell forward and down to disgorge those troops quickly. Drive up to a mud bank, drop the door, and twenty or more heavily armed men could be on the bank in thirty seconds or so. This boat was slower and less agile, but the three boats worked as a team and protected the slower one.

After our boat tours, I was itching to get speeding down the river to whatever new adventures lay ahead, but we were told that the first operation would be tomorrow. We would stop and inspect the small boat traffic on the river, checking for IDs and contraband. Tonight we would form a semi-circular perimeter around the boats to protect them, and tomorrow the fun, if there was any fun, would begin. Therefore, we set up our position, set out the claymores, and kicked back to relax. The sun was low in the sky, so the temperature was getting quite nice. We had C-rations, and C-4 to heat them, and all our friends were here, so we settled in for a nice bull-throwing session. We all felt pretty happy; we had the added protection of the gunboats, and all the free ammo we could carry. If we used it up, no worries mate, because the army always had more, stacked and waiting for our call.

The fun began the next morning, around 0900 hours, but it did not last very long. After a breakfast of C-rations heated over C-4, we washed up, if you could call it washing. We went down to the riverbank only thirty feet away, and filled our steel pots full of water. It was so muddy that you could not see to the bottom of your pot, even though the water was only six inches deep. We all knew that, up and down the river, hundreds of thousands of people were dumping their trash in it, and using it as an improvised toilet. I only washed my hands in the water and wondered if they were now cleaner or dirtier. The river was close to a mile wide here with the incoming tide causing a current of several knots upriver so the water had plenty of flow to clean itself, but even a big river can do only so much with the amount of human waste winding up in it. The boats had fresh water tanks, but they doled it out sparingly for drinking and maybe a little to wash your face. The platoon was so used to being dirty all the time that we hardly noticed it, and when you live and sleep on bare ground there is not much use to try to keep clean.

The boats were pulled up in the shallow water with their bows resting in the mud, but they did not pull out into the river to intercept boat traffic, as I thought they would. The E-6 sergeant in charge explained that with the current, too much jockeying around with the throttles would be required to keep three boats in position, so they would stay onshore. We would work from the rear of the boat, using a bullhorn to call the small motorized wooden boats and sampans to us. It seemed like a poor plan, and I felt like an idiot hollering to the boats. "La Day, La Day," we kept bellowing, which meant "come here" in Vietnamese. Some of the boats were having none of it and attempted to pass by, but we waved our rifles in the air, occasionally firing a few shots upward, and this convinced most of the transgressors that we meant business. On the far side of the river, though, I could see boats bypassing us and some in mid-river steering toward the far shore to avoid us. Oh, fine, I thought, another half-assed idea, just like a lot of others I have been through since coming over here. No doubt, any boats carrying war goods were making for the far side of the river and the news of the interception point would spread like wildfire up and down the river.

The boats that paid heed to our requests were mostly small sampans, narrow wooden boats pointed on each end, from fifteen to twenty feet long. They were designed to carry four or five people and seven to eight hundred pounds of cargo, usually rice in rough cloth bags or bunches of vegetables, to the local town markets for sale or barter. Often there would be a crude cage with four or five chickens in it, and occasionally a squealing pig tied to the bulwark of the boat. Due to the current, the sampans were usually powered by a "mud" motor, a five or ten horsepower horizontal shaft motor bolted to a bracket at the end of a twelve to fifteen foot long pipe. A shaft extended down the pipe to drive the propeller, and it was bolted over the stern of the boat with a counterweight. A flat plate was below the prop, and when it encountered mud or a shoal, the whole apparatus pivoted up to keep the prop out of the mud, and this device would keep powering the boat in very little water. You would often see one powering along slowly, prop half-exposed, showering water and mud to the rear.

The Vietnamese in these boats were not the smiling, happy villagers we usually encountered. They were scowling, and sometimes showed a shadow of fear as we boarded the boats, rifles at ready, demanding their concouk, or ID card. I could understand their trepidation; being stopped and boarded by several dirty soldiers could not be their favorite way of spending an afternoon. As usual, matching the picture on the ID to the brown leathered face was not easy, and we did a search of the boat from stem to transom. We lifted and felt the rice bags, rummaged through the clumps of vegetables, and poked under the seats, all the time with a round in the chamber of the rifle, safety off and your finger out of the trigger guard, but very close to it, just in case. The tension was painful, and the sweat running down your face was not all caused by the sun. We were worried that a wrong movement might cause us to kill what might be an innocent civilian. We were also worried that if he were not the innocent farmer he seemed, a fraction of a second hesitation on our part could make one of us the dead one. All thoughts of fun and games for today disappeared from my mind. The power of life and death could be exciting for some soldiers, but for me it was mentally and physically draining.

The day finally ended late in the afternoon, after we had annoyed thirty or so boat loads of people. We found nothing of importance, and I handled more bagged rice than Uncle Ben could ever imagine. The sergeant finally stopped the day's proceedings, and we returned to the riverbank and our rag-tag camp.

We had a meal of C-rations and four of us got together and combined our food. Two of our friends had cans that contained biscuits, one had spaghetti, and another had a can of hard American cheese. We sliced the biscuits in half, poured on some spaghetti, and topped it with some of the thinly sliced cheese. We heated it up with our favorite explosive, and we had four miniature pizzas. If you closed your eyes and held your mouth just right, it almost tasted like pizza. It had been so long since any of us had seen any real pizza; we could hardly remember what it tasted like anyway, so the poor approximation was quite satisfying.

Our appetites satisfied, we turned now to improving our campsite a little. The area had been a rice paddy at one time, but did not appear to have been used for this for a while. There was a raised area of ground about twenty by twenty feet, and was probably where a hooch had stood at one time, though there was no sign of it now, just dry, hard, sun-baked earth. We had spent the proceeding night sleeping on the hard earth, covering ourselves with our poncho liners to ward off the night dew. It was certainly not the worst place we had ever slept, but we found it less than satisfactory, with the daytime sun shining down making it very uncomfortable.

We dispatched several guys to the thicket of bushes and stunted trees we had walked through on the way to the river earlier, and they returned with a bunch of skinny five foot poles, which we planted in the hard earth and draped our poncho liners over them forming several rude huts with no walls. The boats had a large supply of C-rations, and as they doled them out and we consumed them, the cardboard left over was put down as a floor. It was certainly no softer, but it kept you off the bare dirt at night. As we tracked in dirt, it was a simple matter to pick up our cardboard rug and shake it off. As we stayed there longer and came in possession of more cardboard from the C-rations, we gathered more poles and put up cardboard walls with windows cut in them for ventilation. Talk about all the comforts of home!

As the sun went down for the day, we sat around and talked of home, and wondered when we would get mail next. The higher ups knew how important mail was to the soldier, and often had it carried out on choppers to areas where operations were being conducted. You could be sure of getting mail at least once a week no matter where you were. To make it easier for soldiers to write home, there was no postage required on outgoing mail, and practically anything would be accepted as mail. Since we were often in areas where no paper and envelopes were available, out favorite letter was usually made out of the light cardboard that C-rations came in. We would write on one side, fold it over and secure the sides with a bit of wire pushed through a couple of short slits cut in the cardboard, twisting the wire to secure it. We finished with the addresses and a big "Free" written on the outside, and it always went back to the states just fine.

The first time I sent one of these letters home, I got a box back from my wife full of writing paper and envelopes, and a letter telling me it made her cry to see that was all we had to use for writing paper. She must have put the word out, because within two weeks I had received two more boxes of stationery, one from my mother and one from my mother-in-law. This also happened to a bunch of my friends, and the platoon was soon swimming in more paper than we ever expected. The problem was that carrying writing paper out on operations did not work out very well. The paper was always getting wet, or wrinkled and dirty, and quite frankly, it took up space in your pack that could be devoted to food, ammunition, or tobacco products. We did not want to tell our families back home this, because this made it sound like we were in danger. We would mention that the paper was back in base camp, and we were in another base camp, for the moment.

My friends and I were always careful to make it sound like we were leading a carefree, easy existence without any cares or worries. No use to worry the family back home, we were worrying enough for all of us.

We stretched out on the cardboard in our little camp that night, watching the darkness creep up all around us, masters of our universe. The stars came out to play, the constellations were new and unknown to us, and the show was spectacular. These were not the weak, dull stars of our own county, minimized by the profusion of electric lights, but the brilliant, winking pinpoints of light only visible when there is little electric light for competition. Since we were not out on patrol in the jungle, I fired up a fresh bowl of Cherry Blend, and all around me, friends puffed on their cigarettes. I was almost contented, except for the little matter of being ten thousand miles from home, and missing my wife and family.

We set out guards and retired to our magnificent hovels for the night. It was peaceful and I actually got some good sleep, marred only by being awakened for guard duty in the night. The morning arrived, hot and bright, and after breakfast, we went back to stopping boats. The Vietnamese we stopped today were no more accepting than they were yesterday, but no weapons or ammo were found. This made the whole platoon happy, because we did not have to take any prisoners or shoot anybody, and it appeared that our present assignment was reasonably safe.

On the third day came a change of pace. Sergeant Wainwright called us together in the early morning and informed us that boat interdiction was over for a while. Today we were going out on patrol on the boats and we would be dropped off at several different places to check for signs of VC activity. Intelligence had reported suspicious movement in areas about ten miles southeast on the river. Military intelligence had never impressed our platoon; it seemed their information was often sketchy and often very wrong. I frequently wondered if the two words, military and intelligence, were not mutually exclusive and unusable in the same sentence.

Well, it was a welcome break from sampan duty, so we loaded up in the troop carrier boat, and all three moved out downriver. Our boat was sandwiched between the other two boats and the platoon took up positions on the bulwarks, looking out to see the sights. The only sights were muddy water and thousands of palm trees with ragged little villages coming into sight occasionally. We called for drinks with little umbrellas all around, and some deck chairs, but for some reason we could not locate any stewards, and the social director on our little cruise ship failed to put in an appearance. Not to worry though, we had plenty of tepid water in our canteens.

The sun beat down with its usual ferocity, but the boats were traveling at a good clip and the breeze they generated felt almost like air conditioning, especially since we had been roasting on the riverbank for two days. Just about the time I thought we might just make it out to the river's mouth and get a glimpse of the South China Sea, the big diesel's cadence changed, and we slowed noticeably and headed toward the northern bank of the river.

"Ok, men, this is it," Sgt. Wainwright announced. "The boat is going to nose up to the bank, drop the ramp and we are going to come out fast and low. Hit the jungle and get down in case Charley is waiting around to say 'hi'." Great plan. Big problem. There was waist deep mud just past the ramp and as the platoon rushed off the leading men plunked down in the mud, and the ones following did the same behind them, becoming a major roadblock. The ramp was down, the road was blocked, and if Charley had been around, it would have been a complete massacre. Readers from Deal Island will understand the problem. It was like walking in the marsh and then trying to cross a gut after the tide receded.

We solved the mess the soldier's way. As succeeding men sunk into the gooey mass, they fell forward into the mud. The last six or eight men merely walked across their backs and took a running jump onto firmer soil, and we set up a quick perimeter while the less fortunate managed to extricate themselves. If the enemy had been around, he may have been laughing too much to make a serious attempt at eradicating us. Memo to ourselves; send one man up over the side next time to check the ground in front of the boat before dropping the ramp. That way, only one man would be exposed to enemy fire instead of the whole boatload.

We recover quickly and move into the jungle single file, one soldier out on point fifty feet ahead, checking for trip wires or signs of the enemy. This is a totally new area, one we have never been to before, and we proceed cautiously. There seems to be no one around, and I do not know whether to feel let down or not, feeling like we are crashing a party. We get here and open the door, walk in with a grand flourish, and no one is around. The jungle paths are well traveled, so there are obviously people around somewhere. We cover several kilometers northward, then the jungle thins out and we observe a small village in a large clearing. The clearing is parceled off and planted in rice and the village is about a quarter mile away. Everything looks quiet and peaceful, but something warns us this might not be so, to keep our eyes open and proceed cautiously.

There is no sign of movement in the village, no farmers in the fields, no baby-sans playing under the trees. This is an area not normally patrolled by the Ninth Division, so all of this makes us very careful. We send several men forward over the paddy dikes as we form a line in the edge of the jungle, get down and train our weapons on the village up ahead in the clearing.

The men have barely cleared the edge of the jungle when AK-47s open up on full automatic. I get a quick glimpse of angry red spurts of fire from rifle barrels, and I try to make myself one with the ground. Tracers sail overhead, close enough that we can hear them, and we are showered with leaves and tree bark. There appears to be five or six weapons in use in the village, and that makes me feel a little better. If there were more enemies here, they would all be firing.

I light off the machine gun and run through the starter belt shooting left to right into the hooches, the belt links and used brass expelling in an arc over my right shoulder. The brass bounces off something and onto my steel pot, with several hot pieces of brass landing between my neck and shirt collar. I barely feel this; I am on automatic pilot as I unwrap a belt of ammo off my body and feed it into the machine gun. I chamber a round and rake the village from right to left, watching the tracers bite into the hooches about a foot above the ground, where a man would be, crouched down for cover. To my left and right, my comrades have also opened up on full auto, and I hear the flat, harsh crack of grenade launchers split the air. Popping my head up and down as I see the flash of rifles, I observe a hailstorm of tracers fly through the village, and red explosions as the grenades find their mark. As suddenly as the firing in the village started it quits, and we know the enemy is on his feet retreating back through the village and into the jungle behind him. Evidently, he has been duly impressed with our barrage, and that is exactly the reason we light up the village so heavily, to suppress his fire and convince him that another part of the countryside should be on his bucket list today.

Knowing that Charley is retreating, it is human nature to want to rush through the village and into the jungle beyond, but we know that is the quickest way to get somebody killed. The enemy has a quarter-mile head start on us and he will be running as if his life depends on it, which it does. He may have left one or two men to cover his retreat or possibly a few quickly contrived booby-traps, so caution and a careful advance are called for here. As we form a line and head into the village, we are relieved to find that only one of the two men out ahead is hit, and that is Simpson, with a wound to his lower leg. That has not slowed him down a bit. He comes up from behind the rice paddy dike, face beaming and hopping on his one good leg. He grins widely and hollers to us.

"Million dollar wound, guys, million dollar wound," shouts Simpson. He only has about two months left in his tour, so he knows that by the time his leg heals sufficiently to return to duty it will be time to go home. I never saw anyone who was so happy to be shot, and I feel envy and happiness for him.

We leave him and the Doc on the edge of the village to attend to his wound, and carefully check out the hooches. We find significant blood trails in two of the buildings, so several VC have paid for trying to ambush us. We know that right now they are being piggybacked by their comrades through the jungle as the enemy tries hard not to leave anyone behind. They are taught to leave nothing behind to show us what we have accomplished. No signs of booby-traps, either. They left the village quickly.

Hoping that the wounded or dead are slowing the enemy down, we proceed into the jungle spread out several feet apart, expecting to draw fire from soldiers the enemy left behind. We encountered nothing, and the jungle was sparse, so it allowed us to move quickly. Of course, that meant Charley could move quickly too. There is nothing as fast as a small band of VC knowing a group of U.S. soldiers is pursuing them. All we found were several bloody leaves and a few discarded thatched hats. The sergeant calls a halt on the advance after several kilometers, because we need to get back to the gunboats, so we return to the village. Simpson is now bandaged and numbed a little, still happy as he can be. He assures us he does not need to be flown out, so several men pick him up and carry him, and others carry their weapons. We switch men often as we work back through the jungle and arrive at the riverbank, still carrying a very happy camper. One hit, one run, and nobody left on base. Score one for the home team.

We spend the remainder of the week stopping boats on the river again, finding nothing, and the nights pulling guard duty on the riverbank. On the last day of our duty, we shake hands with all the members of the crew, thanking them for the rides down the muddy rivers, and gather our equipment. We remove the ponchos from the shacks, leaving them roofless and with a final glance at the area, turn and head back to Can Guioc base. We are all one week closer to going home, and in Viet Nam, that is the name of the hazardous game we play.

231 days left in country.

Chapter 13
I Lose A Great Friend

Can Guioc-July 1968.

There is a harsh sound of static on the radio and then a chilling message. It is from Sergeant Reynolds and we can hear the fear in his voice. He is working to control the fear, and the radio transmission comes through loud and clear.

"This is Romeo Recon. Charley has blown a mine, I have one KIA and two wounded. Location checkpoint 2-7. Stand by to send dust-off chopper when contact is broken. Will inform, over." We hear the answering affirmative from TAC. The radio goes silent, a deafening silence.

All of Juliet Recon platoon rises from our mattresses now. We have been half-asleep in the building trying to get a little rest. It is around midnight, or 2400 hours in military time. We gather around the radio, willing it to tell us something. Our brother recon platoon is out there, several very long miles outside the camp. We know all the men in the platoon, and now we know one of our friends is dead. We do not know how badly wounded the two men are.

We turn the radio up and gather our weapons quickly. I slip on my flak jacket and check the two grenades I carry on it. Next, I hang seven hundred rounds of .30 caliber machine gun ammo around my shoulders. I finish with several wraps of belted ammo around my waist to keep the rounds in place. I place the machine gun by the doorway so I can retrieve it quickly. We work by feel and the little bit of moonlight coming through the open windows. This is a sparse forward base and we have no electricity.

All around me, my friends have also been preparing to go out to help our fellow platoon. No one really wants to leave our safe area and go out to the ambush area. It would be much better to stay here and not face the blood and death beyond the perimeter. Our friends are out there and we do not let a fellow soldier down, so we prepare to go when the order is given.

The radio comes to life again. In the background, we can hear several weapons firing on automatic, then a pause. There is a thunk as an M-79 grenade launcher sends a round toward the enemy. Several seconds later, not far away, we hear the explosion. We hear bursts of AK-47 fire interspersed with chattering M-16s. It is hard to listen to this without bolting for the door and heading south toward the firefight.

"Request backup gunship. Two clicks south of base. Home in on tracers. Standing by for orders. Estimate ETA," Sgt. Reynolds breathes into the mike. His voice is calmer now, but I detect the stress in the voice. The sergeant sounds royally pissed off. Someone has hurt his men and knowing him as I do, I suspect dawn will reveal some VC bodies. It will not bring back the dead man, but it might even the score. That is all we soldiers want and expect. Just a little payback and maybe a little more respect from Charley. I wonder who is dead out there. I know all of them and do not want to have to attend another funeral. I wonder who else might also die out there tonight. The abbreviated funerals are horrible. There is no body or casket, just the dead man's rifle with the bayonet stuck in the ground surrounded by a lone pair of boots. We stand there and take off our steel pot. We drop our heads as the chaplain says a short prayer. We mouth our "amen" and it is all over. No chance to say goodbye, the death is final. Any grieving we do is done while we carry on with our job. There is no downtime for death, no recess, no do-overs.

We hear several choppers fly over the base and head south. They are on the ball; the firefight started less than ten minutes ago. Some pilots and choppers are on duty 24 hours a day for just such quick response. Over here, there is no distinction between day and night as far as fighting goes. Action goes on the around the clock, but probably more fighting occurs at night than during the day. Charley knows the darkness evens the odds a little more for him. He needs that advantage because he has no airplanes and no helicopters to call upon for support. He knows we can and will call aerial hell down on him. He counters this by fighting ten minutes, then melting away into the jungle. His mantra is simple; fight, kill, and run for his life. I hate the little bastards, but I respect them. I do my best never to underestimate them.

We clamor to leave base and join the firefight. The sergeant says no to the idea now. He tells us that in the dark and confusion of the firefight we could shoot each other. The gun ships will be over the battle quickly and they will force the enemy to disengage and run. We have to accept his decision and I feel a little relieved with what he says; however, the urge to help my fellow soldiers is strong. By the time we get there, the enemy will be gone and we will have no chance for a payback. My friends and I want to help our men and the decision to stay here is a difficult one to swallow.

The gun ship's co-pilot blares from the radio and we gather close to listen. He is over the battle now, trying to orient himself with the positions of enemy and friendly forces on the ground. This is the most dangerous time for the men down below. The battle scene is very black from the chopper and his only guide is the tracers from both sets of combatants. We hear the co-pilot ask the sergeant to halt all firing for a few seconds and then have his whole line open up to pinpoint the exact positions of his men. We know that in the noise of battle it is very hard for the sergeant to get his orders heard and followed. All of us in this building have been in this situation before.

We hear the commands and responses from the radio with the sounds of automatic rifle fire drowning out some spoken words. The chopper's twin .30 calibers open up. We cannot hear any more of the conversation. I am saying a quick prayer that the gunship will put his fire down accurately. Friendly casualties sometimes occur in the heat and confusion of night reinforcement.

"Dead on target, Charlie has broken contact," Sgt.Reynold's voice comes over the speaker. "Request dust-off four men. Will mark Lima Zulu (landing zone) with red lens, thanks much." We know the Sgt. and his platoon will be moving quickly. They must find a flat area clear of obstructions for the chopper to land, and to mark the zone with several flashlights equipped with red lens. Our flashlights have lenses in several colors along with clear. We change them as needed to adapt to the conditions. We know Charley monitors our radio transmissions. He is not above trying to get a chopper to land with his own flashlights so we specify the colors we will use at night. We have various colored smoke bombs to mark a landing zone during the day for the same reason. This is the reality of combat in Viet Nam. We are dealing with a cunning and resourceful opponent. We have to think every move through carefully.

We hear the throb of the two choppers overhead, heading back toward Dong Tam. We relax slightly. The men will be in the hospital in twenty minutes and maybe the three will survive. Some may even have a million dollar wound, serious enough to get them sent to Japan for convalescence, but not bad enough to incapacitate them permanently. This will get them out of this hellhole, out of this never-ending battle with the elements and a tenacious enemy.

We walk around the building, punching the tin walls to work off the nervous energy we have built up. The fact that one of our friends is dead floods back into our minds. We have almost forgotten during the tension of listening to the battle. We all wonder who it is. Which one among us has had his number come up this time? Well, we will know soon enough. The platoon is only about two clicks (kilometers) away from the base, and they will be walking in by 0400 hours. They will be devastated and angry and will be in need of a few friends. No one is going to get any sleep the rest of the night and so I do not even try. I move my machine gun from beside the door and sit there holding it on the mattress. I am in pain and even my weapon cannot help me with this. It does feel good in my hands as I sit there in the dark and hold it for comfort. I plan how many gooks I will kill the next time I use it. The training did not make me a killer, though the drill sergeants tried mightily. I had no desire to kill someone when I came over here, but this damn country has sent me over the edge. Now, killing does not bother me as it had. I have walked to the edge of the world and looked down into the abyss, where it is deep and dark. My old drill sergeants would be quite proud of me.

I sit there in the dark along with my friends. We wait for the bad news. My mind drifts off to the moral argument that has bothered me since I came over here. Church taught me that it is a sin to kill. I did not always pay attention as I should have, but this lesson was easy to agree with. I never thought I would ever be in a situation that would force me to kill. Now my country has drafted me and taught me how to end a life in too many ways. They tell me it is okay and necessary. How can I reconcile the two different teachings? Does God make special exceptions for a soldier? I do not think it is as easy as that. I know I am wrestling with a problem that has plagued untold numbers of soldiers down through the centuries. Moreover, like those soldiers, I have no easy answer. Forty-three years later, I still cannot provide an answer to this most vexing question.

We pass the time with small talk and long periods of silence. We all want to come up with something to relieve the pain we feel. The jokes fall flat, even the Polish ones. One of our platoon members is Polish, so the jokes usually bring laughter and smiles. They do nothing now and the silence grows more oppressive. I rack my brain for a suitable one-liner. I can usually crack the men up with a suitable one, and at times, they depend on me to lighten the mood. Making them smile makes me feel better, also. No matter how hard I try, nothing comes to mind. We sit there in silent pain and listen to the wind sigh quietly through the window openings and doors. These are openings only and have no actual windows or doors. In a combat zone, these just are not needed, an unnecessary frill.

Then we hear the platoon coming in. We hear the tread of boots, the slight rattle and chink of weapons. We hear the quiet murmurs of dog-tired men, trying to walk off the pain they feel. No one wants to greet them and no one wants to be the first to hear the news. Who is dead and who may be fighting for his life? Therefore, we sit and wait quietly as the men walk in and collapse on the bare dirt floor.

"Who did we loose?" I blurt out. I cannot stand the suspense or the silence any longer. The answer is a while coming. No one wants to talk.

Finally, Jennings says, "The bastards killed Marshall." His voice is shaky and on the edge of breaking. He lies back on the floor, sobbing quietly. One of the men grabs his hand and squeezes it tightly. Sometimes all you can do is hold a friend and keep silent. Half of us have tears running down our faces, so I am glad it is still half-dark in the room. We will sit here in our misery tonight and make our peace with the death. Tomorrow we will be dry-eyed. We will go about our business and try not to mention Marshall's name again. We will attend his mock funeral and store his memory away in our minds. This is what we do in war; it helps to keep us sane, at least as sane as a soldier can be.

The news is even worse than I imagined. Of the men in Romeo Recon, Marshall is one of my best friends. The first time I met him, he was sitting on a bunker and playing a rock song on his guitar. I have played since I was fourteen, but I am far from a virtuoso. I know all of five chords that I can change between quickly. His playing mesmerized me. I sat there for an hour listening, until his fingers got tired. He stopped and handed me the guitar. He could see that I was a fellow musician and was dying to play. I protested that I was far below his ability and would be embarrassed to play in front of him. He fixed me with a big smile.

"McCoy, you said your name was? The only difference between us is five thousand hours of practice. We guitar players have to stick together. Of the hundreds of people I have met over here you are the only other musician I have run across." We became fast friends from that moment on. We would sit and play for hours, when we had the time. He was an excellent guitar player, and he taught me and pushed me to improve. That ragged old guitar became our common bond. It took a lot of pain out of the war and gave us both something to look forward to doing. We gained a reputation in the camp and often played for friends. He would do a complicated song and pass me the guitar to do a simpler one. My playing quickly improved but I knew I would never equal his talent. Some people are born to play a guitar and he was one of them.

Now, my best friend and guitar teacher is gone, cut down in the middle of a performance. I am in anguish. I ask God why he took someone who was such a bright and shining star. Why could he not have taken someone less accomplished? An unfair question, I knew. There would be no answer forthcoming. War picked its victims randomly. It mattered little your status or accomplishments. What mattered is if you were in the wrong place at the wrong time. We were all bit players in the great cosmic scheme of things. One minute we could be shining brightly, the next we met our end, becoming a forgotten piece of history, existing only in the memory of our loved ones.

I shouldered the pain and carried on. I remembered his lessons and I played his guitar until we boxed up his belongings, so they could be shipped back home. I determined that I would find another guitar somewhere and continue to play in his memory. Playing that musical instrument took away a little of the pain. It made it a little easier to accept the war and his death.

We wanted to ask our friends exactly what had happened out there, but they all seemed reluctant to speak about it. All we knew was that Marshall was gone, and Phelps, James and Clark had received wounds. James and Phelps were in Dong Tam hospital. They would recover and would be back on the line in a month or so. Clark has a more serious wound. After a stay in Dong Tam they will fly him on to Japan, and then home. For him, the war is over. Only the memories and a pronounced limp are left of his war experience.

I finally get the full story about a week later from Sgt. Reynolds. A little time had dimmed the memory of that night and made it easier to talk. We were alone one evening and I asked him if I could have twenty-four hours off to go to Dong Tam on the convoy trucks. One of the drivers had told me he saw some guitars for sale in the PX (Post Exchange) on the base. I questioned him on the brand of the instruments, but I knew I would have to take what I could find. Reynolds thought that was a fine idea and gave me the time off. It was not going to be the same, playing without my good friend. He was irreplaceable but I wanted to give it my best shot.

I could tell the sergeant was in a talkative mood. He wanted to unload the story of that night. If you keep the pain in too long, it will not come out. It will stay in there and fester. You have to talk about some things. I was glad he considered me friend enough to hear his story. We talked about everything else for a while and I let him ramble on. I knew the tale would come out when he felt it was time.

"Things were going fine that night, at least at first," the sergeant relayed. "We set up in an ambush position and some VC walked into the trap. We opened up and shot them, but several others ran off toward a village. We followed them with the starlight scopes, and then decided to head into the village to check it out." The sergeant told me that there was a small bridge over a canal going into the village. As the first few men crossed the bridge, the enemy blew a mine. The man on point was far enough into the village that he did not receive a wound. The second man, my friend Marshall, was right beside the mine and had no chance. He died instantly. The M-79 grenade launcher he was carrying even had several jagged holes in the aluminum barrel from shrapnel. The three men behind him were also wounded, one seriously.

"The whole thing is my fault. I should have known they were suckering us into a trap. Marshall is dead because I screwed up," the sergeant said. I told him there was no way he could have foreseen the trap. Charlie had risked losing several men to bait the trap, and that made it very hard to spot. Even after hearing the story, I never blamed Marshall's death on the sergeant. I tried to convince him it was not his fault. I could see that he was not buying my point. He probably carries the blame in his head to this day, and that is sad. Sgt. Reynolds is a fine man and a great platoon leader. He does his best to keep his men safe. I have great respect for him.

That night I borrowed money from one of my friends. Tomorrow was guitar day and I did not want to risk not having enough money to purchase one. When the other platoon members heard what I was going to buy, they walked over and solemnly handed me one or two dollars each in MPC (military payment certificates). I protested and told them I could never afford to pay them all back.

Benson set me straight. "Just buy the guitar and play it, man. That's all we want." A few other friends added that I should also look into purchasing a few lessons. This brought about a gale of laughter. I was glad to see the platoon was mending. These were a great bunch of men and you could not keep them down for long. Everything was going to be all right.

I hopped on one of the convoy trucks going back to Dong Tam that afternoon. It has been a while since I had been on a truck. It sure beat humping through the jungle or rice paddies. I carried my M-16 with me since it was a lot more portable than the machine gun. I kept it in my hands the whole ride and I took three bandoliers of ammo with me, what I used to carry in the field before switching to the machine gun. Some idiots left base with only a couple of magazines, but I felt naked without at least twenty. I did not intend to drop my guard for even one hour until my tour was over. I figured I would hand over my rifle and ammo at the base of the ramp leading up to my flight home.

Sure enough, we received several bursts of automatic weapons fire out of the jungle. We were on the last several miles of "Ambush Alley," which was famous for harassing fire. I heard several rounds thump into the side of the truck ahead of us. I dropped down prone behind the steel body of the bed. No one seemed to be hurt so the escort jeeps did not stop and the convoy kept rolling. We were too close to the main base to open up, and of course, Charlie was between the base and the road. The enemy planned it that way, so we could not return fire.

It was a Saturday, so Charlie wanted a little weekend fun. We have all known a few rednecks that would go to the dump on a weekend afternoon. They take along a few six-packs to drink and shoot at rats they scare out of the garbage. Well, the road was the enemy's dump and we were the rats. Did they carry beer with them? They probably did, which explained the poor shooting they usually exhibited. Alternatively, did they choose to shoot poorly, knowing that their fun might end if they hit anyone? The gun jeeps might halt and lob a few 106mm high explosive shells into the jungle. Our platoon certainly did that at times when we ran the gun jeeps. It usually made the perpetrators decide to find another source of amusement.

We ran into no more problems and we rolled through the base gates around 1400 hours. As soon as the truck quit moving, I swung down and headed for the PX, which was about a quarter mile down the dusty street. Once inside I quickly located a display of cheaply made guitars. My worst fears came true. These instruments would hardly make decent firewood and would be hard to keep in tune. I really had no choice, so I picked the one least out of tune and purchased it. I also bought a couple of cheap plastic cups and returned to the transient barracks at Dong Tam. I spent a couple of aggravating hours getting the guitar in some semblance of tune. I then took out my knife, cut the plastic cups up, and made some picks for myself. It felt good to have a guitar in my hands again, even though it was crude and had poor tone.

I got tired of fooling with the guitar and went to the mess hall for supper. They served up a good meal of beef stew, vegetables and mashed potatoes. The biscuits were excellent and the apple pie fabulous. At Can Guioc, we had been subsisting mostly on C-rations since we were out on operations a lot. We did get a good hot meal most evenings if we got back in time from day recons of the area.

I finished off the meal with a good pipeful of tobacco. The sun was down now and the air was cooling off. It was my favorite time of day. I found a sandbag bunker to sit on while I puffed on the pipe. Other than swatting off the mosquitoes, it was a quiet peaceful evening. I did not have to go off into the jungle tonight to set up an ambush with my platoon. I did not have bunker guard overnight. I had the whole evening and night stretching out ahead of me. No worries mate, as the Australian troops we knew would say.

Alone with my thoughts, I sat there quite happy. It was so peaceful. I found it hard to believe that a war zone existed all around me. I had not heard the sound of small arms fire for several hours. No bangs from mortar shells or artillery blasting their way into the air. The silence was a blessing. I could fall in love with this Viet Nam, at least for the moment.

The sky was turning a deep blue with an overwash of pink translucence. The sun was down behind the horizon, but still fighting the oncoming darkness. Overhead the first evening stars were beginning to wink, high above me in the heavens. I thought of many summer nights as a child, wishing on the first star to appear. Life had been so simple then. I was too old for the bogeyman to worry me, too young to know of the harshness and suffering in the world. I wished on that first star, sitting there on that bunker. I asked that this dammed war would end and that man would find a way to live in peace with each other. I waited but nothing changed. The old world just kept on spinning, and far off in the distance I saw a burst of automatic weapons fire. I watched a line of green tracers climb toward the heavens. I had my answer. It was not what I wanted, but it was what I expected.

I arose early the next morning as I had one more mission in this base camp today. It came to me as I tossed and turned on my cot last night, unable to sleep. I headed to the chow line and had a good breakfast. Then I made a beeline to the nearest EM (enlisted men's) club and purchased a case of beer. I still had plenty of money left that the platoon gave me. The selection was limited and I fretted over my choice. I finally settled on an Australian brand, Victoria Bitter. It came in a distinctive can with green and gold on the label. Most of the platoon considered it drinkable. It would not be cold when I got back to the base, with no way to make it cold there. We could dunk it in some water for a while in the shade and that would have to do.

I lugged the case back to the company area. I found some shade and played that guitar for all it was worth, waiting for the convoy to load and form up for travel. As it got ready to leave, I swung my booty and my weapon over the tailgate. I carefully handed the guitar to a soldier in the bed of the truck, then climbed up and made myself comfortable for the hour's ride. As the convoy rolled through the open gate I loaded my M-16 and chambered a round, making sure it was on safe. Up and down the convoy, everyone else was doing the same. We would be on "Ambush Alley" again in ten minutes so it was best to be prepared. I was quite sure I was the only one on the convoy playing a guitar as we rolled down the dusty road. I placed my weapon on a crate six inches from my hand, just in case.

"Ambush Alley" was quiet and the rest of the trip uneventful. We got to Can Guioc by 1450 hours and I unloaded my stuff and headed to the platoon barracks. The guitar was now precious, even though it was a poor excuse for one. It would likely be a while before I got to Dong Tam again. Even if I made it there, would the PX have any guitars for sale at that time? The loss of our friend and the chance to buy the musical instrument seemed connected together in my mind. Had a higher power, seeing our grief, helped us in the only way he could?

I strode through the doorway of our building with my hands full. My friends were busy cleaning their weapons and removing dust from magazines and ammo. There were mazes of rifle parts scattered over pieces of cardboard on the dirt floor. Cleaning rods protruded from barrels. Little tin cans of gun oil were everywhere. Just the normal thing we did in the evenings before going out on ambush patrol after dark. Tonight, we would be doing the same thing that killed Marshall and wounded three men not so very long ago. The insanity would continue.

The platoon was glad to see the guitar, but happier to see the beer. We stashed it in a ditch behind the barracks. The water was dirty but shaded by a few scraggly nipa palms so it was cool. We figured about sundown the beer would be cool enough and the heat would relent by that time. Therefore, we gathered by the trees that evening and each of us had one beer. We toasted the memory of a good friend and I mutilated a few of his favorite songs. We sat mostly in silence, talking little. It was just easier to think of Marshall and not say anything. We were just eighteen to twenty year old soldiers. We did not want to verbalize our feelings and risk crying in front of our friends.

Marshall was one of the gentlest souls I ever knew. He never complained and he always had a good word for everyone. He was a good soldier, but he did not belong in a combat zone. He might have done well as a preacher. I hope the good Lord forgave him his combat duty and welcomed him aboard. After all, the army forced him into the war, as it did almost the entire platoon. I can picture him now, guitar in hand and a big smile on his face. I bet the string section of that heavenly orchestra sounds especially awesome.

211 days left in country.

Chapter 14
The Patience Of The Vietnamese

Can Guioc-July 1968.

Juliet Recon is still here at Can Guioc and our mission has not changed. We go out daily on operations and sometimes at night. The operations are mostly platoon-sized, but occasionally can be much larger and last more than one day. Our small operations send us out to specific villages or areas of jungle to recon, short for reconnaissance. We are supposed to look for signs of the enemy and report this back to base, but sometimes we bump into Charley and then we can report that we know where he is at the present because he has this disconcerting habit of shooting at us.

The firefights we have with the enemy in these situations are usually minor. He will try to kill a few American soldiers and then fade into the bush. He is smart enough to know that a protracted battle with us never goes his way. We just have the ability to call down too much aerial hell on him.

We are well into the dry season now and it is one hundred and ten degrees day after day. The sun beats down relentlessly on everyone and adds to the general misery of being ten thousand miles from home and away from your families. The platoon stays out of the sun as much as possible, but when you have to walk out into the jungle every day looking for the enemy it is pretty hard to dodge that big bright ball that seems to hang motionless for hours. It seems to be intent on frying your brain right through your boonie hat no matter how you try to avoid it. I have been here almost six months and am used to it, but it still gets to me at times. I pity the new replacements, because some can barely walk a klick before they feel lightheaded and have to rest. All the rest stops annoy me when we are out on patrol, but I wise up and realize that when the new guys are resting, well, I am too.

It is Monday morning, the start of a fresh week. The platoon rarely pays any attention to the day of the week, as this is immaterial here. We are soldiers seven days a week; there is no downtime for good behavior except for the occasional three-day stand-downs we receive. These occur when too many men in the platoon wind up incapacitated by the various ills that happen over here. Immersion foot, malaria, and fungal infections are some of these.

Another is when the sergeant notices that too many men are suffering from a bad case of the nerves. No matter how tough you are, sometimes the conditions just get to you, your nerves go bad, and you get very jumpy. A good platoon leader notices this in his men and tries to help by rotating some of the men off patrols for a few days. Several day's rest often cures the problem and the man returns to normal and resumes his job. It is a little disheartening to be taken off a few patrols since we know the platoon needs us, but we know we cannot function adequately and are a liability to the men until we get that rest.

It is 0830 in the morning and we are going out on patrol once again. Today we have drawn an easy patrol through the village of Duc Lai and out into the surrounding countryside. It will be a ten-click walk conducted at a slow pace, so it will almost be like a mini-vacation. Things are mostly quiet in this area at the moment. Most of the low-achieving VC must call this area home.

Another reason we like this patrol is that we get to stop by what we call "the factory" on the outskirts of the village. This factory is an old French building made of corrugated steel over a wood framework that covers at least a square acre. We do not know the original purpose of the factory, but it is full of old machinery of all types, and long, sagging leather belts from overhead shafts power the equipment. These shafts are powered by an ancient steam engine that puffs smoke and rattles as it rotates. It is a scene right out of the industrial age of the mid 1800s.

It is apparent that the building probably closed up when the French vacated the country in the early 1950s. Some enterprising Vietnamese have cut holes in the walls, and they are using some of the machinery to manufacture simple products and sell them from little stands built beside the factory walls. They also sell the ever-present little balls of cooked rice wrapped in green leaves. Vietnamese buy these as snacks as we would buy a candy bar. They also deal in black market goods such as army C-rations and uniforms.

Several stalls run large sewing machines from the overhead belt and specialize in uniforms. They sell the camouflage ones that we cannot get from supply. These would make us safer on patrols, but are not available in any quantity. This is probably because they come ashore in Saigon Port and are stored in Vietnamese warehouses. The high officials who control these storage facilities charge the army for their use and then run a lucrative black market out the back doors of the facilities. Supplies come in the front door for storage and distribution, and they exit the back door, lining those high official's pockets. In this country, graft is not just a business; it is "the" business.

The mama-san in this stall can tailor your fatigues, getting rid of the standard issue way-oversized fit, and she runs off blackout insignia or the normal colored insignia and all the various platoon emblems as you wait. Just made sergeant? Hand her your fatigue shirt and in several minutes, you have your new emblems made and sewn on for several dollars MPC. (Military Payment Certificates) For the average Vietnamese, the war that is dragging on is a goldmine. If we were to ask them if they want the war to end and for us to go home, we would get an emphatic no!

Other stalls sell American cigarettes, sunglasses, cigarette lighters, and various other items the soldier needs. Do we want a souvenir Vietnamese flag or a rebel flag? No problem, our wish is their command. If we ask for weed, they produce it in profusion. The standard package is a wooden matchbox stuffed full for five dollars MPC. Do you need a woman? They will instantly produce a shy-appearing young girl, her demeanor suggesting she just arrived in the big city and knows absolutely nothing about sex. No one is fooled; this is a carefully practiced act.

The five-dollar price includes a quarter-hour with the girl in a dingy room in the factory. Just make sure they leave their wallet with a friend, as I have heard they have a habit of disappearing in that room. The chance of catching a social disease is high, as these free-lance girls are not checked by medics and given weekly shots. The girls that work the base camps have to agree to this procedure in exchange for tacit permission to carry on their business. It is something that happens in every country, in every war, and will continue to happen. In this country sex is a commodity, to be bought and sold freely, with no social stigma attached.

We get to the village around 0930 hours and begin our patrol. We do not check the hooches here; the people are all pro-government and sometimes show their support by giving us solid information. We see a local Vietnamese friend hurry toward us, giving us his tale of woe.

"Hello, my good American friends," Bai says to us. "Very bad thing happen. VC shoot mortar. Building much damage. Truck no good now." He goes on to tell us that the whole village is sad because the truck that is jointly owned by everyone here is destroyed by fire. The fire spread from the building to the truck and the truck is damaged beyond use.

The whole platoon is familiar with the truck, an ancient French model of unknown year. Even when it runs, it sounds like it is on its last legs. The village uses it to take their wares weekly to Saigon. Every time we see the truck leave the village we figure that will be the last time we see it, but then a few days later we see it back in the village, one more round trip under its belt. Sometimes it refuses to start, so ten or fifteen villagers will push it and it will finally spring to life, rattling and wheezing.

Bai is the unofficial keeper of the truck and under his careful ministrations it continues to serve the village. He occasionally needs a fan belt or radiator hose and we raid the motor pool on base for the part. It does not have to fit perfectly; Bai is very good at modifying things to fit where they have no business being installed. The truck is an amalgam of different parts that somehow continue to work together, long after the truck should be in a junk yard.

There is no such thing as a junk yard in this area. All vehicles here are too valuable to junk; they are repaired year after year until almost everything that wears out is replaced with a new or refurbished part. They rebuild the engines half a dozen times until there is nothing left to rebuild, then they find another engine and make it fit. These men are gear-heads in the finest tradition, not out of love of machinery, but out of necessity. The fact that the roads limit top speeds to twenty to thirty miles an hour probably helps with the longevity of the vehicles.

Bai is genuinely heartbroken because his best friend is unusable now. We follow him to the tree where the truck rests, and it is a sad sight. It has been totally consumed by fire. The truck is a two and a half ton model with a wooden stake bed, and the bed is totally burnt away, exposing the frame rails in the rear. The interior is a mess. The seats are nothing but bare springs, the dashboard instruments melted and the steering wheel plastic is gone, exposing the metal core.

The outside of the truck is even worse. Every panel has the paint burnt off it, and the tires are completely consumed, with only the wires that reinforced the beads visible, wrapped around the rim. The hood is up, and everything under the hood destroyed. The distributor cap and wires are gone, and all the under hood wiring has lost its insulation. The headlights hang out of their buckets, cracked and discolored. There is simply nothing left to salvage. I tell Bai that we are sorry and wish him luck in finding another truck to replace this one.

"Oh, we fix truck," he says. "All village help same-same. Take beaucoup time, but we fix." This man has performed mechanical miracles in the past, but I think-*that truck has seen its last rodeo.*

"We need ten tire, okay, bald no sweat, hole no sweat, we fix. Maybe American mechanics have bad tire throw away. You check, please," requests Bai.He writes down the size on a piece of paper and hands it to me, and I promise him we will do our best to locate some. This is not a one way street, since Bai has furnished information in the past that probably saved American lives. This is probably why he is in the position he is in now, some local VC suspect he is too helpful to us. Bai may be walking a fine line for us, and that worries the platoon. He might not get another warning. The next time his friends may locate him in a ditch with twenty rounds of AK-47 in his body.

The factory building is in better shape than the truck. The two rounds landed in an unused section of the building and the villagers managed to put the fire out before too much damage happened. I know they will tackle the damage a little at a time, working together, and in several weeks, there will be no sign of the fire. The truck though, will be another story.

We finish the sweep through the village and head out through the rice paddies. They are dry and cracked and the sun's heat radiates off them like a furnace. The rice harvest is over for the year and each family has stockpiled enough to hopefully last until next growing season. I think wistfully of the monsoon season and the daily rains. We could sure use some rain now, and I would be glad to put up with the mud to get the rain. That is not going to happen for a long time yet, so I move the machine gun to my other hand and keep on walking. I just put one foot in front of the other and keep on moving since there is nothing else I can do.

We walk in the paddies now instead of on the dikes, but we do have a point man check for trip wires and booby traps, just in case. It is never wise to get complacent in Viet Nam, even in a comparatively safe area such as this. Charley just loves for American troops to get sloppy as this makes his life easier.

We are heading southwest toward a section of jungle where the enemy occasionally is spotted from choppers. Charley will take a few pot shots and quickly disappear, so he may be building a tunnel complex there. I have brought ten pounds of C-4 and some fuse in case we run into a tunnel. Other platoon members are carrying extra grenades for the same reason.

We occasionally visit a small family in this area who has three children, or baby-sans. They love candy, so we always carry some, stop by the family hooch, and share it with them. It is only a little out of our way and we have all day to fill. If we get back too early this afternoon, some idiot with more rank than brains will find us a job, probably filling sandbags.

The sandbag bit annoys the whole platoon. We are grunts, dammit! We go out and mix it up with Charley while the camp-bound men sit and have their tea and cakes. Okay, so maybe they do not have those things, but they still have the soft life. Let them fill the sandbags. We are sure those soldiers should be able to handle the job. A sandbag or shovel will not grab a rifle and try to shoot someone.

We arrive at the familiar little hooch. It is the usual thatched-roof building, but it has a lean-to built on one side to house a water buffalo. This gives the hooch a rather pungent odor and you have to be careful where you step. The family lets the animal droppings dry for several days in the hot sun, and then uses it for fuel. I am glad we never arrive near lunchtime, whenever that is. Rice balls cooked over a fire made with dried animal dung may be a treat, but I think I will pass on that.

Papa-San is off in the distance plowing with the water buffalo, but the kids pour out of the hooch and attack us. We have been here a half dozen times and do not know any names, but that does not seem to matter. The kids jostle to be nearest us, and we hand out the candy to smiling faces. *Do Vietnamese moms tell their kids not to eat candy before lunch?* If so, it does no good, because the kids are bottomless pits. The mom smiles at us and gives a gentle, slight bow to show us she thanks us. She seems to know little English. We give her a new cigarette lighter and a pack of cigarettes we have picked up in the village, and say our goodbyes.

This is the type of Vietnamese that I would like to think we are protecting with this damn war. They are the simple, hard-working family, trying to raise their kids in a harsh world as well as they can. They have no politics, no agendas; they just want to be left alone to farm their little piece of land, to grow enough to survive. If they have a little left over to sell to make the little cash they need, then they are happy.

Good dream, McCoy, but you know that in the end the communists will take over. If this family is lucky enough not to be associated with the U.S. then they may survive and be left to work their land, which is all that they want to do. We may be putting their lives in danger just by befriending them and stopping by occasionally. Sometimes it just sucks to think ahead in this country. Why was I born a deep thinker? I think the happiest Americans over here are the ones who take it day by day and never pause to question the status quo. Does that make us more machine than man? Who knows? I do know that it is time to quit thinking and get on alert. The jungle is ahead of us and we have work to do.

The jungle is a bust. There is no sign of Charley or any tunnels, and we spend a sweaty two hours searching it from end to end. We receive a rare dry season afternoon rain; it comes down hard enough to rattle our brains, and we are all soaked in ten seconds. Our wet clothes bind and pull as we head back for camp. We will walk ourselves dry one more time, and I find it really does not bother me, since the rain is a refreshing treat. The sun will burn off all signs of rain in a short time and the moisture will make it feel like a sauna.

I have learned to turn my body off to the stresses and pains of patrols. My mind stays alert, but the wet clothes, the hot feet, and the incessant walking disappear. The weight of the machine gun is gone, and I do not feel the points of the ammo digging into my skin as I walk. I have reached a peaceful nether land and the spell holds until we walk back into base. Most of another day gone, no problems encountered to speak of, and all our clothes are almost dry.

If we were back at Rach Kein, I could find the solace of our little building. I could put my feet up on the railing and gaze out over the lagoon. I could have a cold drink out of our fridge. Alas, this is not our former base camp, and all of that is gone.

This thought makes me remember the great fridge mystery. When we left Rach Kein in April, we carefully loaded the fridge aboard a truck and made the driver promise to keep an eye on it. It never showed up at Can Guioc, so we know someone has taken it, but we have no idea who, and a complete check of the new base once we settle in turns up nothing. We do not lament its loss too much as we have no source of electricity in Can Guioc. The mystery is solved several months later when the platoon winds up in Dong Tam overnight while we are on an operation. While we are there, I get a summons from my old nemesis, the First Sergeant.

I report to his office and he explains to me that "his refrigerator" is not running correctly and he wonders if I can take a look at it since he remembers that I fixed one back at Rach Kein. Imagine my surprise when he leads me into his back room and there sits our old fridge. The sarge is grinning from ear to ear, and I realize this little meeting is just to let me know I cannot screw with him and come out ahead. The old bastard grabbed the refrigerator off the truck someway, fully knowing that it belongs to O'Brian and me. He has not forgotten our former animosity.

After I leave, I walk down the street aggravated, but there is nothing I can do. As I walk, I start laughing. The man absconded with our fridge and then rubbed my nose in it. I still do not like the man, but I have to admit he bettered me without making my last months here unbearable. The old SOB and I will never be friends, but I acquire a healthy dose of respect for him as I walk down that dusty road.

I smile as I remember that and I head over to the mess hall to have a good supper and wash down today's dust with whatever liquid they are serving tonight. *I just hope it is not that putrid cherry Kool-Aid made with warm water and not enough sugar. I could barely stand that crap when I was a kid, but at least it had ice in it then.*

We do not go back through the village for several days, but when we do, I am shocked. The truck is still sitting under the tree, but it is in pieces. The men have the motor out working on it, the cab is off the frame, and the bare frame is sitting on sturdy sawhorses. Thirty or more villagers are sitting in the shade sanding the various body panels. They do not have sandpaper, but they have sand and water, and they are sanding the rust off the metal with their bare hands. Other men have the rear differential apart and everyone is working industriously. A quiet chatter of Vietnamese comes from the people, and you can tell they are all happy and engrossed in their work.

Well, I thought that truck was forever doomed, but this sight makes me reconsider. These people are rebuilding a complete truck with little more than their bare hands and a few tools. They are using teamwork and a shared desire and this is a powerful tool. The VC we face in the jungle everyday are the same Vietnamese we see in this village. They fight on the other side, but they are Vietnamese. *Dear Lord, how do you prevail over a people that just refuse to give up? How do you fight a people that will disassemble a complete truck and rebuild it piece by piece, and make it whole again?* I have known for some time that the Vietnamese are a formidable people, but this is even more proof.

If the big brass could see what I see, they could not possibly believe we can win this war. Anyone who views this scene, and says the war will be won, is both an idiot and a liar. Send President Nixon over here and let him see this and he will have to face the sad, but inescapable truth. I have known it for some time, but it is perhaps easier to see since I am facing the sharp end of the sword. *I am not a genius, people. If I were, I would not be here. Why is it taking the U.S. so long to figure it out?*

We speak to Bai and tell him the motor pool is working on the tire problem. They have some trucks that use the same size and they have requested tires to replace some that are not quite worn out yet. The process may take awhile, but should result in ten useable tires within a month. We also have some of the convoy drivers checking the motor pools in Dong Tam. It is a much larger base and may already have some worn tires available. They have promised to locate and bring us some tires, and we have promised a couple of trophy AK-47s from the next batch of weapons we find buried. The barter system has been used and fine-tuned by the army for the last century or more.

A week later, we go through the village again, and the progress on the truck is amazing. The frame has been painted black with a brush, several Vietnamese are installing the differential and springs at the rear, and another group is assembling the front suspension. All the parts they are installing are cleaned and repainted and the suspension bushings that melted in the fire are new. Several mama-sans are doing the sand and water job on the seat springs and they have freshly made cloth upholstery close by to install once the springs are finished and painted. There are no arguments as the people work, just gentle talk in that musical Vietnamese way. They work quietly, smile at each other, and appear as if they have all the time in the world. I cannot imagine a group of Americans doing this job and getting along so well while working.

Bai sights us, leaves his work on the front suspension, and greets us. We tell him that we have four tires so far and he points out the stack of ten wheels, freshly cleaned and painted bright red with new valve stems installed. We are going to have to hustle to get him the tires before the truck is finished. These people will not be denied and that truck will be ready to drive in another two weeks or less.

The platoon visits the stalls and everyone buys a little something, even if we do not need it. We know the money to fix the truck is coming from the stall sales as they have not been able to take anything to Saigon for over a month. We converse with our Vietnamese friends and congratulate them on the progress on their truck.

We leave the village again and head out into the country on another patrol, one of many in that long, hot summer. This time we are heading almost north to check another village and the surrounding jungle, so we will not be visiting the Vietnamese family at their hooch. We walk the paddy dikes until we get to the village, a walk of about three clicks.

The shady village is a welcome sight, because the sun is taking a toll on everyone and my machine gun feels like it weighs about fifty pounds now. We have never been to this village before, so it is due for a good check. Several things about the village make us suspicious right away.

No baby-sans tumble out of the hooches to greet us as they usually do. Instead, they hang back in the entrances and stare out at us. Are they shy and waiting to see if we are good guys or not? As we check the various buildings, we note that there are no young or middle-aged men about, only tottering old men who gaze at us unsmilingly as we pass. There are no friendly smiles or greetings from anyone, and the missing men are not out in the fields working. I start to get a bad feeling about all these subtle indications and the platoon discusses it as we finish a simple sweep through the village.

Everything about this village says VC sympathizers run it or the villagers are under control of the local VC and scared to associate with us. Which is it? Are we in an enemy village or just a scared one? Are the men VC and hiding close by in the jungle, weapons ready and sizing us up before making a move?

The platoon confers and we decide caution is called for in this situation. Two-thirds of the men set up around the village in a defensive position. They take cover and face their weapons outward. The rest of us take one hooch at a time and thoroughly inspect for contraband. We do the old familiar routine in the pigpen and the distasteful poking in the toilets. Nothing turns up and we relax a little as we come to the edge of the village and a small graveyard with about twenty graves.

The tone in the village has gone from distrustful looks to something I cannot quite describe. Villagers are very sensitive about their gravesites and we will have to walk a fine line here. It is hard to poke about graves and have the villagers think you are showing disrespect for their dead. The problem is that those same villagers do not mind hiding weapons and ammo in those graves. They figure we will leave their dead alone and thus miss hidden contraband.

A casual search of the burial ground shows a fresh appearing grave. There are wilted flowers surrounding it. Vietnamese often bury their dead in a shallow pit surrounded by a low brick framework and a cast cement slab on top. This is because of the very high water table in the delta area. The slabs are sealed to the bricks with a layer of cement or dried mud. This burial does not have that seal and we are immediately suspicious.

Now we have a problem. We need to slide that slab aside and check the grave. The people here do not embalm their dead; they are placed in the grave to let the normal decomposition process take place. When we move that slab will we face a body and the attendant smell or will we discover hidden weapons?

To show a semblance of reverence to the dead, we surround the gravesite and drop to our knees. We each hold our hands together, close to our faces, and bow slightly to the grave, hold it about ten seconds and then rise again. It is what we have often seen Vietnamese do when visiting a graveyard and we hope this is sufficient in their eyes.

Each man grabs the cement slab, and we push it to one side. The suspense is palpable, and the village has gone deathly quiet. I look over and see at least twenty sets of eyes riveted on us as we move the slab.

Jackpot! There is a sixty mm mortar tube and base plate concealed in the empty grave. It is wrapped in old, greasy plastic and there are seven mortar rounds also, arranged side by side. Next to those is another plastic-wrapped parcel. When we open it, we find a bolt-action SKS rifle in rough condition, with a lot of fine rust showing through a thin layer of grease. The rifle has a loaded magazine in it and a round in the chamber. Whoever placed it in the grave made sure it was ready to fire when grabbed. This is not exactly a treasure trove of weapons, but it probably means that at least several men in the village are VC.

We stare accusingly at the women and children and they stare right back. No one averts his or her gaze. Are they all VC sympathizers and proud of it? We do not know and will never know. We cannot arrest a whole village of women and children on such slight suspicion, and we do not want to. They would wind up being interrogated by the local ARVNs and these men do not do that gently. It is essentially a standoff and we must be happy that we confiscated a few weapons and let it go.

The brass will want to see these weapons back at the base. They will minutely examine them, take pictures, and see this as more proof that we are slowly winning the war. We cut a thick bamboo pole to sling the base plate from, and two men take up the load. Two others grab the mortar tube and the sarge carries the SKS to make sure it does not disappear mysteriously on the trip back.

This is a prime war trophy to take home since it is a bolt-action weapon. It is not an automatic, so it can be registered with the company armorer in the camp, and hand-carried home aboard the freedom plane. The armorer will fill the chamber with melted lead to make the weapon unable to chamber and fire a round. Back in the real world, a gunsmith can remove the lead and the weapon will again be operable.

The walk back to camp is long, hot, and sweaty, but we do it one more time. No taxi is going to show up out here in the rice paddy, so walking is the only way home. We are about halfway back and we take a short rest period to benefit several new men we have in the platoon. They are getting glassy-eyed and stumbling along. We have seen the look and the motions before and know if we do not stop for awhile, we will have two unconscious men. The bitch of the situation is that is hard to recover from heat prostration when there is no shade and the temperature is over one hundred degrees.

We get there about suppertime, but everyone finds a place to fall down and rest first. We do not even take our packs off; it is too much effort, so we lean back against them and catch our breath. Finally, the thought of hot chow gets us moving. We shrug off our equipment and head over to the mess hall. We are sure they will be serving cold milk in quart waxed paper containers, and this is a treat after several days of warm Kool-Aid.

We head back to the metal-clad building that is our barracks. The sun is on the horizon and in another hour, the building will be cool enough for human habitation. Until that happens we sprawl around outside in the shade. The mud we picked up this afternoon is pretty dry now and starting to fall off our clothes in chunks. We amuse ourselves by throwing them onto the metal roof of a building and watching them slide down the metal sheeting and bounce onto the ground. It is a poor amusement, but it suits the day's conditions. We are all tired from the patrol and we can do this while resting in the shade. A soldier rests every time he gets a chance, and conserves his energy for when he cannot.

The platoon grabs its cigarettes and lights up and I pull out my pipe and tamp tobacco into the bowl. I have long ago run out of pipe filters. I have found that a strip of writing paper an inch wide rolled up and inserted into the mouth-piece makes a good replacement for pipe filters. Whatever we run out of, we find something to replace it, and if we cannot, then we do without. We will never again take the little niceties of life for granted as we did before we arrived here.

We talk about the things we did today. Just what did we accomplish? The consensus is that, as usual, we have accomplished little other than to burn through one more day. The two weapons will have no real impact, as Charley will just replace these out of a hidden stockpile. Someone down at the motor pool will attack the mortar tube with an acetylene torch and render it unusable, and someone will wind up with the SKS, a great war trophy that they have not captured themselves.

And us? The men of Juliet Recon will continue with what we are doing, chasing an elusive enemy and eradicating him one at a time. We will use up our days, one by one, and hope they run out before our luck does.

203 Days left in country.

Chapter 15
A Close Friend Is Wounded

Fire Base Moore-August 1968.

Big changes have occurred again, and again the platoon is surprised. We should not be since the army has been bouncing us all over the delta since we arrived in this country. The latest move is from Can Guioc to Fire Base Moore. This base is a really forward base and is within five miles of the Cambodian border. We do not have rough but livable barracks anymore, since our platoon now inhabits some four-foot high bunkers that you crawl into when you want to go inside them.

They are full of dust and loose sand from constant use and no maintenance. Their height means they are useable only for sleeping and storing our possessions. The small interior volume and only two small openings to crawl through means they are stifling hot during the day and become cool enough to use only well after dark. O'Brian and I quickly rig up a small lean-to on the back of the bunker made of bamboo poles with several poncho liners thrown over them to ward off the sun. It is just big enough to place two cots side by side. Over this, we use two mosquito nets to keep off the pests and wind up with shade and a cool place to sleep at night. It offers little protection from rain but we are in the middle of the dry season and rain almost never occurs.

The base is tiny, a rough square about half the size of a football field. It has single story sandbag bunkers every thirty yards along the perimeter and the perimeter is nothing but five rows of concertina wire held up by green metal fence poles. Small flares are wired to the rolls of concertina wire and these will pop and give off a flash of light should the wire be disturbed. There are also claymore mines every ten feet with the "clicker" that sets them off installed in the nearest bunkers. The bunkers we live and sleep in are the perimeter bunkers so we are always on bunker guard, so to speak.

I have never lived right on the perimeter and it is disconcerting, to say the least. Out past the perimeter are only knee high weeds for a hundred feet and then the jungle starts. If Charley wants to shoot somebody, all he has to do is walk to the edge of the jungle and open up. We are only a hundred feet away, so he could easily kill several men with one burst and then disappear back into the jungle. To say we dislike the base would be an understatement, as we positively loathe it.

To make it even worse, this area has the most VC roaming it we have ever seen, and they are not the under-performers we have run across at Rach Kein and Can Guioc. This enemy seems to have a quite personal hate for us and do their utmost to make our life miserable. They mortar us two or three nights a week and continually attack the convoys. This area is quite unsafe, so no one moseys down the road for a look at the new territory. If we go out of camp over a few hundred feet, we go in force, at least ten heavily armed men. We know the close proximity to the Cambodian border is the cause of it since we are not that far from the heavily traveled Ho Chi Minh trail. It is a Communist resupply trail and it snakes down from North Vietnam through several hundred miles of jungle, just inside the Cambodian border. They place it there, because we cannot attack it directly without going into a supposedly neutral country.

Our platoon continues in its job of running daytime recons and setting up ambush patrols at night. Almost every time we go out, whether day or night, we run into some contact with hostile forces. This results in at least a man a week being killed and several wounded. Charley also continues his normal job of picking off a few Americans every day and then running away to fight again later. The losses are mounting, and so is our anger and aggravation. We now go out expecting and wanting contact and we do our best to teach Charley some respect. We are no longer Mr. Nice Guys. If we get a shot or two from the jungle, we do not follow up with small arms fire. We shoot a few LAW rockets into the area and a volley of rounds out of grenade launchers, and then finish up with my machine gun. I am cleaning that gun more than I ever have before, because I use it so much.

We also have listening posts outside the camp every night, usually to the ARVN camp about a quarter mile northwest of base. The platoon takes turns on these so each member is on one every five or six days. As always, they are dangerous and even more so than usual in this area with its added VC activity.

I wonder who the SOB was that decided a base camp here would be a great idea. It was a great idea if he wanted to cause more fighting and that is really why we are here, but us poor grunts that do the fighting are less than pleased with our lot. This leads up to the loss of one of the platoon's favorite men. Thankfully, he was not killed, but he was injured quite badly. I still remember that evening in all its detail, embossed into my memory for all time. It started simply enough, as most losses do, and it started with the sarge calling the nightly listening post crew together one evening.

"Saddle up men," said Sgt. Marsh as he picked up his pack and slipped it over his head. The rest of us followed suit, picked up our rifles and followed him out the door. Our little band, only four strong, are on our way out to one of our least favored jobs, an overnight listening post in the ARVN compound a quarter mile to our north. Every night at dusk, each firebase sends out a small team in four different directions to keep a watch for enemy movement, a kind of early warning device for the camp, but a nerve wracking and dangerous job for the participants. We are out there all night, all alone with only the darkness to shield us.

The only good point to this tonight is that we will be inside sandbag walls and not set up in the edge of the jungle with our butts hung out to dry if the VC spots our movement out of the camp in the gathering twilight. The ARVNs are so trigger happy after dark in this area that we always leave camp with a little light left, even though we always radio ahead before leaving. No one trusts their lives to a Vietnamese that might have a poor command of the English language. It sometimes takes some doing before we are half-sure they understand what we are saying. We, in turn, know little Vietnamese and some pidgin French, so most conversations are conducted in a mixture of the three. This problem is normally handled by our Tiger Scout, a young Vietnamese boy of fifteen or so, paid by the army to act as an interpreter, but Lon also knew when something was not right, so he saved our bacon often in our recons through the countryside. Tonight Lon was helping the rest of our platoon pull guard duty on a small, but important bridge in the local village several miles southeast of Fire Base Moore. The VC keep probing the poor defenses of the bridge at night so several platoons alternated in helping guard the bridge.

We arrive at the compound after an uneventful walk through the balmy night air. As usual, the Vietnamese are happy to see us and greet us warmly, shaking our hands and clapping us on the back, sort of a misery loves company deal. They are glad to have extra troops on hand, because night is upon us and in Viet Nam, extra firepower is always handy. They are especially happy to see the LAW (Light Antitank Weapon) rocket I have slung on my back and quickly set to examining it, handing it around and chattering like happy kids in their native tongue. When one soldier unhooks the end caps and attempts to pull out the telescoping firing tube, I call a quick halt to the show and reassemble it. Accidentally firing the rocket would be bad enough, but the back blast coming out the rear of the tube will instantly kill anybody in a large area behind. I sling the LAW back over my shoulder and make a mental note to keep a close eye on it tonight.

O'Brian has set the radio up, and we each find comfortable places near firing slits in the sandbag walls. It is dark now and all I can see is jungle through the slits. The jungle is way too close to the base for my liking. The VC can get too close using the cover of the trees.

"This is Juliet Romeo one niner, TAC, sit rep negative," intones Sgt. Marsh into the mike. He is issuing our first report back to base tonight.

"Roger that, out," comes from the mike along with burst of static. It is the voice of the radio operator at Tactical Area Command back at base. We will call in every half hour to relay that message which means situation report, nothing happening. If you miss a report for an hour and they cannot contact you on the radio they will assume something bad has happened and send out a platoon to help or drag in your bodies. This is the stark reality of war and something that never leaves your mind.

It is good and dark now, so we set up sleep relays and turn in on the hard ground, one person always awake. The ground smells faintly of urine, so some of these soldiers obviously are not too meticulous about where they let fly. After a few months of combat, you learn to sleep anywhere, but I draw the line at this and move around until I discover a less smelly spot. At least the ground is dry, which is not always the case.

We have an uneventful night, no mortar rounds fired in and no probing gunfire and I wake up with the first rays of morning sun in my eyes. We pack up quickly and say our goodbyes, anxious to get back to base camp. Breakfast starts at 0600 sharp and the thought of coffee to take away the morning chill and stiffness, and a good meal adds haste to our movements

We start home, Horner on point and the rest of us strung out at intervals to make it harder for one burst of automatic fire to take out several people. Just as I am mentally congratulating myself on one more day survived and one less day to go, a loud explosion and a burst of red light suddenly split the early morning stillness. I feel the shock wave of angry, displaced air pass over me as I hit the ground, my finger automatically flicking my M-16 onto full auto. I try to make myself one with the ground and I'm thinking we are out in the open and pretty much dead meat if this is an ambush.

Seconds pass like an eternity, but no shots ring out and Horner is on the ground, moaning and thrashing about. We rush to him and his right pants leg and boot are shredded and there is a lot of blood, but most of the damage seems to be below the knee, I am thankful to see, so maybe it isn't fatal. However, the blood is flowing quickly so Jennings hands me his rifle and slings Horner over his shoulders and we take off at a fast run toward the camp with me just behind trying to get my belt around the wounded man's thigh. We holler out to several sleepy-eyed soldiers on the back gate to get the damn concertina wire moved out of the way and barely slacken our pace.

Jennings is running hard now, gasping for air and the blood is soaking the back of his shirt and pants and flinging off his boots. We do the final sprint to the aid station and lay Horner on the table.

"All right, you guys get outta here, we have work to do and we need the room," the medic informs us. I take one more glance at Horner, he is ashen-faced and breathing shallowly, and I do not like how he looks. I know we have to get out of here, sit down somewhere and talk this out, process this latest gift from Viet Nam, and get on with our lives.

Twenty minutes later we're sitting in the shade under a poncho liner stretched from the back of our four-foot high sandbag bunker and sleeping quarters to a couple of bamboo poles embedded in the ground. There is lots of bamboo around here, more than you could ever use and it comes in handy.

Miller is asking, "Should we get Horner's things together?" We look at each other, not wanting to voice our fears for our friend.

I counter with, "Nah, they'll send for his stuff once he gets better at the hospital."

Parks joins in with, "If he gets better." I shoot him a withering look and hope he will shut up with his negative thoughts. We do not need to hear this today.

I say, "Horner is tough and a month from now he will be back in the real world eating a cheeseburger and checking out the nurses." I am not so sure I am right but someone needs to say that to make us all feel better. We all feel as if we have let down a friend, but I was there and there is nothing we could have done differently. That is just the way it goes in "the Nam," as we say here.

A noise draws our attention and a chopper flies over the camp, coming from the direction of Dong Tam. It settles onto the landing pad and the wind brings us smells of burning jet fuel and hot metal.

"Crap, a dust-off chopper," intones O'Brian. "This can't be good news."

"Don't worry, man. He is gonna be okay, the medics will fix him up just fine," I reply, but I am acutely aware that saying so does not make it so. Just then, the door to the aid station flies open and out comes two medics with a stretcher and double-times it toward the chopper. We jump up and follow out to the pad, the chopper sitting there, the turbine winding down and the blades doing their flick-flick through the air, raising huge clouds of choking dust.

It is the middle of the dry season, when Viet Nam is ten percent solid matter and ninety percent dust. The medics set the stretcher down just outside the blade arc and pull the blanket over our friend's face to keep the grit out, then rise as one and load him aboard, strapping the stretcher down tightly. Another medic in the chopper is already hovering over Horner; we step back as the turbine spools up, the blades accelerate, and the dust cloud gets worse. The chopper raises almost vertically a short distance, then the nose drops and it bolts forward and up, with a long climbing arc out over the road, and disappears behind the jungle. A chopper's blades can only lift it straight up as the pilot feeds in increasing blade angle, then they tilt it forward slightly so the blades can pull it forward as well as up.

The medic says, "Your buddy is going to be all right, we just want him back at Dong Tam where he can get better care than we can give him. We stabilized him and the leg is savable. That air conditioning at the hospital will help him a lot." He pounds me on the shoulder for emphasis and heads back to the aid station.

Dong Tam Hospital has a bunch of forty foot long wards made of rubberized fabric with air chambers built in, equipped with air compressors that run full time to keep the chambers full of air, with air locks at one end to keep the air conditioning in. That really blew my mind the first time I saw them, and on the rare occasion we got to Dong Tam we would often visit a sick or wounded friend, as much for the cool air as for seeing the friend. Sometimes we would make up a name to get in, and then gather around the bed of someone we did not know to stay in. Initially the soldier would be confused by the sudden appearance of people he did not know, but they usually caught on quickly.

Five of the platoon members arm ourselves and head out to where Horner was wounded. It is on the well-worn path between our base and the ARVN compound, and it happened less than an eighth-mile from our back base gates. The little bastards that did it really have some nerve and that aggravates us. Charley is determined to attack us and show us no mercy. We make plans to do the same thing. If he shoots at us twice we will cut down every tree in the area with LAW rockets. If he kills or hurts someone, we will do our best to extract retribution tenfold. We will toss every damn village in this area weekly and if we find one weapon, we will burn it down. If Charley wants to escalate this war, then he will have a fight on his hands. Starting today, we will extract vengeance and teach the little buggers some respect. It is not good to get twenty-two teenaged soldiers pissed off at you with the weapons we have at our command, and Charley will learn this as he dies.

After we calmed down a little and inspected the area, we found that the whole listening post crew, me included, is extremely lucky. A grenade caused the explosion, but it was taped to a large caliber artillery round. The round split open when the explosion occurred and spread yellow powder all over the ground, but did not go off. We are all lucky to be alive. Old, damp powder is the only thing that saved us this morning. The booby-trap was set off electrically with a ragged old piece of wire that is buried six inches below the ground. We pull the wire up as we walk toward the jungle only seventy-five feet away and find an area just inside the trees where one or two men waited for us to return to base that morning.

The weeds are matted down, there are scuffmarks in the dirt, and the butt ends of several cheap Vietnamese cigarettes are scattered around. They probably planted the mine, buried the wire in the middle of the night, and then kicked back for a cigarette break. Then they waited until we came along this morning and detonated the mine. Only luck or perhaps divine intervention saved the four men in the post. I am one of those men who came so close to dying about 0540 this morning, but the news does not shake me up. I am filled with a hate like I have never felt before, and I vow right then and there, that I will do my best to eradicate every one of these little vermin I can in the last five months of my tour. I also caution myself that blind hate can get you killed, and you cannot kill Charley if you are dead. *Be cool, McCoy, watch and wait, bide your time, and show zero mercy when the time comes.* That is the deal I make with myself. McCoy is now officially pissed big-time.

The men who did this have been gone long ago and there is nothing to shoot at here, so we head back to the camp to tell the rest of the platoon what we found. We know we can get them to go along with our new, undeclared zero-tolerance policy on Charley's crap. We sit there in the shade and discuss what to do, and think about heading to the nearest village and inspecting it closely. It is only several hundred yards into the jungle to the south of the back entrance to the camp, but the sun is burning down on the camp and some cooler heads prevail. They know we are too worked up to be objective and careful when we get to the village and we grudgingly agree and back down. The platoon has the rest of the day off, but it will be business as usual tomorrow and most of the platoon still has five months to teach the enemy a little respect.

The last time I ever saw Horner was that final glance into the chopper as it lifted off. I often wondered that year, and later, when I got back home, if he was still alive, if my friend made it.

***

Later on, after the Viet Nam Memorial in Washington opened, my wife Lori and I rode over there and spent several hours in the Smithsonian Institute Museum. We then headed for the wall. I wanted to see if Horner and a few others that were badly wounded had their names on the wall, since after a guy was flown out you never heard anything else about them, even if you tried to get information. It was always, yeah, he is home now and fine and your butt is still over here bugging me, but I never believed their story. I was sure bad news was bad for morale and the army did not want that.

Going to the Wall was worrying me. I wanted to go and I did not want to go. When we got a hundred feet away, my feet started dragging, my legs got shaky, and a bowling ball settled into my stomach, a very large and very heavy bowling ball. The quiet tears started rolling down my face.

"Lori girl, can you wait here and I'll go ahead and come back in a little while and get you?" I asked my wife. I was not sure how I was going to react and I wanted to test the waters first.

She understood, nodded her head and squeezed my hand. I forced myself to move another thirty feet, but when I called down to the engine room for more power to the legs no one was answering from down there. I felt I was going to throw up all over the sidewalk, and defeated, I walked back to Lori, wiping away my tears, unable to say a word. She had seen me fight the Viet Nam demons before, at night or when I was feeling down, and good wife that she was, just gave me a little smile of encouragement and hugged me tight. She somehow knew that it was best to keep quiet and let me work it out for myself, and hand in hand, we went back to the museum and never discussed that painful walk again.

Lori tragically passed away in 2000 and I never knew there could be so much pain in the world. Viet Nam was a cakewalk in comparison. The woman that took away a lot of the residual pain of the war was suddenly gone from my life, and I knew she could never be replaced. I would now have to continue the battle on my own.

Several years before she died, Lori mentioned that vacation was coming up again and since we both really enjoyed the trip to Washington and the museum, she wondered if I might want to go back again for a day or two. I knew the hidden question in her request, however, and after carefully considering it, I told her I was not quite ready to go back there again. I had done some quiet soul searching, trying to figure out why a man who had survived almost a year of combat was so traumatized by a granite wall and oh, so many names. It finally hit me that as long as I did not see Horner's name up there, or Marshall's name, or the others, then in my mind they were still alive. I want to remember them all in that long ago, short moment of time as they were, young and full of life and vigor. They were only eighteen or nineteen, their lives still stretching out far ahead of them, and full of plans for when they got back to the real world, as we called it. Oh, the cars they were going to buy, the girls they were going to kiss, and the food they were going to eat. Therefore, I passed on the idea for that moment, but promised her that someday we will return to the Viet Nam Memorial.

I still tell myself that someday I will go back again. I will not have Lori by my side, so it will be hard to face it alone. Going back is a promise I have made to myself, but a promise so far not kept. Someday... ...

169 days left in country.

Chapter 16
Standdown On A Navy Ship

Navy ship Stoddard-September 1968.

My platoon continues with its daytime operations; flying out on choppers during the day to inspect jungle areas and villages for hidden war material and signs of Charley. Sometimes the routine is changed and we fly into an area to set up ambushes at night, trying to catch some hapless enemy in our net. The rainy season is long over now, making problems with immersion foot minimal. Something else has come along to replace it and our lives are miserable because of this.

The problem is skin parasites that cause a burning red rash in our private areas and armpits, or wherever the skin rubs together. This is almost worse than the problems with our feet. We try the army-issued powder but the only thing that seems to help is ventilation and sun on the affected areas. Half of the platoon is walking around like old men, legs splayed outward and arms held away from the body.

Our platoon sergeant reports to the First Sergeant that almost none of us seem currently fit for operations that require walking. In the bush, all operations require walking. The First Sergeant responds in his normal brusque way. He stops by our company position and berates us for our malady.

"You damn bunch of pansies! I don't know how the hell you managed to get into this man's army. I have seen better men than you at the old folk's home back in the world," says the First Sergeant. He goes on to tell us that we better shape up and stop catching various shit that keeps us from performing our duties. To him, we are the army's possession and our current maladies keep us from fully performing our duties. The First Sergeant is above all, an understanding man, at least in his world.

The platoon is put on light duty, which means we do not have to go out on operations, but they continually order us to unload supplies from convoy trucks and fill sandbags. Understandably, no one gets any better, and I suspect some of the men are secretly abrading theirs to make it worse. Mine is so painful that I have no desire to do this; it is quite painful enough as is.

Someone up the chain of command pulls some strings, and several days later, the sarge gathers us together and tells us that our brother recon team, Romeo Recon and our platoon will be going on a three-day stand-down aboard a navy ship anchored in the Mekong River. This is outstanding news and we all cheer and clap each other on the back.

The promised vacation starts the next day. Trucks roll in at 1100 hours and we gather our gear with everyone carrying their full load of combat equipment. Our weapons and equipment go everywhere with us. The only time we put them down is when we are in our base camp.

We are trucked west past Dong Tam several hours until we get to a gentle bend in the river. We disembark and walk down to the river, which is about a half mile wide here. A navy launch meets us and carries us out to the ship, which is huge, grey and very well kept. The ship is what I think is called an LST. (Landing Ship Tanks) It has a large ramp at the front that has a mechanism that allows the ramp to be cranked down to unload the tanks and other bulky equipment onto a beach. I have seen this type of ship in many of the World War II movies on TV. I am very happy to be heading for this ship since my father served in the navy in the South Pacific during World War II. I have always wanted to look over a big navy ship.

The launch drops us off at a floating barge moored to the side of the ship. It has a steel container on one side and a husky-looking navy man operating what appears to be a small fire hose. We are all dirty and stinking from the last several weeks of combat duty and I can easily figure out why that hose is there.

"Good afternoon men. I am Petty Officer Marlow and I am here to see that you are clean before you board our ship. Put your weapons in the steel container and remove all clothes. Deposit them in the box to your right. Grab a bar of soap and wash once we spray the water. Take only your boots and wash them also, then head up the ramp to the deck. You will be issued new fatigues at the top of the ramp."

We have not planned to get naked in front of a bunch of swabbies, but the ship looks like a haven and we figure well, whatever it takes. *Nothing like boarding a ship in your birthday suit.* We grab the proffered new clothes and put them on as we walk across the deck. I pour the water out of my boots and carry them, wanting to let them dry. I have on my first clean pair of socks in months and I do not want to get them wet.

A navy man leads us below down a series of stairs until we come to the hold of the ship. It is twenty feet high and cavernous, well lit and clean. He apologizes for not having better accommodations and points out a row of the old familiar inflatable mattresses. We tell him not to worry, these are the best accommodations we had seen in months. He then tells us supper starts in an hour and he will come back and show us how to get to the mess hall near the stern of the ship.

The platoon discussed the friendliness of the navy personnel. We were surprised about how much better they treated us than some of our sergeants. After all, we came aboard their ship dirty and stinking, but they seemed to go out of their way to make us feel wanted. I remarked to several of the platoon that I would rather be in the navy, but I figure it is a little late for that. I would also have had to enlist and that would not have set well with me.

The meal aboard the ship was a revelation. The mess was spotless and the food superb. The cooks told us to take all we wanted, but to eat all we put on our plates. Some of us, me included, drank much more of the cold milk that was available than we should. We arrived back at our mattresses stuffed and miserable. We would find that over the next three days it was hard not to overeat.

We relaxed on the mattresses and smoked, luxuriating in the knowledge that we could do pretty much whatever we wanted for the next three days. The medics gave us medicine for our rashes and we greased ourselves up and lay around like bums. We were going to take full advantage of our freedom by doing as little as possible for the next three days. The war faded into the distance and we talked about our families and home until dark.

With the coming of evening and our over-stuffed stomachs relenting, we decide a tour of the ship is next on the list of things to do. We spent several hours traversing the various corridors and decks on the ship. It is a little confusing at times to find our way around, but wherever we go, the navy men are glad to see us and explain the ship and their duties aboard it.

Secretly, I was wondering what the penalty was for disappearing somewhere aboard the ship and never returning to Fire Base Moore. We reached the fantail of the ship on our journey of exploration and found it to be the perfect place to end the day. We sat on the deck, leaning against the railing or the ventilator stacks, and stared out at the sun riding low in the evening sky.

It was that magic time of the evening that I so loved. The ship faced down-river and swung gently on its mooring. The waves on the water were tiny, irregular steps, viewed from the deck height of around thirty feet. A cool breeze is blowing aboard the ship, coming from the northwest. The last rays of the sun had turned the sky a fiery red up the river, and the sun was setting directly into the water far away. It is such a peaceful, beautiful evening and we have heard no small arm's fire for several hours. Looking at the sun drop into the water, I almost expected a sizzle and found that I was holding my breath waiting for one.

We sat smoking, and I lit my pipe and reveled in the taste, holding the smoke in my mouth and savoring it. I missed not having a guitar in my arms for an instant. It was seventy-five miles away and I wondered how I had been stupid enough not to bring it with me. The mood passed quickly, it was just too perfect an evening. I figured I could live without my guitar for three days, but I did make plans to question the sailors tonight about the availability of one on the ship.

As usual, my mind turned to thoughts of my tour here ending. Mentally I ran down the months I have been here, adding up the days and weeks. *Let's see; I have been here two hundred and eleven days, so I have one hundred and fifty four left.* I have been making these calculations for so long that it happens almost instantaneously in my mind. As always, I reflect that this is still far too long. I just have to get back to the real world as soon as possible. The nagging feeling I often feel forces itself into my mind. Could the real world and my past life there be but a dream? Was I born in this place and my thoughts of a better life just mere escapism? I push this thought away harshly. I know that former life was real, and it is there on the horizon just waiting for me.

The platoon and I sat there on that ship, on that perfect evening, until long after dark. We discussed important matters, things that could affect the eventual outcome of the human race. One was trying to decide if a cheeseburger and fries were better than a steak and baked potato. Another was the relative merits of certain cars. Everyone in the platoon had his own opinion and I was verbally silenced when I stated that a Pontiac GTO was certainly better than a Camaro. We finally decided to go back to the hold and get some sleep since breakfast is served at 0600 hours and nobody wants to miss that meal. At base camps, we could always fall back on readily available C-rations, but on the ship, we have no access to them. I expect to have trouble sleeping, but the gentle rocking and quiet hum from somewhere in the ship calms my mind and

I drift off quickly into a deep, restful sleep. I am safe here and my mind allows me the rest I need.

The next morning the bustle aboard the ship wakes us early. We all go to the bathroom where hot water showers, razors and soap are available. *These sailors sure lead a much better life than we grunts do,* I think for about the tenth time. The sailors continued to go out of their way to make us feel at home, and what caught my eye was that they actually seemed to like the navy. I still wanted to switch to the navy for the rest of my career, but I knew that was not going to happen. The army had me for another year yet, and the only way that is going to change is if they shipped me home horizontally.

We enjoy a great breakfast in the mess, and then continued our exploration of the ship, slowed only by our ability to walk long distances due to the rash. We were welcomed all over the ship and explored it from the depths of the engine rooms to the topmost decks. The engine room fascinated me; it contained the largest motors I have ever seen. Everything is clean and spotless all over the ship. Sailors busily chipped loose paint and repainted those areas. I was thoroughly impressed with the ship and the way the sailors kept it well maintained.

As we explored the ship, we ran across the ship's store where we could purchase cold drinks, snacks, and tobacco. They even had a small selection of pipe tobacco with my favorite brand available so I stocked up, buying three pouches. This was the most tobacco I had had at one time since coming to Viet Nam and I walked around feeling as rich as a king. At times it takes very little to make a grunt feel happy.

While touring one of the crew's quarters I spied a beat up old guitar stashed under a bunk and asked one of the sailors if I could talk to the owner about borrowing or buying it. He told me to wait around and he would go and find the owner and bring him back to talk to me. He returned soon with a tall, tanned sailor whom he introduced as Seaman Hodge. I explained that I played the guitar a bit and was hoping I could use his or purchase it if he wanted to sell.

"It's not much of a guitar and I have beaten it up pretty good trying to learn to play it," Seaman Hodge stated. "I could use some lessons and I will let you use it in exchange for them. I don't want to sell it, because there is rarely a place where I could buy another one." We sat down and exchanged what we knew about playing, and I could see that he needed the help that I could possibly give him. It was great to meet another guitar player that knew less about playing than my limited knowledge. He had to get back to his duties, so we made a deal to let me use it the rest of the day and I would meet him back here after supper for some lessons. This was proof that this ship was heaven on earth. I now had everything I needed to make my life perfect for the next two days.

I spent most of the day in the hold of the ship playing to a non-existent audience, trying to remember the twelve or so chords I knew. I wrote down parts of songs and put the chords over the lyrics, so I could help the sailor tonight. He had never met me until today yet he entrusted me with his prize possession. I was determined to help him with his playing and leave a few songs written down that he could practice after I left the ship. I had lost my good friend Marshall two months ago and I was determined that I was going to pass on the guitar training he gave me in his memory.

With a guitar in hand and tobacco in my pipe, the day passed quickly. At 1800 hours, the platoon assembled in the hold and we all went to the mess for another great supper. We met Seaman Hodge and his friend Walston there and they informed us that the cooks aboard the ship always prepared better meals when there were infantrymen aboard. They said that was to thank us for our service and to show us what we missed by not joining the navy. We told them that we were definitely regretting not joining their branch of service. After the great meal, the platoon split up and I went with the two sailors back to their sleeping quarters.

"Okay, you know the C and G chord. You can see where I have drawn them on this piece of paper as they appear on the guitar neck," I said to Hodge. "I have also sketched out a D chord and several other simple chords. With these three main chords, you can play eight or ten easy songs such as *Blowing In The Wind*. Do you like that song?"

I explained that a chord was merely one or more strings held down on the guitar neck and then some or all of the strings were strummed.

Hodge assured me he did like the song, so I had him practice the D chord. He tried to form it and got a muffled sound when he strummed the strings. He tried repeatedly and I had him change his hand position slightly on the neck and press the strings harder. This time he was rewarded with the correct sound and a big smile spread on his face. That was one reason I liked the guitar, you simply could not play one without smiling, no matter your level of expertise.

"Forming a chord on the guitar correctly and changing from one chord to another quickly is the whole basis of playing a guitar," I told Hodge. "Learning a chord is mostly muscle memory, so you must practice that new chord hundreds of times until every one sounds clear and sweet when you strum the strings. Once this is learned, you must practice changing between those three chords quickly until the changes come automatically and the chords ring true. Your fingers will get tired and hurt and you will feel like throwing the guitar overboard, but you have to keep practicing. Like anything else you want to learn, you must want it badly enough and continue practicing. Do you want it bad enough?" I asked him.

He assured me he did, so I had him practice the new chord and changing between the three chords until his fingers were painful. I then picked up the guitar and played *Blowing In The Wind* slowly, showing him the chord changes and then picked up the tempo until I was playing it at normal speed. He told me I was a very good player but I assured him that I only sounded good because I could play better than he could. We discussed the chords and I told him he needed to practice those chords and the changes for at least four hours throughout the day. If he followed my instructions, I would have him playing the song before I left the boat.

Hodge buckled down and practiced as I asked him, though he told me later that he was temporarily evicted from the crew quarters by his fellow seamen, and had to go up on the foredeck to practice by the glow of the anchor light. They could not take the incessant repeating of the chords that he had to do. I told him that was a good sign. If you practice chords enough, people are going to get tired of hearing them, but that is a sign you are practicing well. As with anything in life that you want to be good at, practice can make perfect only if you want it badly enough.

The platoon continued our idyllic vacation aboard the boat. We finally tired of exploring it after we covered every passage and cabin we could find. We never got tired of the hot showers though, and took more in those three days that we had experienced in the eight months we had been in Viet Nam. We were probably the cleanest platoon of grunts in the country as we walked down the ramp to get on the launch the day we left the ship.

That night the platoon gathered on the main deck to walk the ship one more time and to say goodbye to the friends we had made on the ship. Soldiers make friends quickly because we have little time to nurture relationships, knowing that a friend can be a casualty quickly, or our duties will separate us. This is both a good and bad part of being a soldier in a combat zone.

As we walked the deck, we came upon sailors stationed at the bow and stern whose jobs were to occasionally drop a concussion grenade overboard, deterring the VC from swimming up to the hull of the ship after dark and attaching timed explosives. We were all familiar with concussion grenades, because we sometimes used them in tunnel entrances.

The concussion grenades were different from the normal fragmentation grenades. Frags use cast iron segmented bodies that split up into hundreds of small fragments when they exploded. The concussion grenades had heavier non-grooved bodies that split and caused a shock wave during detonation. This made them more efficient in enclosed areas and in the water. When the grenade exploded in the water, the shock wave tended to rupture eardrums and disorient a swimmer, thus causing him to drown. The army had a specific weapon for most specific conditions and this made the average combat soldier a more efficient killer.

We hung around and watched a few dropped over the side of the ship. The sailor would pull the cotter pin from the grenade and that allowed the handle to pop off and arm the weapon. He would then count one second before dropping it over the side of the ship. The grenades had approximately four-second fuses that would explode by the time they reached the water and sank several feet. The effect was like a miniature depth charge. First, you heard a muffled explosion and then a column of frothy water would shoot into the air. It was quite entertaining and safe as the explosion produced little shrapnel, but it was quite deadly to a person in the water.

We said our goodbyes to the navy men and continued our walk around the deck. This was our last night on the ship and we all knew our walk would end on the fantail, high above the water. We timed the walk to arrive there so we could catch the setting sun off to the west, turning the river into a cauldron of fire. Soldiers had few times of beauty in their lives, and this was one that we tried to never miss. The display was an affirmation that God was up there in his heavens, watching over we rebellious and bloodthirsty human beings. Just maybe, he was watching over us and taking pity on us as we continued our lives. We probably looked like a colony of ants from up there, running in no apparent direction and performing no useful functions.

As always, we pulled out the soldier's girlfriend, our tobacco products. Watching a brilliant sunset with a pipe full of tobacco and the conversation of good friends was almost worth the life we had to live. We talked of home, family, and plans for the future. Then the show was over as the sun retired below the horizon to allow the tropical night to approach. The sky spread out its magnificent show of gleaming stars, almost like an encore, and we headed down to the hold and to our mattresses, except for me. I had a final appointment in the crew's quarters with Hodge and that guitar, and I knew that tonight the chords would come together for him. He would play a complete song tonight, maybe haltingly, but it would be a song and his friends would listen instead of banishing him to his studio on the bow of the ship.

He made me proud that night and I could see that he wanted to play a guitar badly enough that he would continue after I left. His friends did gather around to listen and I gave him some songs and chords that I had written on borrowed writing paper. We played until long after lights out, and finally got tired. I shook hands with the sailors and headed down to the hold for what would probably be my last good night of uninterrupted sleep for some time to come. I hope and prefer to think that Seaman Hodge is still playing a guitar and has far surpassed my ability. It would be a small legacy to be sure, but to me an important one.

We were up at daylight for one last sumptuous breakfast and gave our goodbyes to everyone in the mess. These men have become great friends in the short space of three days, and I was not sure if I would miss the navy or the ship more. Army life is a continual succession of meetings and goodbyes, so we take it in stride as we gather up our personal possessions. We climb the ladders to the main deck and trod it one last time, before going down the gangplank and into the launch. We watched the big grey ship recede into the distance and then the launch bumped against the dock, and waiting in all their dirty glory were several army trucks to take us back to base. We have exchanged the clean, grey colored part of our lives for dirty green and now it makes a difference, for we know there is a better existence in this country. Sometimes, it is better not to know.

We loaded up and the trucks rolled off with a grinding of gears. That yellow dust, which we had not missed for three days, slowly infiltrated over the tailgate and settled upon us. I tried brushing it off my clean fatigue uniform but finally gave it up for a lost cause. We were back in the land of yellow dust and nothing was going to keep it from its appointed rounds.

The past three days had cured our rashes and we were feeling much better as the miles rolled behind us. The vegetation was droopy and colorless due to the lack of rain; we were in the middle of the dry season. Torrential rains would not bless this land for another six months and life would have to grind on in the dust. I reflected that I would not be here for another rainy season so I would miss the miraculous rebirth of the vegetation, but I would not miss all that resulting mud. We all slowly turned yellow in the back of the truck as we continued down the road, and we soon made the familiar turn off Highway Four and headed west toward Fire Base Moore.

The trucks rolled through the small village of Moc Hoa and across the short bridge that spanned the river. I was surprised to see the bridge still standing. The VC have done their best to take the village and blow the bridge several times, but the local ARVNs have managed to fight them off each time. Our platoon often reinforced the local militia at night to protect the bridge. Obviously, another platoon had taken over the job during our absence and helped to keep it standing. The bridge is strategically important because it is on the only road leading to the base. Charley would love to blow it up and force us to rebuild.

Before long, the familiar right turn came up, and the trucks exited the road and there stood the dusty base camp ahead of the deuce-and-a-half. It looked ruder and dustier than it had before and no wonder. We are now viewing it through the eyes of ones who have seen the Promised Land, and this is definitely not that land.

As proof that we have returned to the land of toil and sorrow, our platoon sergeant appears at the tailgate as the trucks screech to a halt.

"Welcome back, boys," Sergeant Reynolds exclaims. "I hope you all enjoyed the vacation and are ready to get back to business tomorrow. Charley stayed here and we lost two more KIAs and four men were wounded." He filled us in on the particulars of the losses and we found that a Delta platoon operation had taken the casualties. One of the men wounded was a good friend of mine so I could only hope his wound was serious enough to get him out of the country, but not bad enough that he would not recover. It was harsh to be hit with the bad news as soon as we got back, but I knew the sergeant was using the information to remind us of the serious game we were playing. He wanted to make sure we were jarred back to reality after the time off as he awakened the hate we had for the VC. The hate made us more cunning and careful. We wanted to be around for the payback.

We have a good supper, but not close to navy standards. Then we go back to our sandbag bunkers. They are four feet high and have a quarter inch of dust accumulated from the previous three days. We crawl in and remove our poncho liners that we sleep on, and shake out most of the dust. The bunkers are small, just enough room for two men to stretch out prone at night and a small alcove with the floor dug out to allow one man to sit upright and put a gun through the firing slit. They have a slight smell from years of continuous use and no real way to clean them. How do you wash a sandbag wall? The contrast between our last three night's accommodations and this hovel is pretty extreme. I think to myself, *McCoy, you have spent several months in this hole, and you will be spending more, so suck it up and get on with your business!* There is nothing like giving yourself a pep talk because only you know what your mind needs to hear.

We turn in early and get some sleep because daylight comes too soon and we know there is an operation planned for tomorrow. The platoon does not have bunker guard tonight as they are allowing us our full three days of rest. We do watch the sunset through a cloud of tobacco smoke and then retire to the bunkers, though we know our minds are back on wartime and our sleep will be fitful.

Sure enough, I find myself waking up every half hour on the dot, but I finally settle down for a good sleep in the wee hours of the morning. This is short-lived as the mortar crew has a fire mission about 0400 hours and I lay there wide awake listening to the rounds blast into the night sky and feel fine bits of dust and sand rain down from the sandbag ceiling two feet above my head. Hey, it is great to be back home among familiar surroundings and to wake up in the mornings spitting sand out of my mouth.

We rise early and get ready for breakfast. There is not going to be any soap and hot showers today. After breakfast, the sarge calls us together and briefs us on today's mission. Seems that the big boys think that we ought to fly out, give a certain village a check over, and make sure Charley is not misbehaving. We tell him fine, we do not have any other plans now so we check our weapons and load up, ready for combat once again. We march out through the gate, ready to make our little piece of Viet Nam safe for human habitation one more time.

151 days left in country.

Chapter 17

Charley Is Not The Only Danger In Viet Nam

Fire Base Moore-October 1968.

My platoon, Juliet Recon, is still stationed at Fire Base Moore in what would be late fall in the United States. In this country, we are still in the dry season and it is hot and humid. This country seems to have only two seasons, the dry one where it is very hot and dry, and the rainy season when it is merely hot and wet. This is the ideal country for pursuing that beach tan although we have never been within a hundred miles of a beach.

"Juliet Recon, form up," said Sergeant Reynolds. "We have a mission this morning. This will be a recon in force over near the Cambodian border, north-west of Saigon. Romeo Recon will be coming with us and choppers will be here at 1300 hours."

Okay, that gives us a couple hours to check our weapons, procure extra ammo and decide what we will carry. The platoon is not anxious to be heading toward the Cambodian border again, but we know why we are going there. This is where the enemy calls home.

The sarge has a large-scale map out and I look over his shoulder. His finger is pointing to an area north of the Parrot's Beak. This is great; not only is it way out in Charley country, it is also near that Beak again. If they had asked us where we really did not want to go, we all would have pointed to that general area on the map.

"How long are we going to be gone, sarge?" I ask, hoping this is going to be a one-day affair. I want to fly in, take a quick look around, and get the hell out of Indian Territory.

"Overnight," the sarge answers, "so carry enough ammo for two days." It could have been worse, I reflect, as I head toward the bunker and my weapons. We have had a few longer operations, so I will settle for two days anytime. By the time the choppers get here and then take us to the landing zone it will be late afternoon. That will give us little time for patrolling before dark, because we have to find a good place to set up an ambush site.

The night ambush will be the hairiest part and with only about forty men going, it will be a little worrisome after dark. If the night passes okay then we will only have four or five hours of recon before the choppers pick us up. We could encounter a strong force of enemy and wind up tied down longer. Well, worrying will not make things any better, so I concentrate on making the M-60 machine gun and my .45 caliber pistol clean and ready to rumble. Knowing that both weapons are clean and going to function okay is the only thing that concerns me now.

As we gather outside the gate and wait for the choppers to arrive, the sergeant hands us one more surprise, one that does not make the platoon very happy. He points to a captain that has suddenly appeared and makes our day.

"Recon, meet Captain Evers," Sergeant Reynolds says. "He just got in from Dong Tam and will be head honcho for the platoon. I am sure you men will show him the respect he deserves."

This is another fine surprise. We suddenly have a new officer in charge of the platoon, just before a new operation with no time to observe him to see if he knows which end of the barrel the bullet comes from. The army is always rotating officers in and out of the line platoons to give them some experience in commanding troops in battle. It also allows them to earn the CIB, or Combat Infantryman's badge. You are awarded this the first time you are in actual combat and everyone wants one. This shows you are a real line soldier and are out there mixing it up with the enemy.

Everyone in our platoon has one, of course, and we are not anxious to take orders from someone we know nothing about, and who is not wearing one of his own. The army system of rotating a new officer into a platoon, letting him get a few weeks of action, and then replacing him with another fresh one is a poor system. All we grunts feel this way, because it exposes us to some officers that use us as an experiment to learn how to command in battle. Then, off they go with their shiny new CIB as proof they know all about warfare. You do not learn to command troops in combat in two weeks, or even two months. *Give me an E-5 or E-6 that has six month's solid combat experience and I will follow him into hell, but an untested junior officer, no!*

We have another reason not to trust this captain and we all eye him warily. He is carrying an M-14 and that is no problem. The problem is that he has a full-color VC flag wrapped around the weapon. He has evidently been down to a village and bought it from Mama-San. Now in a show of bravado, or lunacy, or something he has appeared at a new command with the flag wrapped around the weapon. *I wonder how many seconds it will take to unwrap and bring the weapon into use? Does he think Charley will stop and salute his flag and give him time to fire back?*

Another consideration is that we all wear blackout insignia in the field so the enemy cannot distinguish rank from a distance. The insignia is sewn in black thread on a green background to eliminate color and we all wear green fatigues to make us harder to spot in the trees or grass. That colored flag is going to stick out like a sore thumb in the bush. That bit of color can endanger the whole platoon from a distance.

As Captain Evers walks around and shakes everyone's hand I think about pointing it out to him, but it is going to be awkward with everyone standing there. I do not want to get on his shit list the first day, so I remain quiet and give him a firm handshake to welcome him aboard. I tend toward distrust, but I want to give him a fair chance to prove his worth or his worthlessness to us. This patrol will show us the true man.

Standing there outside the gate, another thought crosses my mind. We all know that in an ambush Charley wants to kill the commanding officer and the radioman first, because these two working together can call in artillery or choppers to reinforce his men. Take away the man in command and the cohesiveness of the platoon suffers, which means they fight poorly. We also know the third person they want to eliminate quickly is the machine gunner, because he has the most firepower and can cause the most damage to the enemy. This is why the man in charge and the machine gunner walk far back in the procession and are never at the point or the tail end. As a machine gunner, I always stay well away from the man in charge and his radioman, and this added bit of color from the flag will certainly give Charley added incentive to blast the captain first. *If they are concentrating on him, then they are not concentrating on me, and in the McCoy version of the combat manual, this is page one.*

We hear the sound of choppers coming from the direction of Dong Tam; our chariots are on time and dropping down toward the pickup zone in single file. We hustle out to the field and form two lines for pickup. The choppers whisk us up to fifteen hundred feet, which is low enough to see the ground clearly and high enough to get a little warning if we are targeted from below. We will be flying northeast toward our objective, which should take us very close to the Cambodian border in the Parrot's Beak area. I keep a close watch on the ground though I know all the jungle will look the same from up here. There certainly will not be a big red arrow in the trees to mark the border.

We are in the air less than an hour when the choppers circle a large area of rice paddies several times; the door gunners tense and swing their machine gun barrels as the helicopter circles. Charley does not appear to be home, so we start down toward the ground. It will hopefully be another quiet insertion into the paddy and we will start out the mission with a little luck. Our platoon loves it when Charley is not around to say hi. As we swing around, I see a section of jungle with a wide, denuded swath running down it and off into the distance. It is wider than a football field and I cannot see the length. It appears that all the foliage is dead in this area so I know we are going to be walking through another area where Agent Orange defoliant spraying has taken place.

This is not the first time we have had to do this and I am aggravated once again. The first time you walk through such an area and see the magnitude of damage, you know that a platoon should not be walking here. Every blade of grass, every leaf and vine is dead and shriveled. This is some high-powered crap they are spraying. Even the nipa-palm trees themselves appear to be dying or dead. If this stuff can kill a tree, it certainly has to be bad for the platoon.

The army has an on-going operation called "Ranch Hand" and they spray selected areas of the jungle repeatedly. They figure if they can take away Charley's cover then he is exposed and they can have us fighting men eradicate him. They fail to consider that half this damn county is heavy jungle that gives numerous havens for the enemy. Even if they could kill all the jungle in this country, they cannot do it in Cambodia, and Charley would just go there until the cover grew back. I think the lack of a decent strategy on the army's part could be summed up in one simple phrase, "they failed to consider, repeatedly."

As we drop into the landing zone, I think back to the first time we walked through a denuded area such as this. Our sergeant at that time was named Trivette and he seemed very unconcerned about walking through that mess. When I pointed out that maybe we should stay out of that area I got a quick and pointed comeback from the sarge.

"Whasamatter, doesn't the real McCoy like this little bit of jungle?" he asked. "I can call in a chopper to pick you up and escort you to Dong Tam and they can stick you in the stockade for awhile." In essence, he was telling me to shut the hell up and walk or he would see that I got into trouble. This was a typical comeback from a lifer. This was a grunt's derogatory name for someone who has swallowed the army's hook and line and plans to make the army his career. It is one thing to be ordered to walk into a jungle where a man might be waiting to kill you, but it is another thing entirely to be forced to walk into an area where chemicals can accomplish the same thing over time. We grunts suspected the chemical was bad for our health, but the army maintained it was perfectly safe and only affected vegetation for awhile.

The platoon knows better than this. From the time we got our draft notices until we arrived at this combat zone, we saw numerous instances where the army cared little for our health or safety. The army was concerned only with pumping us through training as quickly as possible and then shipping us off to combat where hopefully, we would kill some of the enemy before we were killed. Why be too concerned, I am sure the army brass thought? The U.S. has an almost inexhaustible supply of mother's sons to carry on the war. They were right and they managed to burn through over fifty-eight thousand young lives before public opinion finally brought the mess to a halt.

The thump of the chopper's skids into the paddy brings me out of my reverie and we jump out into the rock-hard paddy and run to the nearest paddy dike, which is thirty feet away. Things are looking good, no gunfire greets us, and everyone is out and behind a paddy dike quickly. The sun is beating down and we are sweating, but that is a small price to pay for a cold LZ (landing zone with no gunfire).

Once we are certain no enemy is in the vicinity, we form up and head down a well-used path toward our objective. We run into a problem immediately. We are a quarter mile from the denuded wood line, but we have a tidal inlet in front of us. The tide is out and we face an unknown depth of soupy mud around fifty feet across. The first man tries walking through the mud dragging a rope, which he will tie to a tree on the other side. He gets ten feet in, sinking deeper with each step and finally can go no further. He is waist deep in mud and it is apparent his movement is making it worse. We use the rope to drag him out backwards.

Jenks is thin and wiry, so he tries next. He ties the rope to his ankle, puts his rifle on his back, and drops gently into the mud horizontally. He then uses a swimming motion, propelling himself over the surface slowly until he reaches the other side and secures the rope. A safe way found, other men use the same procedure and find that it works carrying their weapon and pack on their backs.

We have plastic caps on our rifle barrels and the M-16 is equipped with a spring-loaded cover over the ejection port so mud stays out of the inner workings. The outside gets muddy however, so we have to use our meager supply of water and shirttails to clean off the worst of the mud. Each man gives his weapon a quick clean when he reaches the other side before taking up a defensive position on the bank. We are vulnerable now and if any enemy is in the woodline, they will pick now to attack us.

When my time comes to cross, I am hesitant since I am carrying a twenty-two pound machine gun and all that ammo. Another man takes my pack, and I have the rope to pull myself through so off I go, raising a bow wave of mud in front of my face. The rope helps and I make the trip with little problem. The rest of the two platoons follow and after an hour of exertion, we are all on the other side resembling tall, skinny columns of mud. It is comical and since we have no way of cleaning ourselves we wipe the worst off, pick up our weapons and head towards the jungle. With walking, the mud will dry and flake off and we will slowly lose our brown armor.

With our point man checking the path ahead for booby-traps, progress is slow and halting. We cross a band of jungle before we get to the dead area and the column halts with a warning from the man on point. He has come across some signs lettered in French and does not know what they are, but they have a red X and that is never good.

The sarge and the captain hustle forward and determine that we are crossing an area the French have mined at one time in the past. It is not shown on our map and we have no idea why the French would mine an area and then put up warning signs. We reason that most likely they placed the mines and later put up the signs, deeming it too risky to search and retrieve them. After a hurried conference between the sarge and the captain, they decide to carry forward down the path carefully. The path shows signs of frequent use and is obviously used daily by the local civilians. This is probably a safer choice than trying to circumnavigate a minefield of unknown dimensions. The path takes us past several hooches and then we break into the desolation of the jungle that received the Agent Orange treatment.

We walk into the area that is eerie and quiet. Nothing is growing and everything is brown and withered. There is no sign of any small animals, no rustling, and no birds flying through the air. No monkeys are chattering, warning others of our approach. The animals are either smart and have left this area, or they are dead. This is not a place fit for human habitation and I try to breathe as shallowly as possible. There is a slight, acrid smell I do not like and I am ready to leave as fast as I can. The other platoon members feel the same way; I can see it in their faces.

We continue onward. With the vegetation so ravaged, it would be easy to spot bunkers or tunnel entrances but we find nothing. If Charley has been here, he certainly left as soon as they sprayed and will not return for a long time because this area offers him no cover. The smart places to look would be the jungle adjoining this scorched earth, because there is cover there. Where there is cover, there is often the enemy. The only question is; has he gone to ground close by in the jungle, or has he moved miles away? I would cast a vote for miles away. Any idiot looking at this mess would want to get as far away as he could.

We follow the denuded area for about three clicks (kilometers) or at least two miles, and then the desolation stops and the undamaged jungle starts again. We have come to the end of the sprayed area. Once the whole line of men enters the jungle, the Captain passes a message forward down the line of men to call a halt. We drop in place and rest, already winded, though the dead vegetation has presented little walking difficulties. That little mud swim earlier in the day did not help, but it is finally drying up and falling off in chunks.

After another discussion, the captain decides we will double back and recon the jungle to the northeast of the damaged area with the assumption Charley might have moved over there. My opinion is that he is several miles away or further, and we need to make a dozen sweeps through the jungle, each one covering a swatch of jungle back to the muddy inlet. Then we should double back and try another sweep further to the northeast.

I keep my opinion to myself for what I have just envisioned are several days of hot, backbreaking slogging through double-canopy jungle. This might result in running into the enemy, but my main desire is to spend these next two days with as little physical exertion as necessary, and to miss running into the enemy. The whole platoon wants to wind down those remaining days in country with as little contact as possible. Less contact means fewer men will die or be injured. I am torn between wishing for contact to eradicate some enemy, and no contact to eradicate some time.

As we make our sweep back through the jungle, we hear the "bam!" of a single shotgun round, and we all go to ground, weapons at the ready and eyes peering intently. This jungle is thick, and you can see no more than ten feet into it. We know Dix, our point man, has a shotgun and he has only fired once so maybe it is a minor problem.

In a few minutes, the men in front pass down the line that Dix had encountered a snake swinging out of a tree and blasted it in panic. I cannot say I blame him; ninety percent of the snakes over here are poisonous, and several species will kill you within several minutes of receiving a bite. The medics all carry snakebite kits, but with the variety and deadliness of some of the snakes, we know there is nothing that they can do for some bites.

The procession moves forward again and we try to spread out to help our chances of finding any bunkers or tunnel openings. This jungle is thick and we have to cut our way through in places. I almost wish we were back in the sprayed area. The jungle appears a little clearer up to the left; we can see sunlight penetrating much better, so we angle over to investigate. Clearings usually mean a village or some kind of enemy installation.

We come out into the area and find it is clearer because it has been bombed in the past. Downed trees are everywhere and the underbrush is burned because of fires started by the ordnance. We walk past numerous holes at least fifteen feet in diameter partially filled with greenish water. The bombing has been at least a month in the past judging from the accumulation of water and the green scum on its surface.

I walk up on some of Romeo Recon's members clustered around one hole and glance down into it. Whew, that is the butt end of a bomb sticking out of the water. The casing is scratched and rusting but is unmistakable. I am not a bomb expert, but I know it has to weigh at least several hundred pounds and maybe a lot more.

"McCoy, front and center," the sarge commands. "We cannot leave this here for Charley to find and make booby-traps out of the explosive. Do you think you can blow it?"

All I can think of is, *oh crap!* This is way out of my expertise and I know right away that we do not have enough explosive and not enough fuse with us. A bomb this size can spread shrapnel and pieces of tree for a hundred yards so I would need at least ten feet of fuse to be sure I would not be killed by the blast. I quickly do the calculations. Nope, ten feet would give me a little less than seven minutes to get away, probably not enough time to get clear in this thick jungle. I know some of the other men are carrying some C-4 and I have three pounds but mine added to theirs likely would not be enough. I am hoping no one is carrying any extra fuse because I really, really do not want to blow this bomb. The explosive we have would likely only move it some and possibly make it more dangerous.

"Sarge, I don't have enough explosive and I am way too short on fuse, I would need at least fifteen feet to get away," I say. This does not make the sarge happy and he and the captain walk off and have a quick discussion.

"Are you sure, McCoy?" asked the captain. I can see he really wants to blow this big hunk of steel. "Don't you men carry enough explosive to do a big job?" I need to do some quick convincing that it is not possible to blow the bomb, because I do not intend to risk my life with a short fuse.

I know that army SOP says that weapons or explosives cannot be left in the field for the enemy to recover and use, so the captain has a problem. We either have to blow it or stay here and guard it until a demo team reaches us. I like the second choice much better. I do not mind spending the rest of the day, and possibly the night baby-sitting a bomb. We have encountered no enemy today so an overnight stay is no big deal, and then we will be flown back to base, the operation over. This is actually a lucky break.

The captain motions his radioman over and reports to base about our find and the need for a demo team. I can tell from his voice that he would rather pull one of his own teeth than have to report what we have found and ask for help. It is great to see an officer in a bit of a bind for once, instead of me. Officers are graded by their commanding officers on every operation, and this is likely a minor black eye for him. Oh well, it is not my problem. I am just glad he listened to reason, because several officers I have known would have been a lot more determined to cure the problem without calling for help.

The sergeant tells us the demo team cannot make it here until morning and we will set up a defensive position around the bomb. Since the bomb craters are partially full of water we take turns digging some foxholes in the ground for cover. Only three men have brought entrenching tools so it takes awhile. Since we have the afternoon to dig, we approach it leisurely, at least when the captain is not looking, because he still looks pissed.

Once we finish the holes, we line them with some nipa palm fronds, as we want deluxe accommodations tonight. We certainly have the time and it makes us look busy to the leader. We retire to the holes for a good C-ration meal and heat the food up with C-4. I may not have enough explosive to blow the bomb, but we have plenty to heat C-rations. I am sure the irony is not lost on the captain. He continues to walk around looking like a dark cloud.

The night passes uneventfully, but we get little sleep. We are right in the middle of Charley country and we are extra nervous. The early morning sun filtering down through the gaps in the trees rouses everyone and we rise and stretch, then prepare breakfast. I go with beef stew, not exactly breakfast food but the C-rations contain nothing for breakfast. The closest thing to breakfast is a canned biscuit with nothing to go on it, but you can usually borrow some jam from another man's rations.

Shortly before 0900 hours, we hear a chopper coming in toward us. The sarge sends some men double-timing through the jungle to the nearest rice paddy to give them some cover for landing and to pop a smoke grenade to mark the landing area. In about twenty minutes, the demo team meets up with us and surveys the bomb in its crater. They have brought enough explosive to split an ocean liner in half and a big reel of fuse.

I feel a little left out at first, but then I realize I can get a very safe distance away with the platoon and watch the fireworks. No sweat, no danger, let someone else do the dangerous work for a change. I still feel a little let down as we head out of the jungle; this is the first time I have had to walk away from a demo job.

An hour later the demo crew bursts out of the jungle, runs across the paddy to a dike, and takes cover. We wait and wait and just about the time I think the team has a bad charge set, the ground jumps beneath our bodies and a big, muffled thump comes out of the jungle. We feel the rush of displaced air and watch bits of trees and dirt blast high into the sky. I feel it is time to get down and then shrapnel and debris splash down into the paddy only a few hundred yards from us. This operation has been somewhat of a bust, but we did see some good fireworks.

The captain still looks annoyed this morning and he puts us to work quickly. We have to return to the bombed out area and finish the sweep that we abandoned yesterday. Then he has us move north a hundred yards and do another mile long sweep. The thick jungle has us panting like dogs on the second sweep, but he does not call a rest period. I suspect the good captain may be taking out a little of his anger by working us harder. *Wait a minute; an officer would not do that to his men, surely?*

The captain finally halts us in mid afternoon and radios back to base for choppers to take us home. We rest for fifteen minutes then make our way southeast to the rice paddy where we watched the bomb explode. Those little green blobs are a welcome sight as we spy them on the horizon. My butt is dragging and I keep thinking of my bunker and some hot food for tonight.

The choppers materialize over us, a most welcome sight and sound. We pop a purple and a white smoke grenade, the agreed on signal, and they drop in and touch the paddy lightly with their skids. All the men are smiling now and we do not need an invitation, we pile in and are whisked into the air. The chopper blades and forward movement are blasting in a gentle cool wind and it feels so good. The jungle was stuffy and airless and this is almost as good as air conditioning. The platoon will be happy to ride this conveyance the rest of the day.

We arrive back at the base in the late evening and stow our equipment, then head for the mess hall. The hot food will do us good, and I have an appointment with at least a half gallon of whatever liquid they are serving today. We are happy to be back behind a solid perimeter. This base camp, as crude as it is, is home and we are happy to be here and happier to be alive one more day.

None of us can know that in the distant future the skin rashes we have contracted will plague us through our lives and that some of us will fall victim to the dioxins we have inhaled and drank during our tour. These will cause cancers in Viet Nam vets in much higher concentrations than the general public. The harm to our bodies will take years to surface, but in the end, they will be just as deadly as Charley.

***

In the last fifteen years, an alarming trend has been noted among sailors that served on ships in the river waters and close to the coast of Viet Nam. These men are contracting rare cancers in frequencies much higher than civilians do. This has been investigated and it is now understood that the rivers and coastal waters of Viet Nam were highly contaminated by the overspray of Agent Orange.

Navy ships do not have a large supply of fresh water, but instead depend upon large desalinators to process the water and make it useable to cook food, drink, and bathe. It has further been determined that this equipment did not totally remove the dioxin from the water so the navy personnel were ingesting it every time they ate food or drank the water aboard ships.

It is pretty ironic that army personnel who left the dangers of the jungle for a few days rest also faced this hidden danger. Thousands of army men did stand downs on navy ships and drank the water, my platoon included. Not only did we have to walk through dioxin-contaminated jungle, we had to drink the poison and it is slowly taking our lives, one by one. The army argued this point for years and only in recent times has admitted there is a connection between Agent Orange and the increased rare cancer rates in personnel that served in Southeast Asia. They have been paying restitution but the process is time-consuming. My own claim has been on-going for over a year now as I write this, and I have no idea when and if it will be resolved. *Viet Nam, the gift that keeps on giving!*

123 days left in country.

Chapter 18

A Christmas Standdown Does Not Last

Fire Base Moore-Dec. 1968.

Word goes around camp that we have received a stand down order for the whole unit stationed here at Moore. Ongoing talks with the North Vietnamese have resulted in a Christmas truce and all operations are suspended for the time being. Yeah, sure, how many times have we heard this same story? Seems there is always a truce going on, but no one tells the enemy. They seem to come out of the jungle and start more trouble during a truce, probably because they think we will not fight back.

I will wait and see what happens, but a cessation of hostilities sure would be nice. This daily grind of operations is quickly getting me down. A few days off for Christmas sounds nice, though there is no way it will feel like a holiday with the temperature hovering around one hundred degrees every day. All over the base, I see happy faces and hear plans for a little rest, but there is also a shadow of doubt on those faces. We have learned to believe little of what we hear from the men in charge, and to believe only part of what we see.

We spend the day replacing rotting sand bags on the bunkers on our part of the perimeter, a job never ending, all over the country. The army used canvas bags for years here, but has replaced them with woven plastic bags, which last a lot longer. We also go out to the perimeter and cut down weeds that have grown too high around the concertina wire there. We do this carefully, as there are trip flares on the wire we do not want to set off, and wires running out to the claymore mines that we do not want to cut.

We post guards in the bunkers to secure the clickers, little hand-operated generators for the mines. A squeeze generates a few volts, which is sent through the wires, and boom go the claymores. The mines are deadly, seven hundred steel balls encapsulated in epoxy, and several pounds of plastic explosive in a molded plastic housing. The housing is curved, which allows the balls to cover more area, and on the bottom are four metal feet that fold out, to be pressed into the ground to secure it. The mine can be adjusted for angle via the feet, which swivel, all designed to cover the widest swath. Some person with a warped mind must have designed this weapon, but it is highly effective. Being out near the mines gives me a distinct uneasy feeling. If one were to go off, a soldier would be dead before he heard the noise.

The day passes uneventfully and slowly winds down into a cooler evening. We grab chow at the mess hall; fried chicken, mashed potatoes and beans, and it tastes all the better knowing that a few days of rest are heading our way. As the sun drops behind the jungle to the west, we sit on top of our sleeping quarters, a sandbag bunker about four feet in height, and smoke cigarettes as we talk of home. Everyone smears on mosquito repellent because as the sun retires, the bugs come out for night duty. The army furnishes repellent, a foul smelling, oily substance in small plastic squeeze bottles which works quite well. I have become used to the oily feel and learned to live with it at night. We all carry at least two bottles with us everywhere. Slapping mosquitoes in the middle of the night while we have set up an ambush position is a hazardous undertaking. They always seem to find a place to bite, so you suffer in silence and oil down the offending area.

We talk late into the night, knowing we do not have to rise early. The stand down takes a lot of pressure off our minds, and sitting there talking with my friends, I almost feel like I am home. I sit there and try to remember how my wife feels in my arms and how it felt to get up clean and go to work, but the feelings just will not come to me. I feel like my country is just a fond but cruel memory, and the things I remember of home are just delusions. I remind myself once again that I had another life far away, and that I will return to it someday.

I try to sleep late the next morning, but old habits die hard and I am up with the coming of the sun. We hit the mess hall, have a leisurely breakfast for once, and then walk back to our company area. We watch the morning convoy pull in, and several escort jeeps are pulling small trailers with canvas tied over them. Son of a gun! We know what that means. The trailers will be loaded with cases of beer and soft drinks and fat steaks, all surrounded with large chunks of ice to keep things cold. Looks like the stand down is for real or they would not be bringing in the supplies. We can look forward to a party day with enough meat and drinks to satisfy everyone until dark. The army does this occasionally, a kind of bonus to let weary soldiers let off a little steam, and I think we certainly are entitled.

Getting ready for the festivities, we set up a tent in an open area, roll the side walls up, and push the trailers under the tent in an attempt to make the ice last longer. By the time we accomplish this task, the cooks have brought out their grills, made of fifty-five gallon drums cut in half lengthwise with pipe legs welded on to support them, and the tantalizing smell of cooking meat is drifting across the camp.

Sgt. Johnson shows up and picks out men for bunker guard tonight, and of course, O'Brian and I are on that list. I knew, stand down or not, somebody had to be on guard at night, and all across camp other men were getting the same message. At least we will be free tomorrow night.

We all started to partake of the beer as we stood in line for the steaks, and I promised myself I would limit my drinking to three beers all day, because I needed to be clear-headed tonight for the guard duty. Nothing is worse than standing guard with a buzz on, for you are awakened every two hours for a one-hour shift and it is hard enough to stay awake completely sober. It is amazing how hard it can be to get to sleep at night, but if you are on bunker guard, all you want to do is sleep.

The night passes peacefully, except for snatches of drunken singing that break out at times. This gave some of the black guys, who are excellent singers, an idea, so they gathered together and entertained us with some mo-town, and a few doo-wop songs. There was some good-natured ribbing, with some asking if they knew any country, but these men were shouted down quickly. We all enjoyed the night, the songs, and the companionship of our fellow soldiers. There is something quite satisfying about being surrounded by a bunch of close friends, partying late into the night, knowing there is danger all around you. A few miles away, someone could be dying, but your base is a happy, secure little island, at least for the moment.

My last shift on guard duty ends at 0500 hours in the morning and I leave the bunker and sack out, trying for some serious shut-eye. The night passed quietly, once the drunks ran out of steam. No mortar rounds in or out, no tracer rounds sparkling in the night sky, a night you seldom see in this area. Soldiers on bunker guard are allowed to sleep late, and with the stand down many men are going to be sleeping late and nursing hangovers today. The army's position on drinking is: drink it if we hand it out, but do not let it affect the performance of your job, or we will be called in and our lapse discussed with the sarge, or in more serious cases, with the LT.

Sgt. Johnson comes around and wakes us up around 0900 hours, and gathers us together and I know this is not a good sign. I know he has some information no one wants to hear. Several men start bitching and the sarge brings a quick halt to this. He goes on to explain that the stand down is over, and that intel has some information about a VC camp hidden in some dense jungle about fifty miles northwest of us, near the Parrot's Beak. This is an area where the border of Viet Nam and Cambodia take a weird kink and on a map, it resembles a parrot's beak. We know this is a bad area and a stronghold of the enemy. The sergeant goes on to explain that the intelligence reports indicate the camp has extensive underground tunnels, housing a hospital for wounded VC, and may have cages where captured American soldiers are being held. We are all quietly complaining about the loss of our stand down, but this last part gets our attention. All right, then. No one wants to go out near Cambodia, but if Charlie is holding some of our men prisoners, then we all agree it is time to go kick some VC butt.

We are told that the choppers will be coming in at 1000 hundred hours, so that gives us precious little time to get our equipment together and our weapons checked. It appears this operation is running on a tight schedule and that gives me pause to reflect. The quick operations are the ones that seem to turn messy at the worst possible time, and I am so glad that my alcohol consumption yesterday was minimal, leaving me quite clear-headed. All around me, I see signs that others cannot say the same thing.

I hustle over to our sleeping bunker, haul my M-60 thirty-caliber machine gun out, and get it ready, making sure the feed tray is clean and my starter belt of eighty rounds is spotless. A machine gunner carries five or six hundred rounds of ammo slung around his shoulders, hanging below his belt, and this is secured against his body by a double wrap of ammo around his waist, Poncho Villa style. It looks bitching, and it is the best way to carry belted ammo to keep it quiet and out of the way. Looks like old Poncho knew a thing or two about carrying ammo!

In belted ammo, each round is held to the next by small spring clips that are stripped off and ejected by the weapon's feeding mechanism as each round is chambered. These clips allow you to disconnect the belted ammo anywhere you want, wrap it around your body, and then secure it by clipping the belt back together again. You cannot fire ammo wrapped around your body, so you carry a starter belt, which is short and will not bang around or hang up on underbrush.

I am left-handed, so I carry the weapon on my left side, supported with the strap around my neck, with the gun angled to the right side of my body. I have found around eighty rounds just long enough to hang over my right shoulder a little. The starter belt gives me quick initial fire capability, then I can hit the ground, unwrap a section from around my body, and clip it to the end of the starter belt. Machine gunners also have an assistant gunner who carries another four to five hundred rounds, and if the operation seems to warrant it, a spare barrel and an asbestos glove, which will allow him to change the barrel even with it red hot. I check with Miller to make sure he has the spare barrel and glove; I do not know what we might run up against on this operation.

M-60 machine guns have a lever that releases the barrel, so it can be changed in thirty seconds or so if the assistant gunner is nearby, which is where he is supposed to be. If contact is heavy, you may be forced to fire too many bullets too quickly, which can overheat the barrel and make it glow red. You try to fire only short, controlled bursts to conserve ammo and protect the barrel, but in an ambush, the machine gun is used to suppress fire from the enemy, and may help break the ambush thus saving lives. I have seen M-60 barrels hot enough to light cigarettes on and if you can do that, the barrel is considered used up, and you turn it in and get a new one. Fortunately, I was rarely in a situation that I had to use the weapon so hard that I had to replace the barrel.

The platoon starts assembling with packs slung over shoulders, last minute checks of weapons being carried out, and with a signal from Sgt. Johnson, we walk over to the chopper pad. All around us, men are forming up and heading in our direction, and it looks like every combat man in camp is going. This is going to be a big show. We gather up near the pad in front of the main gate and groups of men are dispatched forward to wait for the helicopters .There is only room for five or six choppers on the ground at a time, so it is going to take some time to pick up every soldier.

We hear the choppers long before we see them, a massive vibration coming from the sky, and a long line of dark green appears in the sunny, cloudless sky. Out in the field, smoke grenades are being set off to help the pilots position themselves on the ground. We are enveloped in a circular wash of white and yellow smoke and dust as a line of choppers drop in. Their skids barely touch the ground, holding just long enough to pick up a full load of men, and then quickly bound into the air. We do not waste time when a chopper drops in; it is duck and jump in. We try to stay out of other men's way, because we know that the vehicle is only going to be on the ground about ten seconds, and if we are tardy, he will leave us there, staring up and looking like a fool.

I jump in, laying the M-60 flat on the aluminum floor to give more room. All around me, men pack in, and the smoke and dust disappears below us. The chopper climbs and banks to the left. I can see a line ahead of us, and a long line behind climbing into the sky in a graceful arc. My heart gives a little jump as I feel the excitement of a great adventure ahead of me. I hope we will not be landing in a hot LZ, or landing zone.

We are wearing our steel pots today, since it is going to be a daylight operation going in, and a steel pot will usually deflect a bullet that might otherwise enter our head, so they are worth the extra weight. My fellow soldiers and I are also carrying our soft slouch hat in our packs to use after dark. We take our pots off and sit on them for an added bit of protection. We tell new men on their first chopper flight, where do you think the bullets are coming from? From below, right, so we sit on our helmets for a little protection.

Choppers have some armor around the pilot, the copilot's seat, and around the turbine and transmission, but the passenger area has just a thin outer shell and a slightly more substantial load floor of aluminum. The floor may stop small arms up to thirty caliber, but a fifty-caliber machine-gun can make mincemeat of it.

Off we head in the direction of Cambodia and one mile out I can still look back and see choppers dropping down and then rising and falling into line, a neatly choreographed line of green. When we drop in, it is going to be a landing in force, that is for sure. The choppers are breaking their long, straight formation and lining up in rows, so wherever we land there must be plenty of room. I suddenly realize there are no Cobra gun-ships around, armed with mini-guns and rockets to help support a landing. This means, thank God, that the landing zone is likely to be cold; no gifts from Charley zipping up to meet us as we drop down. It is bad enough being shot at on the ground, but in the air, it really sucks. There is just nowhere to hide up there; you just have to grit your teeth and pray.

As we drone along about fifteen hundred feet in the air, the terrain below seems so clean and peaceful. The rice paddies spread out in geometric patterns, and the jungle looks cool and inviting, a picture-perfect post card. *Dear Wanda, I am here and down there is Viet Nam. So glad you are not here, and I wish I were not.*

Love, Randy. We pass over areas that have been shelled in the past and I feel sad to see the destruction. There are circular, irregular holes in the soft ground, full of greenish rainwater, and broken tree limbs everywhere. The place sure took a pasting, and that pulls me out of my reverie.

I give myself a quick inventory; one machine gun, knife strapped to my flak jacket, and two grenades. Check, check, and check. With the ammo wrapped around my chest, my pack on my back, and a twenty-two pound machine gun, I am probably carrying sixty pounds. I am used to the weight, and can move all day like this, as long as it does not entail too much running. I also carry a plastic canteen of water, and in my pack, I have my soft hat, two C-ration meals, and my pipe and tobacco. I also carry a cheap camera wrapped in a plastic bag in the hopes of getting a few "in combat" photos. I have carried the camera before and found that when in contact the last thing on our minds is taking pictures. I usually wind up with a camera and film damaged by water and rendered useless. Maybe things will go peacefully and I will have better luck this time.

Up ahead the choppers are arcing to the left and dropping as the door gunners tense up and swing their machine guns forward. I get sight of a large area of jungle, probably three miles long and two wide, looking like nasty double-canopy vegetation, which is very hard to walk through, and just made to be a haven for VC. The jungle is surrounded by miles of rice paddies on all four sides, so there is no way for Charley to escape during the day. It isn't often you have the enemy all bottled up this way, and I wonder if he made a mistake putting a hidden camp here. Once we drop in and knock on his front door, he is going to have to fight like mad until dark to have a chance to slip away, or take cover in his bunkers until we leave. If we can get men around all four sides of the jungle then he cannot get away; however, this creates a nasty crossfire situation, bullets fired on one side possibly making it through the jungle and hitting our own men on the other side. Most likely, we will cover two sides in an L pattern, and then move in to flush him out. Choppers in the air, working with the men on the ground, will greet him as he tries to flee. I am glad I am not a VC right now, waiting in that woodline. Charlie will probably put up a fight today, but he always, always runs away as we bring on the considerable firepower available to us.

We are going in now, the rice paddies rushing up to greet us. We whip our steel pots on as we see the skids of the choppers ahead of us splashing into the wet rice paddy, that muddy water churning up into the blade wash. We are all surprised to see water in the paddies this time of year. There must be a river or canal nearby for the farmers to pump water from onto their land. There is nothing around us but paddy water and mud. The choppers, not having anything solid to set down on will only touch and hold slightly off the ground, so that means we better be ready to unhorse instantly. We are all tense, waiting to hear gunfire as we propel ourselves out the door and run through the mud and water to a dike about twenty feet away. Rice paddy dikes are merely walkways about a foot wide and two feet off the water, created to hold the water in and give the farmers a path to get to the fields without trampling on their rice plants.

We reach the dike safely and take cover behind it, splashing geysers of water as we drop into a foot of water and mud. Our weapons go on the dike and we aim them at the peaceful-looking jungle, about two hundred yards in front of us. We are all soaked, with only our backs and heads out of the water as we peer cautiously over the dike. Mindful of my tobacco and camera, I pull my pack off my back and set it on the dike in front of me, placing the M-60 on top of it. It will give a little added protection if shooting starts. I find that if I turn my head sideways, I can get the top of my steel pot just below the top of the dike without getting my face in the water. Close, but workable.

I look to my left and right, and as far as I can see down the dike, there is a soldier every few feet, pressed up against the dirt wall. Choppers are now coming in and dropping off men to the right of our position in a line, so it appears we will be covering the east and south sides of the jungle area. Charlie, you had better have your A game with you today!

I remove all my ammo from around my body before it gets too muddy, and lay it carefully on top of the dike, splashing water on the muddy parts to clean it. By now the slightly chilly water has soaked in everywhere, my boots are full of water and my privates are surrounded. As the layer of water next to my skin warms up, the chill goes away as long as I do not move around too much. I just wish I had brought my poncho liner to throw over me, even though it would be soaked quickly. We can see only jungle or the rice paddies, and if we do not take the jungle today, we will be sleeping in this water tonight. I am glad the rainy season is over or it would get pretty cold, sacked out in this water overnight.

Radios crackle up and down the line, and choppers fly back and forth over the woodline. Nothing happens, no firing at us, no firing at the choppers. If he is in there, Charlie is being pretty cagey. I am soon bored, and I find that by turning over and facing the sky, and using my pack as a pillow, I can be fairly comfortable. At least, as comfortable as a man can be with his butt in six inches of soft mud, and his whole body, except for head and neck, in muddy water.

I pull out a box of C-rations and remove a can of beans and franks, the soldier's favorite of the different meals available in C-rations. I use my little P-47 can opener to cut open the can, and use my chest as a slightly underwater table. I did not bring any C-4 to heat it up, but it is just as well, with little solid ground to cook on. I look up at the sky; another brilliantly blue summer day, adjust my sunglasses a little to cut the glare, and have my lunch. I wash it down with several swallows of warm water out of my canteen, the water tasting of plastic from the lining in the water tanks back at the base.

Quite contented, I close my eyes and try to catch up on my sleep. There is nothing to do, I am reasonably comfortable, and if there any action, it will make enough noise to wake me quickly. Down the line, other soldiers have adopted my position and are shading their faces and getting some rest. It is an old soldier's standby, sleep when you can because you may not be able to later.

My sleep is short lived. I wake up with a start. A Sam and Dave song is drifting over the position. One of the soldiers, a couple of places down from me has brought a small transistor radio. Kearney turns it up so everyone can hear and several voices join in. It is a local armed forces radio station, Radio Saigon. My watch says two-twenty, and still nothing is happening. That only gives us about six hours to do something, so we need to get started. As I lie there listening to the song, something does start.

We suddenly hear the rumble and swish in the air overhead. It sounds like it is passing right over us, so I hope they do not have any short rounds. We all roll over and face the wood line as an airburst occurs, dead smack over the jungle area. The yellow burst dissipates and drifts off to the right. Some mortar crew back at some base camp is sending Charley some aerial love letters, and they were dead on with the spotter round. I know that someone is on the radio, calling back to the base, telling them the first round was right on target, so fire for effect, as it is called.

We do not have long to wait; within a minute we hear the rumble of multiple rounds streaking overhead. The jungle is engulfed in red blossoms, tree branches fly through the air, and the ground jackhammers beneath my chest. I figure we are far enough away from shrapnel, so I peer cautiously over the dike and watch the show. Several hundred feet in front of me, the paddy erupts in many small geysers of water from the shrapnel and I decide I was wrong and duck my head down behind the dike. I hate to miss the show, but I do not want to get a piece of metal in my head. This could ruin what has been a fairly nice day so far.

This goes on for over an hour, and then stops as suddenly as it started. I peek over the dirt bank, and the jungle is definitely thinner in spots. There are a half dozen or so small fires burning, trying to get bigger, but finding only green material to burn. After awhile, it turns into thin columns of smoke with no visible fire. In front of us, a line of men rise in unison and move forward to a dike closer to the jungle, the cover running pretty much parallel to the woodline. A little later, the sergeant splashes by behind us, telling us all to move forward to the now unoccupied positions up front.

We leave our little short-lived homes, walk the seventy-five yards to the next line of dikes, and take up our new positions. As I drop down into position, I encounter a hard lump in the mud, and my mind goes cold as I roll to the left several times and hug the mud while dropping my face into the water. All I can think is booby-trap, but nothing happens. After my heart rate returns to nearly normal, I cautiously crawl over and reach toward the object, trying to see through the muddy water. I cannot, but I have to use this area, so I need to know what is down there. It did not explode when I put my weight on it, so I think I can chance it. I finally touch the object gently, and it is smooth and circular. I feel no protuberances on it, no trip wires anywhere. It feels just like a C-ration can, so I lift it slowly, gently, and discover as it breaks the surface, that it is a damn can of C-rations, beans and ham to be exact. Some SOB up ahead of us has left it here and taken two years off my life in doing so. Well, at least I have added to my meager store of food; no telling how long we will be here, or when we will be resupplied.

We get acquainted with our positions, and the day starts to wind down into evening. It is obvious we are not moving into the jungle today. Do they have a night assault planned? It would be nice if they would tell us soldiers what is coming up, after all, we do the heavy work. It reminds me of the line you hear all the time, hurry up and wait. I heard that probably the third day I was in the army, and it is always on someone's lips. Army life in a combat zone is predominately hard exertion interspersed with a lot of waiting, moments of terror, and very little information.

When It Rains In Hell

My friends and I get some more sleep, but when I awaken, it is dark, and a bit chilly in the water. While feeling around in my pack for some food, the night is suddenly shattered by the unmistakable sound of a twenty round burst from an M-16, with a loud explosion right on its heels. I catch sight of tracers flying through the jungle, bouncing off something, and corkscrewing through the night air. The explosion is a grenade, a big red flash that lights up the position for a fraction of a second. There are a few more discharges from rifles, and the night goes silent. The action has occurred in front of us where 'B' company is situated, just twenty feet from the jungle's edge. What happened? Is anyone hurt? I hear the radio chattering off to my right, but the volume is low and I cannot catch what is said. A few minutes later the sergeant passes down the line the info that a VC popped up out of the jungle, arm cocked back, but a soldier that was on the ball sighted and dispatched him with a full twenty round burst. Then, the enemy's grenade, which he did not have time to throw, went off and finished the job. That soldier was obviously on the alert. Now he has a great story to tell and is alive to boot.

The night passes uneventfully. We alternately doze and pull guard duty, but no one sleeps much after what happened a hundred feet in front of us. I consume the offending beans and ham; and a tropical chocolate bar from a box of C-rations with that great favorite, plastic-flavored water from the canteen. At least it is cool now, after sitting in the paddy water all day. I am dying for a few pulls from my pipe, but I cannot chance it after dark. The flare of the lighter can be seen a long distance, and there may be a VC a hundred yards away, rifle balanced on a log, waiting patiently for that flare, or the glow of a cigarette being puffed.

Most of us are awake to greet the dawn, the sun a red orb off on the horizon, trying to peer through a foggy daylight mixed with smoke from the jungle, which has been smoldering all night. We are all cold and stiff, but reluctant to get up and expose ourselves should Charley be watching. I loosen up by rolling around and bicycling my legs, a disagreeable task in the cool water, but I know that in an hour or so, the sun will be victorious over the water, and I will soon be wishing for a little less heat.

The radio blares out again. Sgt. Johnson passes down the line that at 0730 hours, all platoons are going to rise and move forward, and we will enter the jungle and see what we have to face. The prospect of moving into the jungle is both heartening and scary. I want to get on my feet again after lying in the paddy

- 225 -

for eighteen hours, but the idea of moving into the jungle is a little terrifying. Charlie has had a long time to prepare for us, and the thought enters my mind that I could be dead or badly wounded in a little while. I quickly banish it. I have a job to do whether I want to or not, and it will be easier to do if I do not think like that. A soldier does not fight because he is brave; he fights because he does not want to let his friends down. To do so would be worse than fighting, so you get up and do your job.

That time comes and we get up and move forward. I have prepared an extra long starter belt for the M-60, just in case. About three feet long, it loops up over the weapon, down in a loop by my chest, and up over my right shoulder to keep it out of the mud. The army's weapons are designed for right-handers, so my left-handed carry means the ammo belt has to loop up over the weapon from the feed tray, since the ammo feeds in from the left. A bit clumsy, but I have found out it works okay if you flip the belt to the left when you are firing.

Everything goes fine for a few moments, but as we enter the edge of the jungle, rifles open up, and we can tell from the sound that it is AK47's. M-16's answer back and everyone scrambles for cover. I take refuge behind a small palm tree, thankful to be on some dry ground for awhile. The firing tapers off and turns into an occasional shot with the thumps of grenade launchers mixed with the rifle reports. We move forward again, and soon encounter the open mouth of a tunnel with a little smoke curling from it. Looks like Charlie is playing hide and seek, popping out of his underground lair just long enough to take a few pot shots.

We counter with our own tried and true recipe. We gather a few palm limbs with big soft leaves and place them in the opening, then a soldier crouches over the hole, bends down and tosses a CS grenade as far back into the hole as he can. He follows it with a regular grenade and we all take cover. The CS is army tear gas; potent stuff, the grenade is used to force the gas deeper into the hole, and the palm fronds are to seal the gas in the hole. Our enemy probably has a sliding door a short distance into the hole to counteract such measures, but some gas is going to get through to him. He will not be using this particular hole for awhile. Later, once we inspect the whole jungle area and get an idea of what might be hidden here, some poor souls will have to go down the holes to check for VC, hidden weapons and food. They also have to liberate the prisoners, if there are any.

Up ahead we hear more fire being exchanged, and word comes down on the radio that the forward platoons are getting into contact that is more serious. We are told to withdraw to our former positions. We tramp back into the paddies and drop into defensive positions. I was just starting to dry out, and here I sit, a small island surrounded by acres of shallow water again. This is starting to get aggravating. *Doesn't the enemy have anything else to do but interfere with my plans to spend a quiet, serene 365 days here, then go back to the real world and prosper?*

Sitting in the sun again, waiting, but this time we set up and expose ourselves more. Charley did not seem to be out in force near the edges of the jungle, and we are all getting tired of hiding behind dikes. When is this going to get moving again? This question is answered by a sound high in the air coming out of the sun, barely visible and moving fast. The jet drops like a stone, follows a gentle arc across the jungle, and disgorges a string of dark objects that disappear behind the trees. Just as I think they must all be duds, the jungle erupts again, but these explosions are so much bigger than the mortar rounds yesterday. We all drop for cover, and the noise is painful. The shock waves roll across the paddy and we feel blasts of searing air. Dirt, limbs, and water splash all over the paddy, and there is the unmistakable whine of high speed metal fragments, which impact in the water hundreds of yards behind us. I cannot believe they are doing this if they suspect there are American prisoners in there, and I immediately know the prisoner story was so much bullshit. Just another lie to keep us quiet when they told us the stand down was over.

It is fascinating to stare up at the sky and pick up the tiny blob of a plane, then watch it drop and gain speed so that you can barely keep it in sight. When the bombs fly out you know it is time to get down, and you stay down until the shock wave passes and the shrapnel stops hitting the water. Then it is time to pop up and inspect for damage. The jungle is getting thinner with every bombing run, and the piddling little fires of yesterday have turned into infernos, the heat rolling out of the jungle and over us. I am so glad that I am in the rice paddy, and not in that jungle.

The bomb runs go on a half hour, one after the other, and I swear the temperature has risen twenty degrees. The smoke is foul-smelling and cutting visibility down badly. There is a ten-minute lull, and I get ready to move out again, but the sky is cut by more thunder, and another plane drops low over the jungle. This time it is a single bomb, much larger, and it flips end for end as it disappears into the trees. The explosion is quieter, but the fireball that erupts is hundreds of feet long, and so much bigger than the earlier bombs. This is napalm, something we have had classes on, but I have never before seen it deployed.

The bombs contain explosive and jellied gas. The gas sticks to everything and sets it on fire. It also has the added benefit of consuming all the oxygen in the area it explodes in, and suffocating anyone who survives the initial blast and fire. The army has some powerful weapons in its arsenal without a doubt, but I think in the end it will not do any good. The Asian soldier does not plan for today, or next week, but a decade down the line. He will wait, watch, and kill us, one here and one there. He will take his losses, replace them with an almost inexhaustible supply from the north, and wait patiently. He knows that time is always on his side.

The bombing ceases again, and after several hours of waiting to let the jungle burn out, we are ordered to move in again. We walk through a maze of dismembered trees, large open areas with fifteen-foot diameter holes, the earth gouged and still smoking. Everything is blackened and stinking. Nothing moves. There are no bird sounds, no wind, and just total destruction. How could anyone survive in this mess, I wonder.

We spot several tunnel entrances in the burned out underbrush and treat them to our special procedure. By now, the whole jungle area is crawling with American soldiers, but there is little to do, little to see, and nobody to fight. Our platoon, advancing through an area with less damage and no burnt undergrowth, halts for a short time while the procession slows. We are walking on a path single file and the point man is checking carefully for trip wires. We move out again and as we pass around a large tree, we see a tunnel mouth just to the left of the path. Halfway out of the hole is a dead VC, bent over with his face to the ground. There is no weapon around and no blood. Shaw grabs the arm and hauls him out of the hole, the body stiff and unyielding. The only wound evident on his body is a tiny puncture in the middle of his stomach, just a dot with a small blue band surrounding it. Whatever got him was small and did not penetrate through his body. Did he suffocate during the bombing and is the wound only incidental, or did the wound kill him? And why no blood? We will never know, and in the grand scheme of things, it is not really important. What is important is that all my friends and I are alive, and it looks like we will stay that way today.

Orders from the radio halt everything, and we set up a defensive position where we are, and relax somewhat. Tunnel Rats are being sent in, and they go into the openings and check them out. I am glad that I am too big to be a TR, they need to be no more than one hundred thirty pounds and five feet or so tall. My job may be tough enough, but I really feel for those men. The job has to be scary. They climb through tunnels that are kid-sized, armed only with a flashlight and a forty-five caliber pistol. You have to be on the lookout for booby traps and VC waiting in ambush and some of the tunnel complexes are so big you could easily get lost. The men often carry a roll of thin line and some wooden pegs to help mark their way through the tunnels.

We keep our defensive positions set up the rest of the day, as do the other platoons, to provide security while the tunnel rats crawled through the complex. The tunnels were extensive, so the inspection stretched into the night. We were very alert that night, in case our enemy was in force and hiding somewhere in the tunnels. We were all quite relieved that this operation had not turned into a serious firefight.

The night passed uneventfully, and the next day the soldiers continued checking the tunnels, finally finishing around 1100 hours. They found no prisoners, no cages, and only a small quantity of weapons and food stores. The rats reported that the tunnel complex appeared to not have been used much for several months, though it had been set up to conceal a company of men with extensive supplies. There were also several rooms carved out underground, littered with old, bloody bandages, so it had been used to take care of wounded men. The intelligence report had been at least partly right; we may have just gotten there several months too late.

Choppers flew in several hundred pounds of explosives in the early afternoon, and we set large charges at each opening to collapse them. We could not totally destroy the complex, but the explosions meant that a lot of work would be required to make the complex useable again, and that area would be the target of patrols for months afterward.

We flew out in the late afternoon, tired and dirty, and thinking about the hot chow waiting for us back at camp. Total haul for the three-day's work was less than a thousand pounds of old weapons, mostly unserviceable, and food, mostly rice in dirty old bags. We found five VC bodies, and we had two KIAs and three wounded men, none of them seriously wounded. These men will be stabilized, then flown to the Dong Tam hospital to recover from their wounds.

Once they get ambulatory, they will be sent back to their unit until they recover completely then it will be business as usual and they will be sent out to do it all over again. I am sure it is hard to be wounded and then to have face combat one more time.

The three days are a waste of time, having no real effect on the war. We just marked time, and it gets us a little closer to the day when we will go home to the real world. The war is no closer to being over, and Viet Nam's agony will continue, as will ours.

56 days left in country.

Chapter 19
Charley Changes Tactics

Fire Base Moore-January 1969.

"Who is the machine gunner in this platoon?" The question comes from a tall, deeply tanned man wearing mirrored glasses. He is wearing carefully tailored fatigues and his boots have a shine I have not seen since advanced infantry training in Louisiana.

He is wearing no insignia on the fatigues, and I peg him as a CIA man the instant he speaks. There are so many of them running around the delta that we wonder who is running the war, the big brass in Long Binh or the CIA. My personal guess is the big brass; the CIA would be doing a better, if bloodier job.

"That would be me," I answer. Since he is wearing no insignia of rank, I do not have to call this person sir or salute him and I like this. He does not look like the sort of man you would want to screw with, though. We have gathered for a pre-operation briefing, just before the choppers get here, and I wonder about this man's connection to that operation.

He hoists a thousand round box of .30 caliber M-60 machine gun ammo and hands it to me. It looks like every other box of M-60 ammo I have seen here, but I notice right away that it weighs a lot more as I take it from him. Curiosity aroused, I set it down, flip the handles and open it. The rounds look the same as the thousands I have looked at before, the same as the thousands I have fired.

"This is pretty special right out of R and D in the states. You are going to be one of the first gunners to use it over here. Each round has two projectiles, so you will have twice the bullets going downrange. It will kick more and the range will be a little shorter, but you are going to like it," explains Mr. X, as he has not introduced himself. There are no nametags on his uniform, either.

I am not very pleased to have my ammunition changed an hour before an operation. We will be out several days and will be doing a lot of walking. I have two-thirds of a box of ammo wrapped around my torso and I cannot carry a full box on this operation. I will have to use one or the other. Asking this of a machine gunner is like substituting another woman on the day of his marriage.

You get to know your gun and the ammo intimately, and sudden changes are unwelcome. Twice the bullets flying out of the barrel are nice, but not that extra weight.

"Use this ammo and see how it works. I will be back in a week or so to question you on how it works in combat because I have to send in a report to the guys back in the states," my unknown benefactor explains. *Great, I am going to be a guinea pig for the government. This day cannot possibly get any better. That is, unless they send Mr. X with us and give him a close-up look at this ammo in battle!*

We hear the blades then and turn to watch a long thin blur in the air get closer and resolve into individual Huey choppers, the best method of transportation in the delta. I carry the box with me and decide to change to the new ammo while in the air. I can give the door gunners my old ammo and parcel out what I cannot carry to my assistant machine gunner. If Mr. X thinks the ammo is so good, then I should at least try it.

Today we are headed to the vicinity of Chau Doc. It is in the IV Corps area and again near the Cambodian border. Much to the platoon's dislike, our company commanders seem to have a fixation on the border of Viet Nam and Cambodia. We know the reason, though. You are much more likely to run into the enemy over there. We much prefer the jungled areas of Long An province, an hour south of Saigon. It is far less exciting, but much safer. Every time we get out of Long An province we run into determined VC, and that just makes the day no fun at all.

We know we have to get a tough operation occasionally, and today is that day. We will be flying in and doing reconnaissance on a ten-mile square area, and that is a very large area to cover when a third of it is double-canopy jungle. The whole company is going, and the operation will last two days. We like the big operations a little better because we feel safer, but they walk your butt off in the two days. The only drawback is that a company-sized operation pushes the enemy out of areas Charley feels he owns, and sometimes he likes to push back. It then becomes a test of will power and guts. The big brass has the will power, and guess who has to provide the guts?

After I change the ammo, which is quite a chore as we are jammed up in the chopper, I watch the land unroll beneath us. Other than sitting on a bunker and watching the sun go down, this is my favorite view of Viet Nam. Everything is clean and neat from the air with no sign of the war that plagues this country, unless we pass over some hidden enemy and he decides to shoot a few rounds at us. The choppers are high enough to make small arms fire nothing to worry about, but the rockets and anti-aircraft fire are definitely something to command your attention. A rocket can bring a chopper down quickly, and the chances of surviving are slim.

A chopper does have one redeeming feature that an aircraft does not have. If the hit is not too bad and the pilot can retain control, he can use his altitude to perform an auto-rotation landing. This is when he lets the chopper drop fast enough to keep the blades rotating and provide some lift. It requires some finesse and skill, and the chopper will probably crash-land because it will be coming down too fast, but that is much better than just falling from the sky. I have seen choppers that auto-rotated in and almost everyone survived. I like those odds better.

We are in the air an hour or so and then the choppers drop down and head for the landing zone. The door gunners tense up and ready their machine guns and the men aboard ready their weapons and sweat the landing. We never know if Charley is waiting down there for us.

All these choppers make quite a racket as they pass overhead and settle down for a landing, and if there is any enemy on the ground, they will certainly know we are coming. Landing in a hot LZ is pretty much a matter of luck, if you pick the wrong place you are in a lot of trouble. The trouble is, we are not the ones who pick the landing zones. Some fat cat general far in the rear puts his big meaty finger down on a map and that is where we land. The orders are conveyed by radio to the choppers and in we go. The general has never seen the landing zone and will likely never see it, but his order is our command. He makes a promise on that map with his finger and we have to back up that promise.

One hundred feet in the air, a new replacement in the platoon points to two people on the ground and takes his rifle off safe. He leans forward and draws a bead, exclaiming that one of the figures is holding a gun. One of the long-timers stops him quickly; it appears to us that there is a pair of farmers working a rice paddy and they are holding hoes. The soldier is not happy and we explain that we do not just blast people from the air without concrete evidence. He asks us if that is a safe way to operate, and we tell him it is the only way to make sure innocent civilians stay safe. We do not shoot until someone shoots at us.

I think that the soldier needs a careful watching over the next several days; he seems a tad too trigger-happy for a man on his first operation. It may just be that he is new to combat and the next several days will tell us the truth. We have had our share of shoot-first newbys and that is an admirable trait in the thick jungle, where the only inhabitants are likely to be enemy. It is not so great when you are dropping into an area where you can reasonably expect to see civilians. Admittedly, we take a chance in waiting to hear gunfire aimed at us, but if we do not, there will be plenty of dead civilians.

This is a part of soldiering that I dislike. We literally have the power of life and death in our hands in some situations. The fear and the adrenaline can combine to make a split-second decision a bad one. In the states if you make an ill-considered decision someone may get hurt, usually the decision maker. Over here, that same mistake usually kills someone. Many men having to make those quick decisions are only eighteen or nineteen, and that is far too young to face such weighty problems. Only trouble is, this is war and seventy percent of the men on the line are hardly more than teen-agers.

The company's luck holds and it is a perfect landing zone. It is a big grassy field with some sharp elephant grass but no water at all. This grass is five or six feet tall with large, firm saw-toothed leaves and just brushing through it as you walk will draw blood. This is another lovely bit of flora from Viet Nam's long list of things to make a soldier miserable. At least we do not land in a rice paddy with a foot of water and mud, which is normal in the rainy season. The closest rice paddy is a hundred yards away and due to the time of the year it is dry and sun baked. It will be several months before the monsoon rains start and the growing season commences.

We land with no opposition and set up a leisurely perimeter around the field, joining some of the other men who have already landed. I am ecstatic with pleasure; I have a good feeling about this operation. I am a short-timer now, a man with only a month left in this country, and operations that start easy are what I crave. The shorter my time gets, the more nervous I become, but I also get even more careful, if that is possible.

Once the whole company unloads, which takes quite awhile, orders come down the line of men and we form a long skirmish line, five men deep, and head toward the rice paddies. I look at the position of the sun and yes, dammit, we are heading west, towards that border, though it is a long way off. Just one time I would like to step off a chopper and head in some other direction than west. *I know if you want to see Charley, you have to visit his neighborhood, but this is getting monotonous.*

Some inane bit of drivel runs through my mind. Follow the yellow-brick road to Charley-land. There sure as hell is no yellow brick road in this rice paddy, but I have no doubt that Charley-land is somewhere up ahead on the horizon, and probably in any direction we choose.

Three hot clicks later we come to a large area of jungle ahead and the wide formation changes into three long single files of men, which will offer fewer targets in case of an ambush. As the formation changes, I make sure I am at least two-thirds of the way back in the line. This gets me further away from the point man and offers more safety in case of problems. This is one of the few perks of a machine gunner. The men want to protect the gunner because he can lay down the most fire in case of an ambush, which helps to shorten the time when we face a murderous amount of fire.

I wind up behind Sloan, a new replacement, though he is not new to the bush. He has been on the line to the west of Saigon for six months, so he is solid and will be dependable. He is a sniper and he carries a shiny M-14 with a big scope, which he treats with the utmost care. He even talks to the weapon at times but we pay no attention; word is he knows just what to do with that rifle. The platoon is anxious to see him in action, which will be the true test. Just looking at the man tells me we can depend on him. He has that almost indefinable air of a soldier that has seen combat and will not shy away from more.

I shuffle back three more positions in the line because if Charley is looking, he can see that longer weapon and he will know what Sloan can do. The enemy might want to eradicate a soldier who can eliminate him at long distances, so it is prudent to remove yourself from his vicinity. I am practicing a long honored-grunt tradition; cover your arse at all times.

Blam, blam, blam, boom! The fire out of the woodline is sudden and withering. Everyone drops to the ground and opens up into the woodline. We are caught in the open with no cover, so we put out a continuous stream of gunfire. We do our best to chop down every tree around Charley hoping he might decide that a little retreat is in order.

I have started an intimate relationship with my little piece of ground and I do not have time to fold the legs down on the machine gun. I roll like a hooked fish on the riverbank, jerk the ammo loose from my body, and hook it to the starter belt. It is a long practiced operation, and in less than two seconds, a red, continuous line of fire erupts from my barrel. I concentrate on an area just to the right front of me where I see the reddest flashes of rifle fire. The barrel is starting to smoke and I tell myself to slack off, but my finger refuses to let go of that trigger. I swing the barrel slightly left and right, conscious that I am firing only a foot over the head of some of our men, but I have no choice. Something tells me that those men are very, very likely to keep their heads down.

I hear the plop of the grenade launchers to the left and right of me over the sound of the weapons, and red blossoms erupt all over the wood line. The M-79 men are keeping a cool head and firing those grenades as fast as they can load them. The jungle ahead is a solid mass of small explosions and the tracers are ricocheting at crazy angles as I run out of ammo. I draw the forty-five, a last ditch effort in case the VC charge out of the jungle, but suddenly everything is deathly quiet. There are a few more shots and the boom of a few grenades, and then the countryside reverts to its former stillness.

We cautiously rise and run forward toward the jungle. Charley is running and the only cover is in the jungle with him. I see men to the left and right of me circle around and head into the trees. They are trying to flank the enemy and put more pressure on him to retreat. Now is the time to take advantage of the lull in the battle and reach cover. We know we will find bodies; some wounded men and some weapons, because the enemy has not had time to police up the remains of the battle.

I leave the machine gun lying in the rice paddy for now. It is useless without ammo and will only slow me down. The forty-five will be fine for the short-distance fighting in the jungle, and I am so pissed that I plan to shoot anything that moves and then find a gook rifle to continue my quest. I hold the weapon out in front of me, stiff-armed, with a spare magazine in my right hand. With the round in the chamber, and six magazines at my disposal, I have a total of forty-three shots. That is not a lot, but it will have to do until I can locate a rifle.

We comb the jungle and it is anti-climatic. We find seven dead or dying, and I hear the single shots as they are dispatched. The only humane thing to do for a badly wounded man is to put him out of his misery. Otherwise, they will lie here in agony as we now own this little section of jungle and have no immediate plans to move. Charley cannot come back to take final care of his dead if we are here, and we paid for this piece of real estate with blood and lives, so we are going nowhere at the moment.

I sit at the edge of the jungle and watch the medics take care of wounded men. The count is not good, we have four soldiers dead and eleven wounded. The dust-off choppers will be on their way now, and the men will be in Dong

Tam hospital in an hour. It could have been much worse. I think the move into single-file before we hit the ambush saved more lives. Another thing that helped is that we have a full company of men on the ground, so Charley knew he had to hit hard and then diddy-mau (run or go away) before our overwhelming numbers turned the tide.

I sit there and shake a little as I survey the scene. I do not know if it is after-battle nerves or the adrenaline pumping through my body. I do not feel scared; I feel only an overwhelming anger at the VC. I want to run through the jungle, shoot and slice them all until I am covered in blood and not one is left alive. They lay there and watched us walk toward them, and then they killed some of my friends. I try to tell myself that they were only doing their job, the same as we do, but my mind rejects all rational thought. Were the situation reversed, we will do the same thing to them, and possibly do an even better job.

My anger slowly dissipates until it is at a level I can control. Running through the jungle looking for the enemy would be a fatal undertaking and I am angry, but not that angry. It is time to rescue the machine-gun from the paddy and collect the rest of the ammo from my assistant gunner. I am not annoyed at the assistant gunner for not being close when I needed more ammo. When the crap went down it was every man for himself, protect your own butt first and in doing that we can help protect the platoon because we stay alive.

The sarge tells us that we are going to stay here tonight in this bought and paid for piece of foreign land, and I start looking for an entrenching tool to borrow. Digging a foxhole in thick jungle is a bitch due to all the roots, but I plan to be halfway to China before the sun goes down. Nothing feels better to a grunt than a good foxhole after dark, except maybe the feel of a well-oiled weapon. And of course, his wife, but that is not going to happen and I shut that train of thought off immediately. Tonight, Mr. M-60 and I will keep each other company through the darkness. *It is not warm and it does not smell oh-so-sweet like Wanda, but it is the best company for tonight.*

It is late afternoon when I get the hole deep enough and line it with nipa palm leaves. All around me, the men are doing the same thing. Once done, I sit on the side of the hole and have a smoke while it is still light. After dark, there will be no smoking of course, and the smell of tobacco can carry a long way even with the air so still. I pull out a C-ration box and have a cold supper; I am still angry and do not feel like going to any trouble to heat it. At the moment I view the food only as fuel; I barely taste it.

Before dark, the sergeants come around to each foxhole to warn us that four listening posts are going out just after dark and to keep our heads cool and our fingers off the trigger when they go out past the perimeter. I mention that I only have about four hundred rounds of ammo for the night, but he says he can do nothing about it now. They plan to call a resupply chopper in tomorrow. I know I have the .45 pistol to fall back on, and then as a final resort the knife, but this does not comfort me in the least.

Once the sun hides behind the jungle trees, the darkness comes quickly. I hear, but do not see, the men going out on listening post and am glad that I am not one of them. A machine gunner does not have to do listening posts in the jungle; the platoon leader considers him too valuable for that, and the extra danger of being a gunner is paying off tonight. We have little to do but crouch down and listen intently, but the cacophony of frogs and small creatures in the underbrush make that hard.

Around 2200 hours I hear a hiss to my right and a warning that the sarge is making the rounds of the perimeter again. He slides up to my hole and tells me that the listening posts have called in on the radio and reported much movement out in the jungle a hundred yards from our perimeter. He tells me the posts have been recalled and the men will be at the perimeter in five minutes. They have done their job and spotted enemy movement, but if the crap hits the fan, we cannot fight back without risking their lives.

He tells me the posts will call out "Mickey Mantle" and we will answer with "Ted Williams." I hope there are no enemies out there who know anything about American baseball history. I also hope there are no over-achieving North Vietnamese army soldiers facing us; I would rather deal with the usual rag-tag VC we normally face.

I hear "Mickey Mantle" before I hear any noise of movement, so these guys are good. They keep repeating the password though, so they are very nervous. You cannot blame them. Behind them, they have Charley who will most certainly shoot them, and they are entering our perimeter in total darkness with the chance of being shot by friends.

I give them my half of the password and I hear it repeated quietly down the perimeter. The men pass by our holes and head for theirs to start the long, wearisome night. Charley is around and he does not intend to bring us any flowers. The change in tactics worries me quite a lot. I am used to an enemy who fights a short time and disappears altogether. The fact that he has stayed close by and is now moving toward our positions unnerves me quite a bit and I fuss with the ammo one more time. I have it laid out on the lip of the hole on some fronds to keep it out of the dirt. I have prepared the best I can, and now all I can do is wait.

As I wait, I remember a conversation I had with a new replacement about a month ago. He was transferred down from northwest of Saigon and mentioned that they were seeing increased incidences of the enemy moving right up to your positions at night. They named it "skirt-hugging" and believed the change was an attempt by the enemy to limit the amount of firepower we could call in on them. I could see the reasoning in this. In the dark, with the enemy breathing down your neck, it is impossible to call in artillery or gun ships without getting our own men killed. The enemy has found a way to negate the advantage we have with our choppers and artillery. It was bound to happen eventually, but I sure wish he was not using that tactic tonight.

Well, it looks like we have us a standoff. Charley is going to move in on us and see who has the biggest balls. I cannot believe he thinks he can take on two hundred men and best us, but then we have no idea of how many enemies are out there tonight.

"GI, you die tonight. We come for you!" The voice of the enemy is loud and startling in the night. As the voice dies out, I hear the harsh, flat crack of a rifle from our perimeter. It is one single shot, and I recognize the sound of Sloane's M-14. I noticed him before dark placing a piece of bamboo on the lip of his hole, and then covering it with a carefully folded poncho liner. He then laid his rifle gently on the liner and aimed the rifle out into the jungle.

Sloan has probably been waiting quietly for just such an opportunity. It would be a one in a million shot in the dark, in thick jungle, aiming only at a voice. Evidently, he has been close with the placement of his shot, because Mr. Macho of the Jungle shuts up and we do not hear one more peep out of him.

About thirty feet to my right, I hear a clunk and a small thud, and a grenade goes off just outside the perimeter. The soldiers in that area open up with their rifles and I see three enemy illuminated by the muzzle blasts. They are within fifteen feet of the perimeter and throw a grenade, but they do not live to get any closer. It looks like the grenade struck a tree and bounced back, exploding without hurting anyone.

I open up with a thirty round burst directly in front of me, but the muzzle flash shows no one there. I halt to conserve ammo and wait in the darkness, eyes straining. I am wishing for a starlight scope, but I never carry one, they are too bulky and add extra weight. I do know that there are at least half a dozen on the perimeter and I know they are in heavy use right now.

Gunfire erupts on the other side of the perimeter, quick bursts that do not last. I hear the pops of several grenade launchers and the resulting explosions, and everything goes quiet again. Charley is feeling us out, seeing if we are on our toes, and trying to get a feel for our perimeter size and location in the dark. I hope we are sending him a message that we are not to be trifled with because I do not wish to fight off an assault in force on our perimeter tonight. *Some claymore mines would be nice tonight. There are a million back at the base camp but not a damn one out here when we need them!*

The small probes happen all night. Charley wants to mix it up with us, but he is not sure of his chances yet. We all get aggravated with the constant attention he gives us. No one is getting any rest and I am ready for this night to be over, it seems like it has lasted twenty-four hours. We all decide separately, lying in our holes, that we want the enemy to try one more time in a big way, so we can show him who is the boss of these woods.

About 0400 hours things quiet down, but we know this is the most likely time to have an attack start. The sergeants are out again checking the perimeter and they decide to strip some men away from the eastern side of the defenses and move them to the western side, which has been seeing most of the action. This will give more men and weapons on the side we expect to endure most of the attack, but it is a calculated risk.

Things stay quiet for a little longer, but we know that for the enemy, it is now or never. The frogs and animals are quiet, almost as if they are holding their breath, waiting to see what happens.

What happens is that Charley hits the western edge of the defenses, just what the sergeants envisioned. Evidently, they have been back at their position smoking wacky weed and psyching themselves up and they come toward us with no attempt at silence. Some scream and hurl themselves at our positions and they run into a beefed-up wall of U.S. soldiers who are determined and sick of the whole situation. Their own muzzle flashes illuminate them and when we join in, it looks like a red daybreak. There is a solid wall of red fire lancing out into the jungle and numerous enemy fall and their compatriots crawl over them and continue moving forward.

The screaming horde has my full attention and the machine gun jumps in my hand and spits empty brass. Suddenly it quits; I am out of ammunition. I can now hear the scream of bullets over my head and hear the solid thunk as they connect with the trees around and behind me. I am scared, but I have no time for such an emotion. The .45 is in my left hand and I rip the knife out of its scabbard and look for a target. The wall of VC in front of our positions is dropping in the withering fire and none are replacing them.

A screaming lone soldier appears before me in the now advancing semi-light and the pistol bucks twice in my hand. I am surprised when it goes off; I am on autopilot. The force of the two rounds kicks him backward and he falls away from my hole and does not move. In the early morning light, I see one foot hanging over the edge of my hole, a flip-flop still attached. The leg twitches several times and then goes still. I crawl forward, put the muzzle against his forehead, and pull the trigger one more time, just to make sure. I spare only one shot, because this magazine is about half empty and I have only five more full ones. The attack is broken and the sun is coming up, but I do not know if I will need to fire anymore. I hope not, I am sick of this.

We sit in the holes and listen to the moans of the dying and wounded men in front of us. Once we are sure the enemy is long gone, we go out and check the bodies. They are piled on each other and most are dead. This is a sickening sight and I wonder about the sanity of men in general and mine in particular. I look at the dead soldier in front of my hole; he looks no older than a teenager. I notice he has four holes in his chest and I am certain I shot only twice. I have shot a man that was already on his way to dying. Perhaps his scream, which I thought indicated defiance and determination, was only the final scream of a dying man.

We have to check the bodies for any type of ID and any papers that might give us information on units and tactics. I rifle through his pockets and come up with a hand sewn canvas wallet. There is no ID, but there is a wrinkled and worn black and white photograph showing a small, smiling Vietnamese woman holding a baby. I have a bad feeling that this man's family is in that photograph and that they will never know where he died and that he did so bravely. We will leave the bodies here and the VC will come back later and bury them. If he is from this area, his family may hear of his death and even find out where he is buried. If not, he will have a lonely grave here and his family will always wonder about him. He was my enemy, but he deserves better. He has joined that large, but elite group of men who died serving their country, and he deserves much more than a quick, shallow burial a hundred miles from nowhere.

It is full light now, and most of us sit by our holes, numbed by the night's proceedings and the loss of life all around us. I want to feel happy that I have survived another night and another battle, but my mind just feels empty. I can summon no emotions other than a sick feeling and a slowly mounting rage that man is destined to repeat his mistakes over and over until the end of time. I am a single individual and can do absolutely nothing about it.

I sit by a tree and replay last night in my mind. The special ammo turned out to work really well; there just wasn't enough of it. Every shot I fired last night sent two bullets out, so it probably helped more than I will ever know. I know I had better check that barrel over good when we get back to the base camp. I certainly did not worry about it last night. I think I remember it glowing as I ran out of ammo, but I was a little too busy to worry with it. That gun certainly deserves an extra good cleaning today; it did its job with nary a whimper and stayed on duty until I could feed it no longer.

My friends and I finally start moving and gather our equipment together. We glance around the jungle that is littered with bodies and spent brass. There is an acrid smell to the air, a smell of desolation and death. Smoke is still curling up from the underbrush on the outskirts of our positions. This is our land now and we will be abandoning it shortly. I call it ours because this piece of jungle has been bought and paid for in blood and terror, but we will be flying back to Fire Base Moore soon. This area has no name, just a number on the Area of Operations map. No one will remember this bit of ground for long, or the men who fought and died here. It will be just one more tiny piece of Viet Nam that we owned for a short period and then abandoned. We continue to take and then abandon pieces of this country; if that is not the definition of insanity, then I do not know what is.

Medics are tending the wounded men and moving them out to the edge of the jungle to await the dust-off choppers, which are on the way. I see some U.S. army boots sticking out from under poncho liners, but I avert my gaze and turn away. I do not want to know how many Americans died today. I will know soon enough when they hold the mock funerals for the men back at the base camp. I do know that we killed many more VC than they killed of us, but that is no consolation on such a sad morning.

I know the choppers will be coming for us soon, but that is no consolation either. I look up at the bright sun in the cloudless blue sky of this country that I love/hate and try to draw some joy and some understanding of this giant whirlwind that is consuming my young life. No joy comes, and I find no understanding. I know only that this night will haunt me for the rest of my life.

36 days left in country.

Chapter 20
We Lose Our Tiger Scout

Dong Tam base-Feb. 1969.

This has been a really, really, bad couple of days for O'Brian and I. We are back in Dong Tam, the 9th Infantry Division main camp in the Mekong Delta in the southern part of Viet Nam. We are here because we are now off the line and have been sent to the rear, since we only have a week left in our year's tour. We have to get a lot of papers signed, records picked up, and gear turned in before we take that big freedom bird flight back to the real world. In addition, a considerable amount of celebrating will happen.

The paperwork is turning out to be a real aggravation for both of us, but especially for me. Most of my medical records have disappeared sometime in the last year. It is probably connected with being in the hospital for malaria and I walk back and forth numerous times between the medical records filing building and the office of the lieutenant, who is in charge of seeing that we get everything signed and turned in before we leave.

It is frustrating walking around in the hot sun and dust trying to tie up all the loose ends, and the army's position is that since my records are missing, it must be my fault. After a year of combat, I have a low tolerance for official crap, and I find myself wanting to reach over the desk and apply my hands to the officer's throat several times. My position is that the army has ten damn clerks in base camps for every soldier on the line and they should be taking care of the problem. It is just one more turn of the screw, one more chance to jerk me around before I leave.

After numerous trips up and down the dusty roads of Dong Tam, the records finally appear. They are in disarray and missing some reports and I can see the incomplete file annoys the orderly mind of the lieutenant. This fastidious idiot has been shuffling papers his whole time over here and he lets a few missing pages jack him out of shape. I wish he had been with our platoon the whole year to get a taste of the real Viet Nam and its assorted problems. Like a dog with a bone, he plays with the file, shuffles the pages, and finally decides it is complete enough to initial as closed out. I grab the file and give him a quick salute as I can tell he is an officer who expects a salute. I clear out of the building as fast as I can before he changes his mind. This is good, one signature down and eight to go.

I check the list, and the next office to visit is the re-up office. This is so comical I walk down the dusty street laughing so hard I almost run into a pole. After a year in this hellhole, they expect me to visit an officer who will try to talk me into signing up for a couple more years in the army. This is an absolute sign that I am in the Twilight Zone and I have to get on that plane this week and escape.

"Let me save us both some time sir," I say to the officer sitting behind the desk. "I don't like the army and unless you can offer me a tax-free million dollars to re-up, could you please just sign this paper and let me leave." I have to be marginally polite or he will find some way to refuse his signature. He sniffs and peers out through his thick glasses and tells me I am obviously not what the army wants in their ranks. I have been telling the army this for a year and a half, but they refuse to listen.

I walk the streets for the rest of the day getting those forms signed. I do not take time off to eat, because I want all nine forms signed and sealed today. They are my get-out-of-jail forms, so they are the most important paperwork I carry in my life. I finally get the last one signed at 1630 hours and I walk back to the barracks hot, tired and hungry, but it has been a good day.

Only someone who has seen a year of combat, constant battle with the elements, and constant worry can possibly know how we felt that week, at least until the bad news came down. We have clean cots, clean clothes, great chow, and little to worry about, but I just could not relax or sleep properly. O'Brian was having the same problem and we kept waking up at night for our turn at guard duty, even though we knew guard duty was over for us. My nerves are shot and it is going to take a long time to get used to the new normal. A year later, I was still trying to straighten out my nerves.

The morning convoy has come in from our former duty station, Fire Support Base Moore, out on Highway Ten, only a rifle shot away from the Cambodian border. Talking to one of the drivers, we hear that a platoon has been ambushed there last night while they were on patrol and a Tiger Scout named Lon, and a bunch of soldiers have been killed. The news cuts through us like a knife and my head spins. I sit down in the shade of a sandbag bunker to digest this latest piece of crap information. Lon has already lost one arm in an ambush a year ago, fighting with the platoon. He has given enough and now we hear our good friend is dead. It is a cruel stroke of luck that we lose him just before we leave the country.

I still picture him, just a teenager, holding the butt of his rifle in his bare feet, as he ran the cleaning rod through the barrel. We all tried to help him, but he waved us off as he refused help, cursing us in Vietnamese, but we knew it was just for show. We all loved Lon; he was a brother to us, and a combat brother, to boot. There is no closer tie in this world.

O'Brian and I both have tears in our eyes, and we both pretend we do not notice. It is hard to believe that our friend can be dead.

"We must get out there and see if the guys are okay, man," shouts my friend. "This can't be true! We have to find out before we leave this damn country." I am just numb, that old familiar "it doesn't matter" that I have felt too many times before while staring at a bloody friend, or watched them carried off in a chopper while ashen-faced medics work on them.

We look at each other, and our minds have decided, without saying a word. I have spent a year in combat with O'Brian; we do not need to speak too much at times. It is almost like a marriage without sex. My wife and I got married while I was on leave, so I have spent only several weeks with her. I probably know O'Brian better than I do my own wife. Luckily, we have already taken care of most of the processing for leaving the country, except for turning in our weapons and equipment we still need, so we figure we can make ourselves scarce for a day or two.

We grab our rifles, break them down, clean and check them for functioning. We take every round out of the twenty-three magazines we carry, wipe them down to remove the always-present dust, and reload them. We are on autopilot, doing what we have done hundreds of times before. We load .223 rounds into the magazines, twenty rounds each, and seven magazines slid into each bandolier. We sling three bandoliers over our shoulders, and two more magazines are taped together and carried in the weapon, ready to be ejected when one runs empty. We can then remove the magazine, rotate it one hundred and eighty degrees, reinsert it and fire again. This gives us a forty round calling card for Charley. If some of our friends are dead, then God forgive me, but I hope we run into the enemy today. Our minds are already out in the field with our friends and we want to extract some payback for one final time.

We finish off our attire with flak jackets, multiple layers of ballistic nylon sewn together, inserted into a nylon vest designed to stop most shrapnel and small arms fire. We wear them anytime we are out of base camp. We head over to the convoy, knowing that in the last hour it has been loaded chock full of ammo, grenades, artillery rounds, C-rations, and all the other miscellaneous items needed every day by a forward base. The convoys come in every morning from the forward bases, where they have stayed all night, load up, head out again, and do it seven days a week, day after day to keep up with the demand for material to wage war.

All Charley needs each day is several rice balls for food, a little ammo, and a few swigs of dirty water to keep him going, but the way the U.S. Army wages war, it takes probably ten men and several vehicles to support just one combat soldier. Only about fifteen percent of the troops in Viet Nam at a given time were actually used in combat. Had a larger percentage actually faced the sharp end of the sword, the outcome of the war might have been vastly different, if it had been coupled with more sensible tactics.

We climb over the tailgate into the truck, and after a short wait, we take off with a lurch. They must give the drivers special training to make sure they do not take off carefully. I have ridden in these trucks hundreds of times and have never witnessed a smooth takeoff. Is it even possible, I wonder? Maybe these people are just tired, trying to keep up with the job of moving everything. Choppers are essential to carry troops into battle and to pull out the wounded and dead. They are too busy with these jobs, so ninety-five percent of material moves by truck. Of course, a truck is a much more economical way of moving heavy loads.

We are waved through the gate, sixteen trucks and four escort jeeps, and off we go on our appointed rounds in a cloud of black diesel smoke. Down the line, you hear the muted snicks of bolts drawn back and released, kicking rounds into numerous weapons. Everyone has heard of the ambush, and no one is smiling today. We are all ready for a tussle with Charley, and I find myself wishing that the enemy will pop up down the road somewhere. There are about forty extremely teed-off soldiers in this convoy, so Charley had better be on the top of his game today.

My friend and I have picked a truck in the middle of the procession. We know if a convoy is hit, it is usually at the front, or occasionally the rear. We learn quickly over here about minimizing our exposure to danger, that is, if we live long enough early on to learn what and what not to do. A combat zone is a dangerous place to be, and not all of the danger is from the front. Sometimes some of the soldiers around me handling loaded weapons worried me more than the enemy did.

Quite a few accidents happened in Viet Nam that had nothing to do with battle. I personally observed Parks, one of my friends, shot right in front of me through the back by an idiot clearing his rifle as we came off bunker guard. Then there was a soldier setting himself on fire with diesel fuel while he was burning the refuse in a toilet, which was an approved way of disposing of it. There was the tracked vehicle that flipped over behind us trying to swerve away from stopped traffic on Highway One, and the explosion of a claymore in a burning trash barrel in Baker platoon. How that got in the barrel, no one could figure out.

There was the light observation plane that took off from Tan An one morning as we were bringing a convoy in along the runway. It took off normally, but suddenly climbed straight up until it stalled, flipped over onto its back and plunged to the earth near the end of the runway. Mechanical failure or the pilot being a cowboy, I do not know which, but we had to remove the two pilots from what was left of the fuselage, still alive but very seriously injured. There were other incidents also, and if I saw all these in a year, I have to conclude a considerable amount of death and injury resulted from accidents. Of course, this was not reported to the relatives, just a telegram informing them that their loved one was killed or injured in battle, which is probably a more humane way of handling it, so I do not blame the army for this. Every war has losses like this. If you teach thousands of teenagers to handle loaded weapons, all types of explosives, and all kinds of things designed to kill human beings, you will see this result.

During the tour spent all over Viet Nam, I often thought of the Boy Scouts and the local troop I was a member of for several years. I came to realize that the overnight camping and marches we did helped to prepare me for the rigors of combat. I met many people in training and in combat that had never spent a night outside in a tent or cooked their food over a fire until they wound up in the army. New replacements that showed up in our platoon were usually petrified when they found we were going out at night into the jungle and I would have to explain that the night was their friend. Sure, they could not see Charley but then, he could not see them either. Set up a defensive position, keep quiet, stay awake, and do not do something stupid like light a cigarette or loudly slap mosquitoes, and they will hear the enemy coming. We could see him with the starlight scopes if the sky was clear, as the scopes magnified moonlight and starlight and Charley would show up as a dark shadow on a lighter green background. Of course, if we were moving around after dark, Charley could hear us coming too, no matter how careful we were.

When I got back from the war, friends often asked me what Viet Nam was like. I would tell them it was like the Boy Scouts, but with guns and people who wanted to kill you. Anyway, a big thank you to Scoutmasters Gene Webster and Brooks Carew for your careful training, it was much appreciated on the long nights on ambush patrol with nothing but a poncho liner thrown over your shoulders to keep out the damp and chill, and a rifle to ward off the enemy.

We are getting close to Firebase Moore now and I do not know what we are going to find, but I know it is not good and I work to insulate myself from the bad news that I know is coming. I am gripping my rifle so tightly my knuckles are turning white from the pressure, but that rifle feels good in my hands. It is my rock, my protector, something to anchor me in this world of uncertainty and discomfort. Shit always happens, but your rifle is ever true, ever ready to help if you get in a tight spot. I have turned my machine gun and .45 pistol back in to the armorer, but will keep the M-16 until I leave the country.

Up ahead we see a little column of dark smoke rising from a burned-out hooch, a Vietnamese house that once had a thatched roof and walls. They always have a bunker inside made of hand-applied mud over nipa palm logs, at least a foot thick, capable of stopping small arms fire. The occupants sleep in it at night if there are any VC or U.S. troops around because they know if we meet Charley, there are going to be some bullets flying around. Not much is left of the building, just ashes and the lump of the bunker showing.

Crowds of soldiers are digging through the remains, shovelfuls of ashes flying over their shoulders. There are green rubberized body bags in the yard and on the back of several jeeps, and some obviously contain bodies. Though I don't think it's possible, my gut lurches and that chain tightens a little more and I wonder if I can make it over the tailgate to the ground. My anger rises quickly, engulfing me in a tide of emotion. I am glad to feel it coming, an old welcome friend. I'm angry at the VC, I'm angry at the army, I'm angry at this stinking little country, and I'm angry at the bastardly old men that start wars and send young men to fight them. If I get angry enough, I cannot feel the pain as badly, and in a combat zone, not feeling the pain makes it easier to function. It allows you to face the impossible and keep moving. I became an expert at getting angry this past year and I could dial in just the perfect amount to suit whatever conditions I faced.

Off the truck quickly, we need to get this done. I have learned the anticipation of bad news can be worse than the news itself. Vietnamese are standing around watching the scene, and I know one or more of them may be responsible for this. It is daylight so they have hidden their weapons and turned into the friendly old rice farmer.

I shout at them, "Diddy mau, diddy mau you bastards," and stick my rifle in their faces when they do not move fast enough. Most of our old platoon has rotated back to the states or are in base camps like us getting ready to go home, but I recognize Phillip Miller in the crowd.

He comes up and says, "Let it go, McCoy, let it go. It don't matter none, man, it don't matter. You are a short timer now so don't worry about it." I want to feel that way but is does so much matter.

"Where is Lon?" Miller poses a single question to the soldiers busy zipping a body bag closed. The soldier points to the bag on the back of the jeep and we walk over. I grit my teeth and zip the bag down. The body is barely recognizable as a human form, all features burnt off, a side of beef too long on the barbie. The body has only one arm. Embedded in the blackened flesh around the neck is the chain and dog tag Lon had made in the village. He wanted to wear a dog tag like his American friends. I can still make out the stamped letters on the discolored metal. No doubt now, but I feel strangely calm and emotionless, no tears forthcoming. The anger is still working and I am in that painless zone for the moment.

"They really screwed up man," says Miller. "Phillips and I talked before they flew him to the hospital. He said they set up a listening post in the hooch. He was outside on guard when the gooks shot a B-40 rocket in and the bunker set it off, and the building exploded. Phillips managed to crawl out to the road with his machine gun before he passed out, but no one got out of the hooch."

"How is Phillips?" I ask. Miller told me that Phillips would survive and recover, but would probably be in the hospital for a month at least with shrapnel in his chest and legs. Only one man has survived the ambush.

"I can't believe this crap, man, the guys knew better than to set up the post in a hooch," I say.

Miller comes back with, "Our old platoon would never have done something that stupid."

"Well," I retort, "our old platoon is all gone now, but I thought that we taught the guys better than that." If we set up in a building at night and send only one of the men outside to cover 360 degrees, then we are asking for it. That is the whole idea of hunkering down in the open, we are not in a fixed position the gooks can pinpoint, and in addition, we have full visibility all around us.

I am angry with the platoon now and their asinine mistake. I barely know some of the dead soldiers, but I know Lon, and he should have said something. He certainly knew better. However, he did not and now he is dead, along with three compatriots, and three Vietnamese that were in the hooch. Charlie never minded wasting a few civilians. They just got in the way when he was killing Americans.

We load up the jeeps and proceed up the dirt road to Fire Base Moore, only a quarter of a mile away. Sergeant Wilson tasks the platoon with the job of rounding up the dead soldier's belongings. The army will fly them back with the bodies to Long Binh, and then home to their families. I know that as we work, someone somewhere is composing a telegram and sending it across the Pacific Ocean, and three families are going to have their lives shattered.

Sorting the belongings is onerous but important because you do not want anything sent home that could cause the families further grief. We burned compromising photos, dirty letters, drugs, or pictures of dead bodies. The hardest is letters the soldier saved to reread when things are quiet. We have to screen them carefully. If the soldier is married, we make sure the love letters are only from his wife. If he is not married, we make sure the letters are from only one girl. It is a distasteful job, but a necessary one. You would want it done for you, God forbid, if your own number came up.

The bodies go across camp to registration and final prep, and we sit in the shade of a bunker and steal glances at the one bag left on the back of a nearby jeep. O'Brian and I volunteer to deliver Lon's body back to his village, since we know where it is; about eight miles back up the road in the direction of Dong Tam. We both feel this is a sad end to such a good person, a friend who saved lives often with his knowledge of the area. He had friends and contacts all over our area of operations and could often sense when the VC were around, and whether the information we were getting from a villager was of use or so much hogwash. We struggle with his loss, and how to give him a final goodbye. We have worked with Lon almost a year, and when we leave to go home, who will remember him, and know of his value, except for his family? We do not want him to be just one more Tiger Scout, used by the army, and then buried somewhere in a lonely grave, remembered only by his family.

We go to chow and force down food we barely notice or taste, and work on our problem. We want Lon remembered as a hero, a man of worth to his village, despite his young years. After mulling it over, we hit on an answer, a solution to our problems. Several weeks ago, the 3/39th Division of the Ninth Infantry Division was awarded a Unit Citation, a medal to mark their operations for the last three months. Nothing big, just an accolade to remember that time of service in Viet Nam, and to be proudly displayed down through the years, alongside the citations from the Korean War and World War II, and every action it had been involved with back through time. Every soldier in the unit received the medal in a plastic box, complete with a small award bar to be worn on your dress uniform when you got back to the real world. We decided to use these to award Lon an impromptu medal for bravery. I hope that the villagers will not know our little secret, and will revere our friend as a war hero, which is what we think of him.

Our two medals are back in Dong Tam, packed up in our duffel bags, but we make a deal with two soldiers in the camp to borrow theirs, and replace them with ours, which we will send out on the convoy when we got back to our main base. To further our preparations, we practiced a manual of arms with our rifles, something we had not done since training, until we became passable at it, rather than the feeble attempt we first did. Being able to manipulate the rifles crisply to their various positions was important, as it was a part of almost all award ceremonies.

Next, we borrowed an AO map, or area of operations map from a squad leader so we could make sure which direction we could fire our rifles without risking hitting anyone when performing the ceremony. A rifle bullet can travel pretty far, even when shot at a high angle, and there are no blanks in Viet Nam. Technically we needed to get permission to fire our rifles while awarding the medals but we knew that would not be forthcoming, so instead we gave ourselves permission. We would be in hot water if anyone found out, but hey, what is the army going to do? *Send us to Viet Nam, maybe?*

The plans and practice took our minds off the pain of losing Lon and his fellow soldiers, something to keep our minds occupied. We decided a little alcohol might help, but a search of camp turned up no source of a few beers. We had no way to cool them down, anyway. In larger base camps, where they had an airfield, you could go down to the airstrip and liberate a few fire extinguishers to spray them, and beer treated thusly would have a close approximation of cold, but no such possibilities existed in a small forward base camp like this. I had to seek solace in my pipe, breathing in short puffs as I was about out of tobacco, and my friend sat in the shade of a bunker, furiously chain-smoking cigarettes.

We turned in early, exhausted from the day's activity. We bedded down on top of a low sandbag bunker, a lumpy bed, to be sure, but at least dry. We borrowed several poncho liners to ward off the night dew, as we had left the main base with nothing other than weapons and ammo. In our hurry, we had not planned for an overnight stay. We both spent a restless night and awoke early the next morning from the noise of an already bustling camp. We grabbed chow quickly, as we needed to get Lon's body to his village, say our final goodbyes, and get back to Fire Base Moore in time to leave on the 1000 hours convoy back to Dong Tam. We wanted to get back before some non-com noticed we were missing. If that happened, we might get in enough trouble to delay our departure back to the real world, and we did not want that to happen.

Checking out our rifles quickly but carefully, we went by the ammo dump on the backside of the camp and picked up a few grenades each, and a LAW, or light antitank weapon, a small shoulder-launched rocket, to supplement our other hardware. Bless the army, they always had plenty of munitions available in base camps, and no one questioned the quantity you picked up. The rule seemed to be, if you can carry it, you can have it.

We were not expecting any trouble in daylight, but it was only the two of us, and the extra armament could help in a pinch. We turned the radio on and did a radio check with TAC, and rolled out the gate. The two soldiers on guard duty gave us salutes and thumbs up signals. They did not know us, but they knew who was in the body bag on the back of the jeep, and they knew we were on a short, but painful mission.

Down the road we rolled, on the alert and turned east in the direction of Dong Tam. Dust billowed up behind us, and though my heart was heavy, I could not help but notice the beautiful sunny day, the crisp morning air, and the birds everywhere, wheeling and circling in the sky. The sun was on its appointed arc through the sky, a fiery jewel rolling through a perfect china blue bowl above us. The rice paddies were blooming, so the local farmers had been busy pumping water out of the canals. I could see the promise of a coming heavy harvest, and the greens of the trees were so bright it almost hurt my eyes. Viet Nam could be very beautiful in its own simple way, and even the dangers lurking around a corner could not take that away. I remember thinking that no one should be dead on such a beautiful day, and how I both loved, and hated this backwater little country.

We reach the turnoff; take a left up a rough track, hardly more than a footpath, and see signs of the recent passing of a water buffalo, large circular brown mounds left on the path as a smelly reminder. The track ends after a quarter mile in a grove of nipa palm trees with twenty or so thatched houses sprinkled around, well shaded by the trees. The houses are interspersed with pigpens, and chickens are strutting around, scratching in the dirt. Kids, or in Vietnamese, Baby-Sans, appear in the open doorways and dart out to us, faces beaming, arms waving. Overall, this is a typical Vietnamese village, very rural but well laid-out, and well-kept.

Crowds of people are arranged around a wooden platform built in the middle of the village, and as we come to a stop, the women put their arms in the air, start a strange and disconcerting wailing, and head toward us. They march around the jeep, no crying but the strange wailing builds up into a crescendo, and I have my first taste of a Vietnamese funeral. I am relieved to find the bad news has already reached the villagers, and we are relieved of the duty of explaining our presence, something I had been dreading.

We pick up the stretcher with its burden and the men and women touch it gently in turn, as we walked to the platform and gently deposited the body on it. All of the villagers show grief in their brown, furrowed faces, and they gently touch us on the shoulders, and the body bag, and murmur quietly in their language. I think they are thanking us, and it suddenly occurs to me I do not know the Vietnamese word for that, and the rest of the words go over our heads. We do not have Lon to translate for us any more. The Vietnamese link arms and march around the platform, moaning in unison. They look to the sky, raising their arms and swaying their bodies back and forth. No translation is needed; the grief and anguish are visible on each lined face.

O'Brian and I exchange glances and know it is time for our show to begin. I say a quick prayer to God, asking him to get us through our brief ceremony with dignity and grace. I reach in the jeep and remove the medals, and my buddy and I march slowly in unison to the platform. I pin the medals on the body bag, and O'Brian pulls a piece of paper from his fatigue shirt pocket and reads our speech, painfully written and rewritten last night in camp.

"The Ninth Infantry Division has the honor to award, on this fifteenth day of February, 1969, two awards for bravery and service to the United States Army, to Lon, who distinguished himself during operations against a hostile force in the Republic of Viet Nam in the preceding year," read Cavanaugh solemnly. I fervently hoped that someone there understood enough of what he said to know we were honoring Lon and his memory.

We then proceeded to the jeep, picked up our rifles and marched back to the platform, careful to stay in step. We raised the rifles in unison and fired into the air in the direction we had earlier determined was safe. With no one to give us fire orders; we knew we could not fire in unison cleanly, so we had decided in advance to fire one after the other, each firing seven rounds. We then dropped our rifles to the side arms position, and immediately snapped off salutes, the sharpest and most heartfelt salute I ever gave in my military career. I was amazed to realize that our ceremony went off smoothly, and was ready to head for the jeep, but before I know it, we are walking around the platform and gently touching it as we walk, like the villagers. We touch it one last time, and I bend over and kiss the bag, and see O'Brian do the same, and the silent tears cascade down our faces. We will be home in a week and will never see this village again, but our friend will be here a long time, and it just does not seem fair. Still, I know we have given our fallen comrade the best sendoff we can with what we have to work with, and that comforts me a little.

We take one long, final look at the platform and head back for the jeep. The village is silent now, so quiet and peaceful, and I realize that this is a good place to be buried. Many a soldier has had a poorer place to lie. The Vietnamese are in a line now and they carefully shake our hands and murmur quietly as we climb into the jeep. *Goodbye, Lon, we love you, and we will miss you, man.*

This all happened forty-three years ago, and I still miss Lon at times. I have a picture of him, faded and worn with time, and I take it out occasionally and remember my friend. I hope those two medals are a treasured possession of his relatives to this day, and that he is still remembered and honored in his village as a hero. To our platoon, he was a hero, and for me, time will not erase his memory.

6 days left in country.

Chapter 21
Goodbye To Viet Nam

Bien Hoa Airport-Feb. 1969

I have signed every piece of paperwork and turned in every piece of equipment necessary to leave the country. The final day in Viet Nam is upon my friends and me. I am still alive, but just a little scarred. I walk out onto the tarmac and the heat shimmers above it in long, undulating waves. Our long awaited freedom bird is sitting there, blue and white paint glistening in the bright sunlight. It may be winter at home, but the temperature is over one hundred degrees here.

Without a doubt, the plane is the most beautiful sight I have seen in a long while. It rests there on the taxiway with its four turbines humming a sweet song that promises freedom, a release from my long sentence of combat. This is the second airplane I will board today to get out of Viet Nam and it is taking me to the edge of my comfort zone.

I think back to the flight that some fellow soldiers and I took early this morning out of Dong Tam and inwardly shudder. This base has a small runway built of steel SPS sheets laid down over a sand base so the airplane we used was small and far from what is sitting on the runway here at Bien Hoa. I don't know what I expected to see carry us north to our debarkation point, but it was not what we actually received. I knew we were in trouble when I heard the plane fly over the airport at a low altitude, then describe a big circle in the air and drop down onto the runway.

What rolled up to us was a tatty old C-47 twin engined transport right out of World War II. Its two radial engines were rattling, clanking, and trailing smoke with each misfire. It bore the colors of a civilian airline that the government paid to fly soldiers around the country. It appeared to be a few years behind in its maintenance schedule, and even further behind in its outward appearance. This is not the first of their airplanes I have seen here, but it is the first time I am a customer of theirs.

The pilot climbs out, kicks a couple of wheel chocks under both main gear, and heads towards us. It is about one hundred in the shade and this pilot is wearing a leather flight jacket, a pair of faceted lens leather flying goggles, and is trailing a white silk scarf from his neck. For a moment I feel like I am somewhere in North Africa in 1943 on an allied airbase. Behind him the plane sits on the tarmac, both engines running at a ragged idle, and occasionally one or another cylinder will miss and the exhaust will belch a bright blue flame and a copious amount of smoke.

The most alarming thing, though, is that engine oil is running off the trailing edge of the wing and dripping onto the runway. I let my eyes drift farther back, and I see the vertical stabilizer and horizontal one covered in the same oil, and it is also dripping and blowing back in the propeller air stream. I have spent a year in a combat zone, and now the army is determined to kill me off on my last day in this country. I do not want to get on this plane, not even to get to Bien Hoa, where they have real airplanes.

The pilot swaggers up and asks us if we are the men going north to catch our freedom flight and I ask him if this poor imposter of an airplane is capable of doing so. I point out the clanking engines and the dripping oil and tell him I have serious doubts about my safety.

"Don't you worry none, man; this baby will get us to Bien Hoa with bells on. She has twin thirty-five gallon oil tanks and I personally topped off both of them before I left this morning," the pilot tells me with a big smile. The information and the smile do not help, but I know this is the only thing I have to get me north and I really have little choice. I have risked my life for a year so I roll the dice and risk it one more time. I do promise myself that if this plane goes down and I have time, I will personally choke this SOB to death before we hit.

We all head for the loading door on the side of the plane and the pilot turns the handle and yanks on it with no results. I hear a banging from inside the plane and watch the thin aluminum door bulge outwards from the blows. It finally relents and swings back, and the co-pilot hands down a tattered ramp and we load up. Talk about a bare bones operation, these guys do not even have a ground crew.

The inside of the plane is no better than the outside; it looks like it has had a long career of carrying everything. Every inside aluminum panel is dented and scraped and there are no seats to speak of, just brackets riveted to the inside skin and wooden planks to sit on. There are no seat belts, of course, and it is unlikely this plane has ever seen a flight attendant. I reluctantly sit down and notice my feet are sitting on a pair of doors in the belly of the compartment and they work as well as the rest of the plane. They rattle around and bang against each other in rhythm with the motors. Neither door closes all the way, and as they vibrate around, I can see a three-inch gap that changes to a one-inch one and back with movement of the doors. Okay, I am in this piece of crap and it is too late to back out because I hear the motors winding up. I do not let all my weight down on that seat for the hour we are in the air and when I see Bien Hoa under us, I am ecstatic.

I feel like kissing the tarmac when I get off that contraption, but the pavement is too hot and I have to wrestle that duffel bag to the bus. It takes us into the base where we do our final processing. It is mainly having our possessions checked by non-smiling sergeants. They turn out our pockets, pour out all our possessions onto white-painted tables, and go through them. They warn us that if we have any ammo or explosives we better let them know now or we can be facing stockade time. They also check for pictures of dead bodies, damaged buildings or equipment.

The final hurdle is our MPC. They count it and replace it with good old American money but do allow us to keep small amounts of MPC as souvenirs. I am pretty nervous as I have several pictures of damaged equipment hidden in the lining of a medal case, but they do not check that. I also have the two bullet points from one round of that special machine gun ammo the CIA guy gave me taped inside the toes of my combat boots, but we are not asked to remove our boots.

I know that ammo is rare and I just have to carry a sample home as a war trophy. I am afraid to carry home a live round since they warned us about severe penalties, but I figure I cannot get into too much trouble if they find the bullet points in my boots. It is a calculated risk, but I leave the county with my rare points. We load our duffel bags back up and go through a gate to the airstrip. I cannot believe it; this crap is finally over for good.

I join a long line of soldiers heading toward the ramp that leads into the plane. All around me, I see excited faces and big smiles. I am so happy to be heading home to my family. I am also so nervous that I am quite sick to my stomach. I hope that I will not have to use one of the airsick bags aboard the plane.

The flight attendant at the base of the ramp is young and pretty. It is so great to see a real American woman for a change instead of those flat-faced

Asian women. The Asian women can be beautiful, but I prefer a good "ole U.S. of A" woman anytime.

She has numerous army patches sewn all over her outfit from every army division fighting over here. I see the Big Red One patch, the First Infantry Division. They are all there, the 82nd Airborne, the 25th Infantry Division and all the others. Bless her. She has included us all. On her right shoulder is my patch, the 9th Infantry Division. I feel very proud for a moment, but the feeling is fleeting. I remind myself that I hate the army and what combat forced me to do. The patch is not my patch. It is only a patch I had to wear on my sleeve.

She also has sergeant's stripes sewn up and down her sleeves, the bars and rockers in profusion. The gold colors glisten in the sunlight. It appears her fanciful rank is somewhere around an E-32. My old First Sergeant would be green with envy.

She welcomes each of us as we step to the ramp with her face so appealing in the morning sunlight. I tell her she is a beautiful angel sent from heaven to rescue us, and her smile lights up the area. She gives me a quick hug as I head up the steps and into the plane.

With the engines running the air conditioning is on and the plane actually feels cold inside. I find a seat and savor this feeling, looking at the aisle lights shining down the rows of seats. It has been nine months since I have felt such coolness, and I am reminded of that long-gone refrigerator we had in Rach Kein. The effect is quite like a dim, secluded cave, but this cave is taking me home.

I lay my head back against the seat and feel the thrumming vibration of the engines through the floor and seat cushion. This baby is straining to take to the air. The engines hum "home" to me and I am ready to go. My earlier queasiness has relented and I can enjoy or at least endure the flight.

The plane fills up quickly. There are many men ready to say goodbye to this country and head across the Pacific. I introduce myself to my seatmate and we discuss our duty stations. We talk about what we did here but it is just small talk to calm our nerves. Our minds are already ten thousand miles to the east. We are all jittery, wondering if we will make it home and what changes we will find when we get there. *Can I fit back in, I wonder?* My mind immediately tells me yes. After this country, the rest of my life will be smooth sailing. At least that was what I thought at the time.

"Gentlemen, welcome aboard Orient Air Flight 242. I am Captain Paul Stubbing and my crew and I are happy to be flying you boys back home. We will be taking off shortly and will be heading across the Pacific at 32000 ft." The message came across the intercom and his second statement disappears in the cheering from everyone aboard.

We shout and pound the floor with our feet. I am leaving this country today and I will never see it again. I pound the floor extra hard, I want the very ground to feel my happiness at leaving.

At last, we are airborne and the pilot circles the area above the base. Evidently, he has this planned. He must sense that we want a long, final look at the land that has been our home for the last year. I look out the window as we circle, willing my mind to remember this scene below me.

I take my camera and snap pictures through the windows as I did when we arrived that long year ago. As always, the country looks so clean and peaceful from the air. There are no signs of any damage or the life and death struggles that take place here every day.

I stare until the land disappears beneath the plane and the blue of the Pacific Ocean comes into sight. It is so big and beautiful. It promises better days ahead and living with the people I love. It is the end of the ever-present pressure to stay alive and of the pain I feel for a country that I can never truly help.

As I stare out of the window, I feel the doom that Viet Nam is rushing into. With our help, this country has kept its head above water. When we leave, as we will in time, the country will quickly fold. I have made many good Vietnamese friends and I worry about what will happen to them when the communists take over. The VC shows the people little mercy, but the NVA (North Vietnamese Army) will be even worse.

Enough of these gloomy thoughts, now is not the time to feel this way. The mood in the plane is light and everyone is talking happily. As we head east across the Pacific, the flight attendants are laughing and telling jokes. Amelia Earhart went down in this same general area and I do not want to suffer the same fate. I worry that this plane will not get me across the ocean. It would be terrible to survive a year of combat and be lost forever in the vast reaches of the Pacific.

There is also another nagging feeling in my mind that I cannot understand. I work at it, trying to figure out what is bothering me. I finally realize what it is. Human beings are such complex creatures. I am so happy to be rid of Viet Nam, yet part of me is so sad to be leaving. *What perverse part of a human mind can want it both ways?*

The trip across the ocean is long and monotonous, broken only by a re-fueling stop in Hawaii. It is mid-afternoon now, not three in the morning as it was when we stopped here on the way to Viet Nam. At that time, all I saw were a few palm trees blowing in the wind outside the terminal. They told us not to go outside and a few officers kept a close watch on us the whole hour we were there. Now, why would someone think that a drafted soldier would wander off and disappear on their way to a combat zone?

This time we get to see the big island spread out before us as we head down for landing. No one is keeping an eye on us so we wander outside. We do not venture far from the terminal, however. We do not want to take a chance of missing the flight homeward. What little I could see looked a lot like Maryland, but with many tall palm trees and much lusher vegetation.

The rest of the flight is uneventful and we do arrive safely in Oakland, California. We climb off the plane expecting to see a group of war protesters. Some of our friends who have gone home earlier have written us and mentioned that it happened to them. We have talked about this as the U.S. coast came into view, and we decided that we just might have to do a little butt kicking. This is a full planeload of vets and the scene would not be pretty. I am relieved to see no one waiting for us; I did not want to spend the first couple of days home in jail, but I was willing to if necessary. After Viet Nam, an American jail would probably have felt quite plush.

We check into the base and they run us through quickly. We get our leave papers and orders for our next duty station. They issue us new green fatigue outfits and dress uniforms with the correct patches and service medals already installed. We receive travel vouchers then board buses to the airport. It all hap-pens in several hours and I am amazed that the army can move this fast. Up until now, any movement I saw in the army has been lethargic at best.

Once safely aboard the plane headed east I look at my orders. I have thirty days leave then have to report to Fort Riley, Kansas. This is great. I have only five months left in the army and they are flying me all the way across the coun-try to get home. In a month, they will fly me half way back across the country to my new duty station. Then a few months later, they will fly me back to the east coast when I leave the army. Who is in charge of such things? Does no one keep an eye on the waste of taxpayer's money? They could have stationed me on the east coast and saved the airfare. Multiply this times the hundreds of men coming home every day and the waste of money must be staggering.

On the plane east I again wonder if this contrivance will get me home. I look out the window at nothing and wipe the sweat off my forehead. I squirm in the seat and am generally miserable

"What is the matter, son? You look very distressed." This comes from a portly but quite pleasant looking person seated just to my right.

"I just got back from twelve months in a combat zone and I am afraid this damn plane won't get me home," I answer.

"Now son, there is no need for that kind of language. I am Pastor Jacobs and I am quite sure the Lord is watching over you and will get you home safely," he says with a kindly smile. "Would you like me to pray for you and your safe return?"

"That would be great, sir," I reply. He takes my hand and prays, and I suddenly have the feeling that I will make it home safely. The Lord has been watching over me all these long months and he may have arranged to put a preacher in the seat beside me. I do know that there are no atheists in a combat zone. This is especially true late at night, out in the jungle, when you can see enemy movement toward you through that starlight scope.

The plane lands safely in Baltimore. I know my wife and family will probably be waiting for me, because I called from California and gave them my arrival time. As I descend the steps, I hear a shout and see Wanda running across the pavement towards me. She runs to me and jumps into my outstretched arms so hard we almost fall down. She smothers me with kisses and I return them. I have been married to this woman for over a year, but have only spent several weeks with her since getting married. Near the terminal I spot my brother Steve, my brother Bob, and my parents who have come to meet me. We exchange hugs and talk excitedly to each other. I am so happy to be home with the people I love. It has been a long year and I have survived the combat and made it back. My life will be one happy day after another now. I do not suspect that the combat experience may not let you go that easily. You do not fight and then turn a switch and walk away unscathed.

We walk through the terminal and head toward the car. Wanda has a surprise for me. We do not walk up to my parent's car, but a new 1968 Pontiac GTO. I glance inside and she has bought one with a four-speed, just what I would have purchased. I am doubly surprised. Is this a woman worth keeping, or what?

My brother Steve drives home and Wanda and I sit in the back. We are jammed so close together that my mom has plenty of room on the seat. He cranks up the radio and all the songs are new to me. Radio Saigon in Viet Nam was always three or four months behind the U.S. with its music.

My mind is in a whirl. The sights and sounds of my old life assail me, and everything seems too noisy and crowded. The car feels like it is going way too fast and all the vehicles seem to be crowded far too close together. There are way too many buildings crowded together and they seem too garish. There are too many signs and the lights are blinding, even though it is only late afternoon. The sparseness and simplicity of Viet Nam has altered my way of looking at things and I realize right then that adjustment is going to take some time.

We arrive at Deal Island and my mom prepares a good home cooked meal. I see that the army food, good as it was, does not approach the level of expertise of my mom. I have merely forgotten how good my Mom's meals taste. Moms have a special ingredient that the army cooks do not have in their kitchens. If you look for it in the grocery store, it is in the "L" aisle and the can will say "Love."

The next week passed in a whirlwind of love and trying to synchronize with my new environment. Wanda has taken a week off work and we spend all our time together. We take long drives in the new car and I try to get used to driving sixty mph instead of thirty. After the jeeps, the GTO feels like a rocket ship. We meet old friends and have lunch, and sometimes we just sit quietly and hold each other.

During this time, I worked on trying to be stationed on the east coast instead of halfway across the country. When I was in Oakland earlier, I mentioned my problem. They gave me the phone number of someone at the pentagon in Washington that might be able to help. Sure, and the Easter Bunny will come by and fill up the gas tank in the GTO tonight as I sleep. Still, I tried it and the lieutenant at the other end of the line gave me an appointment with him in several days time.

I spent three hours driving to Washington and another hour in finding the Pentagon. Another hour passed by the time I threaded the labyrinth of the parking lots and made my way to his office. I was very late and figured this was a wasted cause. The LT. was very pleasant and easy-going. Quick, should I report this man? Does he not know that army officers are supposed to be aloof, uncompromising, and unfriendly?

The officer very pleasantly surprised me. He listened to my story, looked at my orders, and made a phone call. He agreed that it was simpler to station me on the east coast for the remaining five months of my army career. In a short span of fifteen minutes, he told me that I would be receiving a telegram in a few days informing me of a change in my orders to somewhere on the east coast, the location to be stated in the telegram. I thanked him profusely and headed back home. That caring officer had just made the next five months of my life much simpler. Should that person still be living and happen to read this book, I bless you, sir. I cannot remember your name, but you taught me that an army officer could also be a human being. I ran across several outstanding army officers in my career, but they were rare.

As promised, three days later, I received a telegram from the Pentagon and Wanda and I quickly read it. I had orders for Fort Gordon, Georgia. It was not exactly in my back yard, but it was only eight hours away, which was much closer than Kansas. Wanda and I discussed this information and decided that I would go there first. If I found that I could live off base, I would learn my way around and look for a small, cheap apartment. She would continue working until I contacted her, and then would give two weeks notice at her job at the hospital. She would load the GTO and head south to join me. We had been apart so long we just had to be together.

The month's leave went by quickly and we drove to Princess Anne to catch that old bus. Our parting was again tearful, but at least we knew we would be back together within a month. That eased the pain somewhat as I watched her disappear when the bus pulled out of town and headed south.

Fort Gordon was nestled close to one side of Augusta, Georgia. The town was made somewhat famous by a singer of that era, and his famous line that stated, "And the name of the place is Augusta, Ga." A somewhat sleepy southern town, it depended mostly on the base for its livelihood. In more recent years, it has become quite famous for the golf tournaments held there.

I reported to the base, one of many young soldiers coming back from the war zone. It appeared that the army had more soldiers coming back than it could use. If you had more than a year left of duty, then you were still a useable commodity. After spending a few months stateside, they would ship that soldier back to the war zone. Since you still had a use to the army, these soldiers got better treatment than we "short-timers" did.

We soldiers that had less than a year of duty were not going back overseas, so we were yesterday's news. The First Sergeant and some of the non-coms in our company did their best to make our lives miserable. On the days we had nothing to do, they were always calling us over to the day room and giving us oddball jobs, mostly just make-work.

We soon learned to get up very early and join the mandatory formation every morning at 0600 hours. We would then eat quickly and clear out of the company area for the rest of the day. We did not have any transportation, so we would walk around the base, or go to a movie at the theater on the base. There was also the EM (enlisted men's) club that has a bar with a few snacks and beer available.

If you were unmotivated enough to hang around the company area during the day a sergeant would grab you to do jobs that really did not need doing. They carefully picked jobs that you could easily see were worthless and put you to work. It was just another twist of the army screw. They were telling you that they had more rank than you did, therefore you had to do what they said. I really relished this scut work handed out by someone with more rank, but about two-thirds the IQ of myself. I was out of combat but things really were not much better. It seemed that the bases were a haven for a less intelligent species that shunned all work, but delighted in making life miserable for men of lower rank. Of course, not all soldiers were that way. There were patriotic men among us who loved their country and were willing to fight for it. The men I just accused, you know who you are.

I found that it was permissible to live off base, so I found a small apartment about five miles from the base, close to the golf course. Without transportation I could not live there yet so I called Wanda and she loaded the car and came down to Augusta. Life was good again. We had our own little love nest, the first place we had to ourselves since getting married. It was tiny, but it was ours.

We bought a five-dollar television from a soldier that was getting out of the army. It had a bad picture tube and the picture was very faint. The only way you could make out an image on the screen during the day was to turn off all the lights and hang blankets over the two windows in the room. We sat there one day and watched our men land on the moon. The picture was black and white and so faint we had to sit within a foot of the screen. We did not feel poor or disadvantaged sitting there. We had each other, after a year of separation, and that was really all that mattered.

With Wanda here I had transportation and a vehicle that half the soldiers on base coveted. I had gone from another faceless soldier to a heavy hitter within my company. This heavy hitter proudly drove up to the front gate in his car. The MPs (Military Police) on guard at the gate promptly stopped me. I did not have a sticker on the vehicle so I could not drive it on base. To get a sticker I had to have the car inspected on base first. However, I could not drive the car on base without a sticker. This was a classic catch 22 of which the army had plenty.

I had to park the car just outside the gates and turn the keys over to the guard. I then walked two miles to a phone and called Wanda. I explained the situation to her and had her get a cab and come rescue the car. I then walked the final mile to the company area and faced the wrath of the First Sergeant. I was an hour late for the morning formation and he was livid. To think this little pipsqueak of a soldier had the effrontery to miss his formation call. I explained the situation but it had no effect.

"You get the hell out of this day room and if you miss formation again I will have your ass," he yelled. I thought about starting a new- "I want to kill this man at a non-specified later date" list. It was only a thought. My killing days have ended.

I managed to find a sympathetic Second Lieutenant who wrote a pass to get the car on base for inspection and to receive the necessary base sticker. On my second attempt to run the front gate gauntlet, the guard stopped me again. I showed him my temporary pass and thought I was home free. He asked me for my driver's license. Oh-Oh. This was going to be a problem. My Maryland driver's license had disappeared in Viet Nam and it was never found. I did not think to apply for a new one while I was on leave. Guess who had to park his car again and turn over the keys. I showed him my army driver's license but it was to no avail. I had to have a Maryland license even though this was Georgia. This time I ran the three miles to the company area to attend the morning formation and got there on time. Then I called Wanda and had her rescue the car again.

I called the Maryland DMV and talked them into letting me apply for a lost license over the phone. After all, I was off fighting for my country when I lost my license. I doubted this approach would work, but thankfully, the DMV was a little more flexible than the army was. Wanda delivered me to formation every day and waited for me if I was off that day, then we went back to the apartment. We had to get up every day at five to be at the formation at six even if I was off that day. Such was the inflexibility of the army. How would a civilian like having to report to his place of work every morning at six even on his days off? The army taught me to kill and then brought me back home. Then they continued to do things that made me almost want to kill again. I wonder if there is anything in the Bible about this problem? Is there any scripture that says "Thou Shalt Not Kill Thy First Sergeant?"

I continued to work three days a week helping give training to new re-cruits heading for Viet Nam. I often wanted to tell them how it really was over there. I wanted to take them aside and tell them I would pick them up after dark in my car and carry them to the bus station and then they could disappear. A lot of them could tell I was a sympathetic ear and they often asked me for the "real story" of the war. A year and a half ago I often asked war returnees the same question. As the returnees did, I kept the true story hidden and told them to learn all they could in their training, because it could save their lives. I knew that nothing I said against the war would really help. I also knew that trying to help them escape their combat duties could only result in them and me winding up in the base stockade. Like me, it was now their turn to pay the piper.

That last day of my service finally came. I turned down all monetary of-fers to re-up, or enlist for more time. They offered me three thousand dollars to sign up for another three years. At that time, the money would purchase a new car. These people do not learn, they still think I have "idiot" written on my forehead. I drove out that front gate one last time and gave the finger to the MP standing there on guard. I did not look back.

I drove to the apartment. Wanda was waiting with our few possessions packed. We loaded up, left that hated base, and turned north for Maryland. We did not look back. After two long years, my slavery was over. I was a free man.

Chapter 22
Adjusting To Peace Is Hard

Eden, Maryland Sept.1969

After we left Fort Gordon, Wanda and I headed up the interstate toward home. I kept that big engine in the car humming along at seventy miles an hour. The sooner we got out of Georgia the better. We did not stop for food, just gas and a few snacks we purchased while refueling. The closer we got to home the better we felt. When evening came, I flicked the lights on and bored a hole through the oncoming darkness. I kept the hammer down until we got to her parent's house a little before midnight.

We roused her parents, had a late night reunion followed by a simple meal, and then went to bed. We were both dead on our feet but could not get to sleep so we lay there for several hours talking about the future. I was still trying to accept the feeling of being totally out of the army. I had been on leaves before, but this was different. This was complete freedom in not having to worry about returning in a set amount of time.

We took the next day off to rest and then we went to see my parents. The following day we decided that it was time to start making our mark on the world. To do that we both needed jobs. We knew Wanda would have no trouble because she was an LPN and the hospital had asked her to call them when she returned to Maryland. We were not sure that I could find a job easily. I was confident no one in Salisbury needed an ace demolition man and the other skills the army taught me would not be of much use here.

Some of my best friends worked at Wayne Pump in Salisbury, so I called and made an appointment for an interview that afternoon. I did not mention the army or combat duty, because I had heard that such information shared with a prospective employer hurt your chances. I made sure I was well dressed, my shoes shined, and my hair neatly trimmed. I showed up a little early and waited until they called my name.

"Mr. McCoy, I see you have a two year gap in your employment record according to the information on these papers you filled out," said the female who was interviewing me. She was a very prim and proper middle-aged woman, glasses perched high on her nose. She was polite, but her tone said she would find the underlying cause of everything eventually.

"Yes ma'am, I just got out of the army after serving two years. I received an honorable discharge and you won't have to worry about me being drafted if I work for you," I said as I gave it my best college try.

"I see," she said. "Were you stationed overseas?" Her voice was picking up a slightly frosty edge. I knew I was in trouble now and I felt like getting irritated but I gave her my best smile. Maybe I should have brought some flowers.

"Yes, I spent a year in the lovely little country of Viet Nam," I answered her. That frosty edge in her voice ramped up a notch or two.

"What did you do there? Were you in any combat?" she said. She was now eying me very closely and I was sure she had quietly pushed her chair back just a little to get further away from me. I thought, come on son, you can handle this.

"I was in a recon platoon for a year. We mainly gathered information and turned it over to the intelligence people on base," I explained as I thought that sounded better than telling her we tramped around the countryside until someone shot at us and then we shot back. Civilians could never understand, anyway.

"Well, Mr. McCoy, I am sure your service was appreciated, but I do not see that your experiences will be helpful in working here. Have you any machining or tool and die experience?" she asked. I noticed she did not say she appreciated my service for my country.

I came back with, "No, but I am a quick learner and I am very mechanically inclined." I could see she did not intend to hire me. To make it worse, she picked up my application with two fingers, acting as if it was dirty. She leaned to the side of the desk and deposited the form in her wastebasket. She gave me an icy stare that I did not feel I deserved.

I got up then and turned to leave, but I just could not resist rattling Miss Priss' cage. I was not getting the job so why not do so.

"Oh, I forgot to tell you some of my other skills. If you need a hole blown in the building, I can do that. If you have any personnel problems I can kill silently without a weapon," I told her. I could see she was not impressed, but my statement did have the desired effect.

Miss Priss jumped up and headed for the door behind the desk, her face ashen. She slammed the door so hard I saw dust swirl out from behind the molding and drift slowly to the floor. Oh well, you win some and you lose some.

I started the car and headed over to the hospital to wait for Wanda. I was sure she would have better luck than I did. I waited a little while and Wanda came out with a smile on her face. She told me she had a job and would start in a week. I told her it did not look like I would get the job, but I did not give her specifics. I did not want to worry her.

Since we were in Salisbury, I decided to apply for unemployment in case it took me awhile to get a job. I was ever the optimist, so after signing up, I went back home and applied for several other jobs over the phone. My optimism paid off, because several days later I got a call from a man that owned Eastern Shore Oil in Fruitland, Maryland. He was the one I leased my station from and he said he heard I was back in town. He told me he had a proposition for me and would I come by and discuss it. I drove there immediately before he could change his mind.

The man told me he had a new station almost finished and would like me to lease it. I was flattered, but told him I was not quite ready to commit to another twelve hour a day job. I knew it would take long hours to make good money, and if I took the job, I would not be able to resist working those long hours. Wanda and I are finally able to be together as we want to be and I do not want to jeopardize that. He said that he understood and I could think about the station, as it would be awhile before it was ready to open. Meanwhile he needed someone to do finish work at several stations and to drive a fuel delivery truck.

I started work several days later. It would not be a well-paying job, but I figured I could get into working again and make a decision on the station later. I planted shrubs, installed signs, and did finish painting. I also helped level the lot so the paving company could get started. When I was not working at the stations, I drove the truck and made fuel deliveries to various businesses all over the lower shore.

I soon received my first unemployment check, which surprised me because it came sooner than I expected. I called the unemployment office and asked about returning it since I now had a job, but they told me to keep it since I was out of work a week.

With two incomes now, we started looking for a place of our own. We soon found a small, inexpensive apartment in Eden, Maryland. It was not fancy, but was only about five miles from where we worked. We now had our very own love nest again and we were quite happy.

After moving into the apartment, I started having trouble sleeping at night. I would wake up often, get up, and roam the rooms. I would rattle the doors to make sure the locks were set and peer out the windows. I do not know whom I thought I would see out there but I could not stop myself. It is sometimes worthless to argue with your own mind. It will not listen and it has its own agenda.

Wanda took this all in stride and never complained about her loss of sleep because I always awakened her. She soon named my excursions "walking the perimeter" and understood I had to do it. I certainly had an understanding wife and I felt blessed to have her. We thought my nightly excursions would get better in time, but it slowly seemed to get worse.

I decided the lack of a weapon at home bothered me, so I went to Pocomoke and filled out papers to purchase a .45 caliber pistol. A week later, a police officer at the Salisbury Barracks called and said he was reviewing my pistol application. He asked me why I wanted such a large caliber handgun and I explained I had carried one in Viet Nam and gave training on it for four months. It only made sense to me to own a weapon I was familiar with, and he must have agreed. Several days later, I got a call to pick up my new pistol.

Having the weapon at home definitely helped my sleeping. I was much less nervous and my nightly patrols through the apartment dropped off considerably. I still felt the need for something in my life, something extra but I could not figure what that could be.

One of my friends at work told me about a cheap motorcycle for sale that had a bad engine. I went to look at it and the motor was out and apart and most of it in a tomato basket. The price was only seventy-five dollars, so I thought that the cycle would make a good project that I could later sell and make a profit. I purchased it, cleaned it up, and then rebuilt the motor in our unused back bedroom after I put down some cardboard. I also repainted it, but Wanda drew the line on painting in the house so I did that on the back porch. I had an understanding wife and she probably thought it would take my mind off the army.

Once I got that cycle running I spent many weekend afternoons screaming down the back roads behind Allen. I had no tags and no insurance, but things were much simpler in those days. At that time, all you needed to ride a motorcycle was a car permit. Wanda surprised me by wanting to learn to ride the motorcycle so I gave her lessons. There was a large field between our apartment and U.S. 13 southbound and we utilized that for lessons.

She would start out in first gear and ride slowly around the field and I ran along beside her in case she lost her balance. As she got better, she speeded up and I had to run faster. After two days of this, she could ride the motorcycle and I was worn out with all the running. I came home in great shape and I was lucky that I was, because she ran me ragged, but she learned to ride that motorcycle.

I really enjoyed that motorcycle, crude piece that it was. I did not realize it at that time, but that motorcycle added some danger to my life, danger that I had been missing. Flying down the back roads was exhilarating and all thoughts of war and the army disappeared once I let the clutch out. Combat had turned me into an adrenaline junkie and this was my "fix."

That motorcycle led me to the next branch in my road. I heard that the local Honda shop was looking for a new mechanic. Ironically, one of its mechanics received his draft notice and was now undergoing basic training prior to heading to Viet Nam. I stopped by and talked to the service manager and he gave me a couple of simple jobs to do one Saturday morning. Evidently, he was pleased with my mechanical ability because he hired me and I gave notice at Eastern Shore Oil. I hated to leave there, but I had decided that another gas station lease was not in my future.

My new attraction was now motorcycles and I knew a new Honda was in my near future. I was a good mechanic and the head mechanic there became a best friend. Vernon Marshall taught me all he knew about working on cycles and he knew a lot. I absorbed it like a sponge and the boss sent me to Honda training schools to further my education. I loved working on cycles and meeting the interesting, and sometimes colorful people that rode them. Not many people rode motorcycles then so we all stuck together and became one big extended family. There were always rides on the weekends where we would gather at the shop or someone's house and ride all day. I met many people who became good friends and still ride with some of them today.

Vernon quit to open his own shop so I became head mechanic. A year or so later the service manager left to take over his retiring father's business and I was suddenly the service manager. I was moving up faster than I had expected. I loved being around cycles, so it was not so much a job as a daily adventure.

With both of us making good money, we decided it was time to buy a house. We started looking and Wanda's grandmother retired and decided to sell her house. It was in the Pocomoke Forest close to Salisbury and she gave us a very good price. This was great for off-road riding and I was quite pleased with the location.

I started building a three-car garage soon after we purchased the house. That had been a dream of mine to have somewhere to work on cars and motorcycles. My life was complete. I had a great wife, a job I loved, and a building to work on my various projects. I though everything was great, but Wanda noticed that I still had not made it all the way back from the war zone. I was aloof and moody and could not explain my feelings. It was simpler to go out in the garage and work on something. I did not have to explain my inner turmoil to something mechanical and I really could not put my problems into words. I withdrew from the world in the evenings and on weekends and sought refuge in the garage with something mechanical.

Part of the problem was the nightly news reports that I avidly watched. I came back from Viet Nam hating the army and annoyed about the civilians who were protesting the war. I could also see that the news reports misstated what was really happening in the war zone and seemed calculated to make the population hate the war. That angered me greatly. I felt my country forcibly drafted me, made me fight a war and through ineptitude was making the war ineffective and unsupportable. My country had abandoned my friends and me and now our fellow citizens were abandoning us too. I knew that every protest on TV and every wild-eyed mother marching down the street showed the enemy that the country was not supporting the war. This would make them hang on, knowing that public opinion would end the war. The only problem was that every protest made the enemy hang on more tenaciously and that was causing soldiers to die. How ironic! The protesters were trying to end the war and save men's lives but each protest caused more men to die. *Could no one see this? Did anyone care?*

The whole mess caused such a conflict in my mind. Deep down I knew the protesters were right, but I had served at the sharp end of the sword. I knew the sacrifices my fellow soldiers and I had made. The fact that we were expendable cut me deeply. Our war was not like World War II, a necessary one. Soldiers fought in that war and came back to the acclaim and thanks from a grateful populace. Our war was a worthless one and we came back to meet scorn and abuse. It took me over twenty years to get over this fact and I will harbor some resentment to the day I die.

I still hate the army. I know it is a necessary evil as long as men cannot live in peace. I respect the young men and women that enlist and fight for their country, but I can never respect the army. I feel it is still the same old unchanging system, secure in the knowledge that its ideas and decisions are always correct.

I kept looking for ways to remove the pain and survivor's guilt from my mind. I thought that maybe writing a book about the war, a scathing expose, would ease my mind. The more I wrote the harder it became; the memories were just too fresh. I put the uncompleted manuscript on a shelf in the back bedroom and forgot about it for a while. The thoughts and memories refused to die, however, and when strong feelings popped up, I would grab a piece of paper and write them down feverishly before they faded. I wound up with many writings interspersed with sheet music in the notebook I kept. One thing I wrote stuck with me through the years. It is perhaps a mirror into the soul of a man struggling to forget the past and face an uncertain future.

How can you explain to someone who was never there, that the saddest, loneliest sound you have ever heard is the sound of a chopper's blades echoing into the night, bearing out brave young men and bringing back twisted, broken souls? I sometimes think the lucky ones came home in flag-draped caskets. For them, the war is over. As for me, I have fought it forty-three years in my mind.

I tried to find solace and peace in my mind. I kept looking for something else, something new that would interest me and take my mind off the war. A friend of mine had a dune buggy he used in the woods near his house and I had hundreds of acres of forest with many trails surrounding me. I figured a dune buggy was the perfect vehicle for me.

I purchased an old car; removed the body and shortened the frame. I then welded it back together; built a framework to hold the steering column, and added a roll bar. I mounted the exhaust up high and finished with a pair of bucket seats perched over the rear axle. Presto, I had a dune buggy only twelve feet long and weighing around twelve hundred pounds. It was highly maneuverable and would go practically anywhere. I could now carry Wanda along for a ride through the woods and the total cost was only several hundred dollars. We rode that vehicle all over the Pocomoke Forest with a slow moving vehicle triangular tag on it and the cops paid us no attention as long as we stayed on the shoulder of the road.

Both the buggy and the dirt bike presented me with a problem. Within fifteen minutes of getting in the woods my skin would start crawling and I kept stopping, looking for that VC behind a tree somewhere. I knew this was very idiotic and kept telling my mind that, but the phobia made my rides hard to enjoy. I experimented by carrying my .45 pistol in one chest pocket of my field coat, with a loaded magazine in the other pocket and found I could stay in the woods as long as I wanted. It seems I was happy only when I had a weapon close by. I was glad I felt no need of one at work; my employer would not appreciate it. I lived with a weapon nearby for a year, and now I could not do without one for my piece of mind. I detested this part of me; Viet Nam had made me hate weapons. I now felt that a weapon was made for only one reason, to kill someone or something, but I found it necessary to own one.

I had been home from the war four or five years when something happened that really scared me. It was a dark, rainy night and I was out in the garage working on a car. Unbeknownst to me, a friend had stopped by to see me, and Wanda sent him back to the garage. Due to the rain, he ran around the house toward the garage. Meanwhile, I had decided it was time to quit work for the night and left the garage, locking the door behind me. As I turned around a dark figure materialized in front of me and my army training took over. I dropped to one knee and let out a blood-curdling yell as we learned in training. I intended to throw my assailant over my shoulder, then turn quickly and deliver a blow to his windpipe.

"What the hell is wrong with you, McCoy?" my friend screamed. I recognized his voice and halted, so scared I could scarcely speak. I do not know how badly I might have hurt him and I do not want to know. I explained that his sudden appearance, looming out of the darkness, had put me back in Viet Nam again. I asked him that instead of running out to the garage after dark, to have Wanda go to the back porch and call out to me that I had a visitor. He assured me that the next time he would call first, then have Wanda announce him before he went to the garage. What happened really disturbed me. I wondered if I was a menace to my friends. The army teaches you to kill, puts you in situations where you may have to, then brings you home and waves goodbye. Sort it out yourself, soldier, you are not our problem any longer. Is there such a thing as teaching people not to kill after they leave combat?

The soldier that returns home from a combat mission today has all kinds of help since we understand the problem much better now. My friends and I received nothing. I did not get a thank you from the army on that last day on the base, and I certainly never got a thank you from any civilians when I got home.

Wanda and I traded the GTO in on a used Corvette convertible and that became another interest. We joined the Delmarva Corvette Club and I got into Corvettes heavily. I bought good clean cars that needed detailing and a little work and corrected their problems. I then sold each one at a profit and found another. In the next four years, I bought and sold four Corvettes. I made enough to allow us to buy a new silver 1975 Corvette coupe, my first new one. Then I rarely drove it, because I did not want to get it dirty or wet. This exasperated Wanda but she tolerated me. She put up with a lot because she did not understand just what was wrong with me. I thought I was normal, just a car nut taking it perhaps a bit too far.

The sad truth was that I was badly broken and there was no medicine to cure my particular ailment. I can remember that I could not feel elation or joy over anything. Music that used to make me happy did little. I dearly loved Wanda, but I could not show enough emotion to her. The cars and motorcycles were just something that I thought could fill that empty place inside me. I did not know at that time that I had that empty place or that I was searching for something to fill it. Thinking back, I am sure that I was also experiencing depression. It can be hard to find a cure when you know you are sick. When you think you are normal then you do not even go looking for one.

So there I was, "Mr. I'm normal," rushing headlong through life. I wasn't looking for any answers because I did not have the sense to ask the right questions. Wanda was wondering what happened to the happy-go-lucky man she married five years ago. Where was the man who wanted to make a million dollars? He was a victim of Viet Nam. His name was not on a headstone and no one had to cry over his memory. Nevertheless, he was still a victim.

Wanda kept trying to reach me. She decided she wanted to have a baby and approached me with the idea. I am sure she thought that a baby in the family might bring me around, might make me whole again. I did not think too much of the idea, because my mom had her last child when I was in high school. I saw the work and pressure that comes with a new child. Wanda persevered and I finally said yes. After all, I had a garage full of toys and I could not turn her down.

So, we had a new non-mechanical addition to our family, our daughter Christy Lynn McCoy. I fell totally in love with the tiny bundle as soon as I saw her in the hospital. I was almost afraid to hold her; she seemed so tiny and delicate.

After she was a few months old, we continued our Sunday afternoon drives in the Corvette. We would wrap her up carefully in a blanket and place her in the back compartment behind the seats. We would then place pillows around her so she could not slide around. On the first trip, I was worried the side pipes on the car might scare such a young infant when I started the car. Christy took it in stride and seemed quite contented in her snug place behind the seats. She fell asleep before we got far down the road and continued to do that on every ride. I was already thinking ahead fifteen years when I could teach her to drive a four-speed car.

My daughter seemed to take my mind off the mental chaos I was experiencing, but it did not last very long. I soon returned to the peace and quiet of the garage. Working on something mechanical distracted me from the inner turmoil I was experiencing. Wanda complained that I was spending too much time in the garage and not helping with the baby. To be truthful I wanted to help with the baby, but I was a little scared of her. She was such a delicate and precious gift that I was afraid of handling her too much. Too often, when Wanda worked the night shift and I should have been in the house taking care of Christy, I was in the garage working. We hired a baby-sitter on those nights. I understood anything mechanical, but I was quite helpless with a baby.

At the time, I was finishing a five-year project. I had been restoring a 1931 Model A deluxe coupe with a rumble seat and taking pains to make it as perfect as I could. I applied numerous coats of black lacquer and then wet sanded the paint and finished it with several days of mechanical buffing. The paint glistened in the sun and looked a mile deep. It was so nice I would not let anyone climb into the rumble seat for fear of scratching the paint. I removed my wallet and belt, then my shoes, and climbed into the seat to see how it felt. I realized then that I had created a car so nice that I would always be scared to drive it.

Since the Model A was almost finished I bought an old 1965 Pontiac GTO that needed a complete restoration and had the previous owner deliver it to our house, then returned him to Salisbury. I parked the car beside the garage and went over it, making mental notes of what work would have to be done to the car, and estimating how long it would take me.

"Why is that GTO sitting out by the garage?" Wanda asked when she got home from work. "Are you working on it for someone?"

"Ah, well, not exactly," I said to her. She knew what that meant and the look on her face told me I had made a grave tactical error. I tried to explain that once this car looked good again, it would replace the car I had lost when the army uprooted me seven years ago.

I am sure Wanda thought I would take a garage break after the Model A was completed, but I just could not stop buying cars. I did not understand that this compulsion was rooted in my hate for the army, war and the loss of close friends.

My latest purchase put more strain on our marriage. Wanda could see that I was not going to change, and me, I did not understand that I needed to change. We went on for awhile, Wanda taking care of Christy and me out in that garage, seeking solace I could not find.

Wanda finally loaded the car up one day, strapped Christy in the front seat and drove away. I was devastated, my wife and little girl were gone out of my life. Suddenly, the garage full of toys did not seem so important, and I found it almost impossible to go out there and work on anything. My haven of peace and tranquility had turned into a torture chamber. We talked about getting back together several times, but it never seemed to happen.

Many Viet Nam era marriages ended this way. The scenario may have been a little different, but the results were the same. There were many mentally wounded veterans facing a single life, trying desperately to figure out what went wrong.

***

Things were tense for about ten years between Wanda and I, and I saw very little of Christy because it was just too painful. As we aged we got smarter, and both of us realized that we had made mistakes. We were both too young and inexperienced to sort out our problems and make a go of our marriage. We have apologized to each other for our shortcomings, and become good friends after all.

I still regret not being able to hold the marriage together, and I doubly regret all the time I missed in my daughter's life. I have grown older and a lot smarter, and I am doing my best to make up for those losses. We see each other often and text back and forth all the time. In the end, our marriage was not a failure because it produced a daughter that I am quite proud of, and that I love with all my heart.

***

So, what has our country learned about fighting other people's wars? I fear it has learned little. The authorities still feel we need to jump in with both feet into the internal affairs of other countries. We waste our young men's lives and spend huge amounts of money trying to make them democratic. They need to understand that some countries just do not have the necessary leadership and infrastructure to become free. Freedom takes huge amounts of time, charismatic leaders, and the will of the whole population to attain that goal. We argue incessantly about the public debt and ways to minimize it. Our leaders find new wars and spend money we do not have. We will pass that debt on to our children and to their offspring.

What have I learned about fighting other people's wars? Disappear quickly when the army wants to draft you and send you to places where "it does rain in hell." Few wars are necessary and most rarely solve any problems over the long run. Examine the war closely that your country wants you to fight, and make a sound decision based on the information that you accumulate. Ask yourself if it is a just war; will it free a people from oppression or is it just another way for your country to spend money and ruin the rest of your life? Remember that older, rich men run the country, and own or control many large companies that benefit from war contracts. Ask yourself if you think there is a connection there.

I failed to ask myself these important questions and went off blindly to do my country's bidding. I did not stop to think that my country could be so wrong. I survived the war when many men did not, and I am eternally grateful for that, but I paid a price far too dear.

Think carefully, young man, before you play at war. Read this cautionary tale and fully absorb it. Remember that no one comes home from combat without a wound. The wounds that cannot be seen, and therefore cannot be healed, are perhaps the cruelest of all.

Epilogue

The war is long past now, and it has become mostly pleasant memories in my mind. Years passing have that effect. They burnish off the sharp edges and make those memories less painful, and eventually even pleasant. Hidden down deep, though, are some bad memories. I rarely go there as the passage of time also allows me to repress those feelings, to keep them where they can cause no pain. Those memories are of the past, and they are no longer important in my life.

In spite of the war, I became a productive member of society and worked hard through the years. I have had only two employers since coming back and worked at those two jobs a total of thirty-eight years before retiring.

I have not had a recurrence of malaria for over ten years and hope that this continues. I have had enough "upper respiratory infections" for one lifetime.

My hate for the army has mellowed a little. Now I only dislike it, though I know it is a necessity in this harsh world.

My disappointment in my country for forcing me to fight an unnecessary war has also changed. I no longer dislike my country. It is after all, my country, right or wrong. I only wish the decisions our leaders make were right a little more often.

I no longer hate the protesters and war activists of the 1960's. I can see now, quite clearly, that they were right in their actions. Their efforts ended the war quicker than it would have happened otherwise. However, I am still not "fonda" Jane.

We still fight questionable wars, but I did support our actions in Iraq and Afghanistan. I feared they would turn into the same quagmire as Viet Nam, and they have to a degree, but I believe I see light at the end of the tunnel and that our soldiers can return home to peace. We have proven our point in those countries, and given our enemies an important lesson. It is now time to turn the burden over to those countries and let them sink or swim in the doing. We cannot continue to police the whole world forever.

I enjoy my retirement immensely and try to fill each day with some fun and a challenge or two. One big challenge has been this book, but it has been a labor of love. We must never forget the men who have given their lives in war, be it a necessary war or one less so.

I sit here and write the last words of this book that has, in its writing, taken the final pain out of my war. Perhaps all wars are necessary, if only to teach stubborn humanity an important lesson. Can we heed that lesson, and more importantly, will we?

I have learned that love and family transcend all else, and that the bad things that happen in your life are but a footnote in your past history. Love, indeed, does conquer all.

Thank you, ABT. You know who you are. I could not have done this without your help and guidance.

34357020R00168

Made in the USA
Middletown, DE
17 August 2016